SHERBORNE ALMSHOUSE REGISTER

SHERBORNE ALMSHOUSE REGISTER

Edited by

ANN CLARK

DORSET RECORD SOCIETY

VOLUME 17

2013

Published 2013 by Dorset Record Society
Dorset County Museum, High West Street, Dorchester, Dorset DT1 1XA

Typeset in ITC New Baskerville by John Chandler,
and printed by Henry Ling Ltd., The Dorset Press, Dorchester, Dorset
on Chromomat 100 gsm.
Cover case bound in Wibalin over 3mm boards

British Library Cataloguing in Publication Data:
A catalogue record for this book is available from the British Library.

This volume is published with assistance from the Marc Fitch Fund and the Simon
Wingfield Digby Charitable Trust, whose help is gratefully acknowledged.

ISBN 978-0-900339-18-9

CONTENTS

LIST OF ILLUSTRATIONS

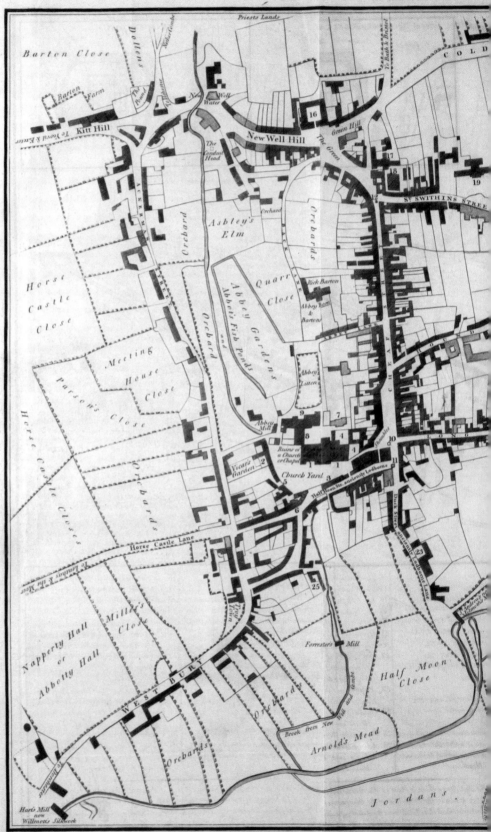

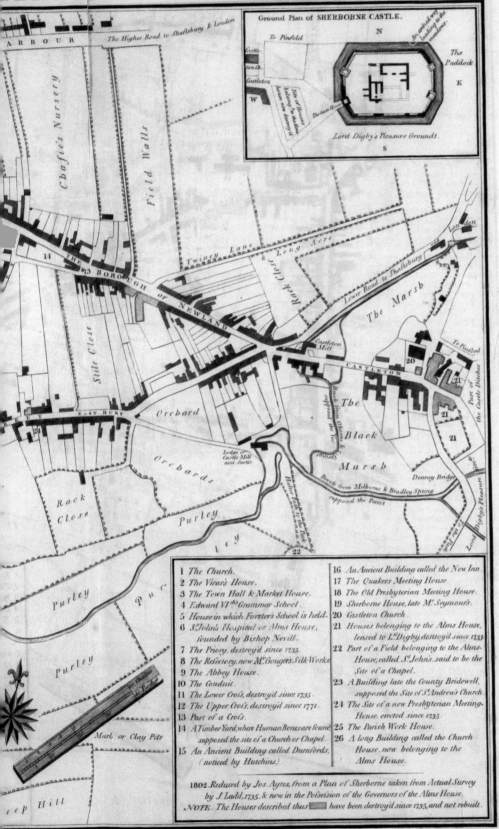

ACKNOWLEDGEMENTS

Dorset Record Society would like to thank the Simon Wingfield Digby Charitable Trust, Sherborne and the Mark Fitch Fund for grants without which the publication of this book would not have been possible.

Many people have generously contributed their time and expertise. Particular thanks are due to Dr Mark Forrest, archivist at the Dorset History Centre, for his patient and expert help to the editor with the transcription of the earlier sections of the text and deciphering 'impossible' words. He contributed the sections on the scripts and hands used in individual records, revealing approximate dates for their entry into the *Register* where this was not apparent. He also re-wrote the transcription in the accessible form in which it is presented in this book and translated from Latin the text of the terrier. Graham Hoddinott reviewed in detail the final transcription and Sam Johnston and Ann Smith read the introduction. Angela Blaydon allowed a preview of her work on Almshouse rules, due to appear in another publication. Brian Miller contributed local colour from newspapers and detail on almspeople's occupations from his research in nineteenth-century censuses. Janet Cumner and June Palmer also contributed from their own research. Special thanks go to John Chandler who has given helpful advice on editorial issues and has typeset the volume. Mr Jonathan Stones, Master of the Almshouse, and his colleagues have kindly given their approval for the publication of this volume and for the use of pictures relating to the almshouse.

Others have been generous in contributing illustrations. Particular thanks go to Rachel Hassall, archivist at Sherborne School and Elisabeth Bletsoe (curator) and David Tuffin, at Sherborne Museum Association for so actively seeking suitable material. Images are reproduced by kind permission as follows: Dorset History Centre, the frontispiece and Nos. 1-2, 4-8, 17, 19-20, 23, 27, 30, 33, 40; Sherborne Museum Association, Nos. 9–11, 15–16, 18, 21–22, 25, 28–29, 36; Sherborne School, Nos. 12–14, 31–32, 34–35; Brian Howson, No. 3; Liz Burt (photographer) and *Dorset Life*, No. 24; and Dovecote Press, No. 26. The editor provided Nos. 37–39.

Finally, Dorset Record Society expresses thanks and appreciation to Mr Jonathan Stones, for welcoming a visit to the Almshouse and allowing photographs to be taken.

INTRODUCTION

The Sherborne Almshouse Register, or the 'Almshouse Register', is one of the documents among the extensive muniments of an ancient Dorset almshouse. The document itself does not bear a title, beyond a faint and inadequate contemporary list of its contents. The word 'register' is used in its wider sense, meaning a book in which official records are kept. This volume stands out from the series of other similar books which record the day-to-day business of the Hospital of St John the Baptist and St John the Evangelist, or 'Sherborne Almshouse'. In contrast, the Almshouse Register houses a collection of records including copies of the royal licence by which the house was founded and documents concerning the governance of the almshouse and its endowments. Contemporary entries include revision and extension of some of the earlier rules for the management of the house and details of land and property held by the almshouse. In addition there are continuous lists, which could of themselves be called registers in the modern usage of the word, detailing the elections of brethren of the almshouse from 1582 to 1863 and admissions of almspeople from the same date until 1866.

The registry book was purchased in the late-sixteenth century, at a time when the paper and parchment rolls together with the large and often folded documents traditionally used for keeping official records were giving way to the more convenient book format. The book provided the almshouse with a means to bring together in one place a selection of important records which might need to be readily consulted at a later date. But this collection of records, when pieced together, presents so much more than a mere business record. It provides a window into the management and conduct of the almshouse, together with glimpses of daily life of the residents, over a period of almost four centuries. The contents hint at the far greater role of the almshouse in Sherborne and provide signposts to other records that provide confirmation of this deduction.

The body of this introduction has four sections. Firstly, drawing mainly on secondary sources, it places the Hospital of St John the Baptist and St John the Evangelist at Sherborne in context by outlining the developing English history of almshouses which evolved over centuries through changing attitudes and beliefs. Then, it sets the almshouse within the framework of Dorset's almshouse provision. Thirdly, it outlines the foundation and administration of the almshouse at Sherborne and, through cross-referencing with records from the collection held at the Dorset History Centre and with other primary sources, it expands on the almshouse as a conduit for more general private philanthropy towards the townspeople. Then it brings to life some of the day-to-day experiences of the people involved in its management and of those living in the house.

The introduction itself finishes by highlighting the significance of this group of records and suggesting possibilities for their use in further research. Then follows a description of the Almshouse Register, the documents it contains and the hands and scripts used in recording them together with editorial issues. Next, the transcription of the records is presented in an easily accessible format, and the final section of the volume offers a glossary and index.

Influences on the almshouse concept

Sherborne Almshouse is one of many hundreds of almshouses which were founded in England after the Norman Conquest, but care for those in need was not the preserve of England, nor of the second millennium. The almshouse concept of residential care is rooted in distant times. There is evidence in classical and other ancient civilisations of a tradition of caring for the sick, the poor and travellers. Followers of Islam, for example, made practical provision for both care and accommodation for those in need. The words *eleëmosunë* in Greek and *elemosina* in Latin mean *alms*. However, these words were not to be used in England until the twelfth century. Latin also included the word *hospes*, the right of hosts to provide and guests or travellers to receive hospitality and the Latin *hospitium* described a place where care and accommodation was provided, such as an inn or a hospice. Archaeological evidence in Perthshire has shown that the Romans brought hospitals to Britain. There, a linked courtyard complex indicated a sophisticated level of care for about 250 soldiers but their efficient organisation in this respect did not outlive the Roman occupation of Britain. Nevertheless, the word 'hospital', derived from *hospitium*, appeared in English at a later date, as did the functions it implied.[1]

In early Anglo-Saxon times provision for the needy in England was probably informal, royalty and aristocracy catering for their own households and retainers and sometimes giving help to outsiders seeking alms. Christianity brought an ethos of charity in the sixth century, along with monastic life and, in some places, hospitals.[2] The town of Sherborne became the episcopal see, or seat, of the Bishop of the ancient West-Saxon diocese of Sherborne in the eighth century, when an abbey church was built for secular canons. By charter of King Ethelred in 998, Benedictine monks had replaced the canons in the monastery.[3] Since the sixth century this Order had been committed to providing hospitality and charity for travellers, the sick and the poor.

1 B. Bailey, *Almshouses*, (London, 1988) p. 15; B. Howson, *Almshouses: A Social and Architectural History*, (Stroud, 2008) pp. 14-15: N. Orme and M. Webster, *The English Hospital, 1070-1570*, (London, (1995) pp.15, 35-41.
2 Orme and Webster, *The English Hospital*, pp. 15-17.
3 Page, W. (ed.), *The Victoria County History: A History of the County of Dorset*, Vol. II (London, 1908) pp. 62-70; J. Fowler, *Mediaeval Sherborne*, (Dorchester, 1951) pp. 60-61.

The Benedictine doctrine was formally imposed on English monasteries (and nunneries) in the tenth century, in a set of rules, the *Regularis Concordia*. All such institutions were required to provide care for sick brothers in separate accommodation and to establish a lodging house for guests. In the eleventh century these rules were extended by the adoption of the *Rule of St Chrodegang*, requiring shelter to be provided in the monasteries for infirm clergy and alms to be given to the poor. This appears to have been the first recognition of the need to provide residential or hospital accommodation for older people, albeit clergymen, who were unable to care for themselves independently.[4]

Secular charity had also been increasing from the late Saxon period. Monarchs had begun to extend their liberality to the poor outside their own households, the Pope expected bishops to do likewise and others were encouraged to follow their example, either individually or collectively. From the tenth century, guilds or confraternities of members with common interests supported each other in times of need and gradually extended their charity to other good works.[5] Such charity began to take the form of hospitals which could include provision for a wide range of need – care of the poor on a daily or longer basis, care of the sick, orphans, foundlings, the infirm, lepers and the insane – although not necessarily under the same roof.

There is little evidence of free-standing hospitals before the Norman Conquest although their functions were being carried out in monasteries. Orme and Webster report the earliest hospital standing independently to have been that of Lanfranc, Archbishop of Canterbury, in the late-eleventh century. Just outside Canterbury a house provided accommodation and care for infirm men and women in poor health. It was sub-divided to prevent fraternisation between male and female residents and was under clergy control from the nearby priory. Further from the city, Lanfranc provided for lepers in small buildings, some for men and separate ones for women. Because of anxiety about contagion lepers were the first to be accommodated and cared for separately. Such shelters were known as lazar houses, many of which were to become almshouses when leprosy declined. Thus the pattern for future foundations was set.[6]

Attitudes to poverty
This differentiation of need together with changing social circumstances began to affect attitudes to poverty and the separation of functions into different establishments widened the scope for charitable giving, houses or hospitals for infirm older people being a popular choice for benefactors. The Hospital of St Cross at Winchester, built in 1136 on a grander scale than Sherborne Almshouse, accommodated thirteen poor 'impotent' almsmen in what is believed to include the oldest English almshouse still in use, though not in its original building. Also on the site was a large hall where

---

4 Orme and Webster, *The English Hospital*, pp. 17-18.
5 Orme and Webster, *The English Hospital*, pp. 18, 143-144; Howson, *Social and Architectural History*, p. 27.
6 Orme and Webster, *The English Hospital*, pp. 19-23.

out-relief in the form of daily food was given to another hundred poor men 'of good conduct of the more indigent classes'.[7] The different wording of these criteria for admission to that almshouse and for out-relief is significant. The terms 'impotent', or unable to work, and 'indigent', meaning destitute rather than 'indolent' or unwilling to work, indicate the growing distinction between the 'deserving' and 'undeserving' poor. Those qualifying for out-relief were perhaps of a lower order or less frail, but of good conduct and not undeserving.[8]

This dichotomy was soon to become entrenched. Almost simultaneously with the Black Death of 1348-9 the Statute of Labourers (1351) decreed that almsgiving to the able-bodied poor was forbidden – they had to work if they were to eat. The pestilence had so reduced the population that many of the twelfth- and thirteenth-century hospitals had to close or combine together, thus reducing the traditional provision for the poor at a time when so many were impoverished by the disruption. Private philanthropy was reduced for the same reasons and recovery was slow. Not until 1388 did legislation recognise that those truly unable to work should be helped.[9]

The words *domus elemosinarie* and its English translation *almshouse* had crept into the language in the thirteenth and fourteenth centuries respectively.[10] As the economic state of the country improved, the late-fourteenth century saw some revival in foundations, only to be set back again by further economic depression during the mid-fifteenth century.[11] From that time many charitable foundations were specifically for older people who had fallen on hard times.

Individual founders had their own attitudes, beliefs and interests which were reflected in the style of their almshouses, the criteria for entry and the rules they set for the residents. William de la Pole, Duke of Suffolk and favourite of Henry VI, with his wife Alice, Chaucer's grand-daughter, founded an almshouse at Ewelme in Oxfordshire in 1437. As befitted their status it was designed as part of a collegiate complex of buildings. It accommodated thirteen men in two-roomed homes, one room on each of two floors, around the four sides of a quadrangle. Three passages opened into the courtyard and another led to a flight of steps up to the church. A free grammar school, with staff accommodation, was constructed beyond the almshouses on the opposite side from the church. In keeping with the time, all residents had to attend daily church services.[12] In Shropshire, John Hosier, a Ludlow draper and member of the religious guild of Palmers, founded almshouses in 1462 for guild members. Details of the original building are few but in 1551 there were said to be thirty-three chambers, each with its own fireplace against a wall. There was also a

---

7 Bailey, *Almshouses*, pp. 14, 24-26; Howson, *Social and Architectural History*, pp. 26, 95-97.
8 P. Slack, *Poverty and Policy in Tudor and Stuart England*, (London, 1988) pp. 22-27.
9 Slack, *Poverty and Policy*, pp. 22; Bailey, *Almshouses*, p. 45. Slack dates the Statute of Labourers as 1349, Bailey gives that date for the Ordinance of Labourers and 1351 for the Statute.
10 Orme and Webster, *The English Hospital*, p. 38.
11 Orme and Webster, *The English Hospital*, pp.129-131, 138; N. Goose and L. Moden, *A History of Doughty's Hospital, Norwich, 1687-2009*, (Hatfield, 2010) p. 7.
12 Howson, *Social and Architectural History*, pp. 94-95; W. Page (ed), *The Victoria County History: A History of the County of Oxford*, Vol. II, (London, 1907) p.156.

chapel to which almspeople were summoned for daily prayer.[13] Ford's Hospital was founded in Coventry in 1529 by a local wool merchant, William Ford. A half-timbered building with a slightly overhanging upper floor, it framed a narrow enclosed courtyard with a chapel at one end and a communal hall at the other. Accommodation was on two floors and originally it housed six residents.[14] In each of these examples, though the almshouses were differently designed and founded by benefactors from different backgrounds, the almspeople were required to undertake religious observances.

Religious beliefs
Contemporary religious beliefs strongly influenced almshouse provision at this time. Under the influence of the Catholic church it was commonly believed that the living could assist their passage to heaven through philanthropy and that the recipients of their charity could help by remembering their benefactors in their prayers. The foundation of an almshouse could achieve these aims and, at the same time, make provision for the care of the souls of the beneficiaries. St Cross, already mentioned, had been founded by the Bishop of Winchester, Henry de Blois, a brother of King Stephen. There he required the thirteen poor almsmen to pray in the chapel, not only for themselves, but for his soul and also for the souls of his predecessors and the kings of England.[15] In similar establishments chantries were often provided, a priest supplied and residents required to pray for the souls of their benefactors.[16] In France, such a house was known as a *Maison Dieu*, a name applied to some early English almshouses such as those founded in Dover in 1221, at Northallerton, Yorkshire in 1476 and, much later, in Melton Mowbray in Leicestershire in 1640. The English version, *God's House*, was used occasionally, at Ewelme in Oxfordshire (1437) and Beaminster, Dorset (1630) for example, as was *House of Mercy*, used in Fry's foundation in Bristol (1778), or *Bede House*, as at Higham Ferrars in Northamptonshire (1423).[17] The almshouse examples given here were founded over more than three centuries. Within that time span England underwent a significant religious upheaval which placed some almshouses under threat.

The 1530s and 1540s saw the Reformation, when Henry VIII established himself as the head of the Church of England. The Dissolution of the monasteries followed. The result was the sudden loss of the greater proportion of the country's hospitals and almshouses founded on the basis of Catholic beliefs, although some, like St Cross at Winchester and Chichele's Bede House at Higham Ferrars escaped. Of around 800 mediaeval hospitals only a very small proportion were left, re-founded on a secular basis. Secular establishments were more likely to survive the dissolution but inevitably there was a dramatic increase in the number of homeless and poverty-stricken as the

---

13 A. T. Gaydon and R. B. Pugh (eds), *The Victoria County History: A History of the County of Shropshire*, Vol. II (London, 1973) pp. 108-109; Bailey, *Almshouses*, p. 70.
14 Bailey, *Almshouses*, p. 78.
15 Bailey, *Almshouses*, p. 26.
16 Goose and Moden, *Doughty's Hospital*, pp. 3-7; Bailey, *Almshouses*, pp. 16-17, 79.
17 Howson, *Social and Architectural History*, pp. 118, 124, 127; Bailey, *Almshouses*, p. 68.

charitable support of so many was once again lost.[18] A contemporary foundation in 1541, the Sir George Monoux Almshouses in Walthamstow, Essex, was visited, like many others, in the late 1540s or early 1550s by the Chantry Commissioners whose task it was to root out chapels founded by benefactors who paid for a priest to pray for their souls. George Monoux had set out extensive rules for the almshouse which included daily prayers to be said for him, his relatives and all Christians. On the day of admission almspeople were to say five *Pater Nosters*, five *Aves*, and a *Creed* in the parish church and then to repeat them each morning on rising. They were also to hear Mass daily in church. Monoux provided for a *Requiem Mass* to be said in the church annually on the anniversary of his death. This was an almshouse in the tradition of the Catholic teaching. Nevertheless, the Sir George Monoux Almshouses survived the Chantry Commissioners' inspection, possibly because its founder was a lay person and because it had no chapel within the building.[19]

Poverty after the Reformation

The Protestant view of poverty was that only those who were 'impotent' or victims of circumstance were truly poor and should receive alms while a growing sense of respectability marginalised those seen as undeserving.[20] Charitable endowments were again slow to make good the losses of the Dissolution, and benefactors favoured the deserving poor by founding almshouses or providing relief in the form of clothing, food, fuel or money for those at home rather than providing for the 'undeserving'.[21]

Early parish relief had generally been funded through church collections and, in some towns, a poor relief fund. By the beginning of the sixteenth century, many parishes and towns had already developed church or town 'stocks' of money, land, property and animals with which to provide help to the poor by means of loans or gifts. Attempts to legislate for the giving of alms for the common good rather than to the individual failed in the 1530s. Nevertheless by the 1550s the practice had developed in London of charitable bequests being controlled by bodies of governors of certain institutions, members of the élite, but separate from the civic administration.[22]

From 1572 magistrates were legally empowered to appoint overseers of the poor and impose compulsory tax collections.[23] Then the law began to tighten the traditional acceptance of family responsibility for relatives. In 1601 lineal kin, grandparents, parents and children, became legally responsible for supporting each other under the Poor Relief Act. In reality, adult children with their own families were

---

18 Bailey, *Almshouses*, pp. 81-83.
19 J. M. Gibson, *The Walthamstow Charities: Caring for the Poor 1500-2000*, (Chichester, 2000) pp. 5-11.
20 Slack, *Poverty and Policy*, pp. 23-24.
21 Bailey, *Almshouses*, p. 83; Slack, *Poverty and Policy*, pp. 18-27, 164.
22 Slack, *Poverty and Policy*, pp. 117-120.
23 K. Wrightson, *Earthly Necessities: Economic Lives in Early Modern Britain, 1470-1750*, (London, 2002) p. 215; Goose and Moden, *Doughty's Hospital*, p. 11; Howson, *Social and Architectural History*, p. 31.

often unable to accommodate elderly parents, who had to resort to parish help. Those who lived in the vicinity of an almshouse were fortunate if there was a vacancy when they needed it and if they met the selection criteria. Both location and criteria varied considerably since they were determined by private charity and often by the whim of individuals.[24] It has been estimated that approximately ten per cent of English parishes benefited from almshouse provision by 1660, still mostly to be found in the towns.[25]

Almshouses after the Dissolution

A positive effect of the Dissolution had been the widening of the location of almshouses as lay founders increasingly made provision in small towns and villages with which they had a connection. These were almost exclusively for local elderly residents who had fallen upon hard times after a lifetime of work.[26] Examples from the late-sixteenth century include Waldron's Almshouses at Tiverton, Devon founded in 1579, and Frieston's Hospital, dating from 1595, in the village of Kirkthorpe in Yorkshire. John Waldron was a wealthy merchant who provided a weekly allowance, an annual amount for milk and an annual monetary gift for each of the eight poor, aged almsmen.[27] John Frieston, Esq. provided a single storey building of seven rooms with a central area or hall, lit from above, and a garden. It accommodated seven men supported by a pension, milk and produce.[28]

Apart from the Civil War period (1642-51), almshouse foundation flourished during the seventeenth century. The legal process had become more accessible through the courts, rather than by royal licence or Act of Parliament as previously, and successful tradesmen increasingly demonstrated their philanthropy through endowment of almshouses. One such was William Cleave, alderman and resident of Kingston and liveryman of the Haberdasher's Company, who bequeathed land and money to provide accommodation for six poor men and six poor women. His row of twelve two-storey terraced cottages with a central hall for shared activities was completed in 1688.[29] A more modest row of single-storey brick cottages for six poor widows was founded and endowed in Berkhampstead in 1684 by John Sayer, a cook for Charles II, friend of Samuel Pepys and a prominent citizen of the town.[30] The row, with the central area dedicated to various purposes, was to become a common building plan.

24 Slack, *Poverty and Policy*, pp. 84-85.
25 Goose and Moden, *Doughty's Hospital*, p. 14.
26 Bailey, *Almshouses*, p. 90; M. K. McIntosh, 'Local responses to the poor in late medieval and Tudor England', *Continuity and Change*, (1988) Vol. III, (2), p. 220.
27 Howson, *Social and Architectural History*, p. 34.
28 H. Caffrey, *Almshouses in the West Riding of Yorkshire, 1600-1900*, (Kings Lynn, 2006) p. 86.
29 Kingston United Charities, *Cleaves Almshouses: Our History*, http://e-voice.org.uk/ kingstonunitedcharities/our-history/ Accessed 04 October 2012; Howson, *Social and Architectural History*, p. 142.
30 Howson, *Social and Architectural History*, p. 122; Bailey, *Almshouses*, p. 128; *Berkhampstead Heritage Walk; a Glimpse of Our History*, URL http://www.berkhamsted.gov.uk/download/ Heritage%20Leaflet.pdf. Accessed 04 October 2012

During the seventeenth and eighteenth centuries the cost of parish relief was escalating rapidly, a matter of great concern to parish ratepayers and causing discord amongst the vestry members whose task it was to set the local rate. Disputes, appeals, concealment and evasion were widespread.[31] Against this background almshouse foundation continued on a more modest scale throughout the eighteenth century, although many reflected the elegance of the period. In 1721 a successful Yorkshire timber merchant, Richard Fountaine, erected a stylish hospital comprising only six units, but allegedly designed by Vanbrugh who was working there at the time. In contrast, Mary Lowther's Hospital near Pontefract, founded in 1741, was a modest row of single-storey almshouses.[32]

The Victorian period saw a revival in almshouse foundation and Howson reports that about thirty per cent of almshouses surviving today had been built during Victoria's reign. Historically, there had been a number of scandals relating to the misuse of charitable funds in some of the older almshouses, hospitals and other establishments. The *Statute of Charitable Uses* (1601) had defined the nature of a charity and a body of Charity Commissioners had been appointed prior to Victoria's accession to systematically investigate the conduct of such institutions. Corruption was found in the management of some charitable provision, including almshouses, resulting in the establishment of the Charities Commission in 1855. The earlier Commissioners' Reports provide much information about almshouses in existence in the nineteenth century and present-day almshouses are administered in accordance with the scheme later set up by the Commission.[33]

As in the eighteenth century Victorian almshouses tended, with some exceptions, to be modest and possibly less elegant architecturally. They were more often small single-storey units built in groups of between four and twelve, some with a tiny chapel, many in villages. Some, like those founded by Mrs Esther Greenwood near Camden Road in London, blend in with other houses in the locality. Others were more distinctive. Some conscientious industrialists established model villages for their workers, as at Sir Titus Salt's model village of Saltaire, started in 1853, which included forty-five almshouses in the style of Italian villas with parlour, bedroom and pantry. Mill workers had priority. A few wealthy manufacturers, such as the Quaker Cadbury brothers, followed suit. The almshouses in their model village at Bourneville (1879) clustered around the traditional quadrangle.[34]

Other benefactors, both individual and institutional, favoured specific groups as recipients of their charity. In Hackney in 1812 Samuel Robinson provided twelve almshouses for 'widows of Dissenting ministers professing Calvinistic doctrines'.[35] In Whitby Sir George Gilbert Scott, an architect, designed the Seamen's Houses in 1842

---

31 Howson, *Social and Architectural History*, pp. 55-56; S. Hindle, *On the Parish? The Micropolitics of Poor Relief in Rural England, c.1550-1750* (Oxford, 2004) pp. 365-378.
32 Howson, *Social and Architectural History*, pp. 56, 59.
33 Howson, *Social and Architectural History*, pp. 59, 61-64.
34 Howson, *Social and Architectural History*, pp. 59, 65-68.
35 Bailey, *Almshouses*, pp. 30, 38, 129-130, 158.

and in Bradford in 1856 the Tradesmens' Homes Charity built accommodation for impoverished retired tradesmen and their families.[36]

Almshouse foundation declined in the twentieth century as the Poor Law was replaced by the welfare state. Many smaller foundations have been discontinued and the almshouse buildings are now in private ownership. Some trustees continue to manage individual foundations and their endowments while in other cases funds are managed collectively by municipal charities. The National Association of Almshouses provides an umbrella organisation representing their interests.[37]

For almost six centuries, the almshouse at Sherborne has survived changing attitudes and belief, fluctuations in national and local economic prosperity and the increasing involvement of the state in local affairs and provision for the poor. It was founded at a time when charity had been rapidly changing from the monasteries' open giving to those in need to the increasingly prescriptive nature of individual benevolence. It was also a time when the secure foundation of an almshouse was an expensive matter of legal complexity. With qualification from other records, the Almshouse Register will show how financial security and a sound basis for administration was established by the brethren, enabling the almshouse to weather times of crisis and to take a significant role in the life of the town.

Almshouses in Dorset

Over forty almshouses have been identified as existing in Dorset between the Middle Ages and the early-twentieth century. Together they form a microcosm of the national picture in terms of variety of founders, architecture, purpose and groups of residents.[38] Sherborne Almshouse is not the oldest in the county. The *Victoria County History of Dorset* indicates that at least ten mediaeval hospitals had been established in or before the thirteenth and fourteenth centuries. Of these, two have survived. Both were lazar hospitals and both were originally sited well outside their nearby towns, as was usual with hospitals for lepers. St Margaret and St Anthony's Hospital at Wimborne, known now as St Margaret's, was probably founded in the reign of King John (1167-1216) according to deeds found in the chapel.[39] Buildings on the site, taking the form of a cluster of small houses and an adjacent chapel with a cottage attached, are still used as almshouses today. Extensive records have survived in collection D/SMS at Dorset History Centre and await research. The other, St Mary Magdalen's Hospital, a name commonly used for leper hospitals, was founded at Allington near Bridport before 1240 and although the foundation has continued to the present day, it is not certain whether

---

36 Howson, *Social and Architectural History*, p. 67.
37 Howson, *Social and Architectural History*, p. 72.
38 Short descriptions of most of these almshouses can be found in E. O. Cockburn, *The Almshouses of Dorset*, (Dorchester, 1970).
39 W. Page (ed.), *A History of the County of Dorset*, (1908) Vol. II, pp. 106-107.

the modern almshouse accommodation is on the original site.[40]

In common with the national picture there are no known new foundations in Dorset following the Black Death of the fourteenth century and only two in the fifteenth. The first, St George's Almshouses in Poole, dating from the reign of Henry V (1413-1422), is attributed to the Guild of St George, a religious fraternity. Surviving the Dissolution, it passed first to the Crown in 1547 and then to the Corporation of Poole in 1550.[41] With some modifications the building still functions as an almshouse. The second, although not generally known as a guild almshouse, is the Hospital of St John the Baptist and St John the Evangelist at Sherborne, dating from 1437. The Almshouse Register hints at the presence of a religious guild providing early financial support and this is confirmed in the accounts of 1446-7.[42] As will be seen, Sherborne Almshouse was typical of its time, a bede house in all but name, but it too survived the religious upheaval of the fifteenth century.

New foundations followed in Dorset until the twentieth century. Reputedly founded by the Mayor of Lyme Regis in 1548, Tudbold's Almshouse for four aged people had two rooms below and two above, accessed by outside staircases. It appears to have been managed by parish officers. The almshouse at Corfe Castle was in existence before 1621 and originally housed six poor people on two floors, also accessed by an outside staircase which remains in place today. This almshouse was not properly endowed and the management fell to the churchwardens, to whom the nineteenth-century Charity Commissioners suggested that priority should be given to the 'second poor' so as not to encourage paupers.[43] This almshouse is still used for its original purpose.

The seventeenth century also saw the establishment of four different types of almshouse in Dorset. At Beaminster in 1627, Sir John Strode founded the small single-storey God's House which was built in the churchyard with easy access to the church. With three 'tenements' it accommodated six poor people to be selected by Sir John's heirs. Generally these were 'distressed people of the better class' who had not received parish relief.[44] In Blandford, Baron Ryves of nearby Damory Court endowed a long single-storey almshouse of ten rooms for ten poor single people who were independent of parish relief. Still in use, having survived the Blandford fire of 1731, this building has a central gable displaying the coat of arms of the Ryves family and an inscription concerning its completion in 1683.[45] The third Dorset example relates to the Daniel Taylor Almshouse in Bridport, founded in 1695. Daniel Taylor was a merchant whose Quaker belief of valuing all people equally would have influenced his decision to give by indenture, during his lifetime, a dwelling house to be converted

40 Page, (ed), *A History of the County of Dorset*, Vol. II, pp. 98-100.
41 Cockburn, *Almshouses of Dorset*, pp. 36-37; Plaque on building.
42 The Dorset History Centre (hereafter DHC) D/SHA/A19.
43 Charity Commissioners Reports: *The County of Dorset*, (London, 1895) pp. 123, 129.
44 Charity Commissioners Reports, *Dorset*, p.260.
45 Cockburn, *Almshouses of Dorset*, p. 11; J. Hutchins, *The History and Antiquities of the County of Dorset*, Vol. I, (Wakefield, 1973) p. 238).

to an almshouse. The picturesque building faces onto a narrow open-ended courtyard with the Meeting House opposite and the Quaker cemetery to the rear. The almshouse had ten apartments, most capable of accommodating couples, who were to be from Bridport, aged, needy and deserving. The almshouse is still managed by the Daniel Taylor Trust.[46] Then, at Pamphill, near Wimborne, a long row of almshouses with a school in the centre, a form commonly used elsewhere, was endowed in 1695 by will of Roger Gillingham. Like many other founders Roger Gillingham, treasurer of the Middle Temple in London, remembered his birthplace when he died. Four men were to occupy the cottages on the left side of the school and four women on the right. All were to be, and to remain, single or widowed. Four were to be from the tything in which the founder was born and the others from nearby.[47]

Village almshouses built by local squires featured in Dorset in the nineteenth century, at Witchampton built in 1831 by H. C. Sturt, MP and at Frampton in 1868 by R. B. Sheridan and his wife, for example.[48] The Frampton almshouses are now in private ownership but still have religious texts carved in stone on the gable ends. Each of the four cottages originally had a verse from a hymn over the fireplace but now only two remain.[49] Dorset also had its own model village, including seven almshouses. Georgina Talbot and her sister, daughters of a baronet, were shocked at the rural poverty they found among working families when they moved from London. Georgina acquired land and created what was intended to be a self-supporting village comprising farms and smallholdings together with the almshouses, a school and a church. The criteria for admission to the almshouses were specific. The provision was intended for widowed or single agricultural labourers, gardeners or poor mechanics earning less that £1 per week and aged over 65, or married couples who must be of any Protestant denomination. Clear rules were to be followed.[50] At the edge of Hazelbury Bryan churchyard, the Reverend Henry Walter founded a row of almshouses for widows in 1842. A lengthy poem, 'Church-Yard Thoughts' based on Matthew, Ch. 17, v. 4, is inscribed on the wall facing the churchyard. The house is now in private ownership.

Finally, master mariner, Captain Nicholas Marder endowed five houses in Lyme Regis for retired men who had been seamen or fishermen. They were to have been of good character during thirty years of employment. Endowed in 1899 these apartments on two floors were completed by 1903. Two years later, in 1905, Owen Carter of the Quaker tile manufacturing company, later to become Poole Pottery, built homes in the town for ten former employees.

Sherborne Almshouse is the least altered of Dorset's ancient almshouses continuing in its original building, changed only by sympathetic nineteenth-century

46 Cockburn, *Almshouses of Dorset*, p.18.
47 DHC: PE/WM/CH/1/1/1; Charity Commissioners Reports, *Dorset*, p. 161; Cockburn, *Almshouses of Dorset*, p. 34.
48 Kelly's Directory of Dorsetshire, 1880.
49 Information from owners, Peter and Audrey Cox.
50 M. Gillett, *Talbot Village: a Unique Village in Dorset 1850-1989*, (Bournemouth, 1989), p.19.

extension and some moderation of the rules. It is a picturesque building and a feature of the environment of the Abbey.

Sherborne Almshouse and its place in history

Sherborne is a small market town in north Dorset. It stands on an ancient Saxon settlement and grew up around the abbey, which was founded in the eighth century AD. With a twelfth-century castle intended as a residence, a sizeable monastery and its location on the main road to London and Exeter, the town was well placed to profit from trade and services. Sherborne must have been a bustling place by the fourteenth century, when agriculture and cloth making required mills for corn and for fulling or compacting cloth for the cloth trade, respectively. Quarries were also being worked to extract the attractive stone seen today in many of the older buildings.[51] One of these, the almshouse, was founded in 1437 by letters patent from King Henry VI, a process which Slack described as 'cumbersome and expensive' and which involved days of travel to and from London, but the initiative was supported by a strong popular movement within the town.[52] The letters patent granted a licence of special significance, not only for the almshouse and its residents but also for the town, because of the role it enabled the almshouse to develop in relation to a wider range of poor townspeople than those who were to become its residents.

Sherborne has its place in the early evolution of the almshouse. A monastic charitable establishment was mentioned in close rolls of January 1222-3 concerning building works at Sherborne Castle. Authorising the purchase of materials, Henry III included an order for twenty timbers to be supplied for Brother John's *domus elemosinarie*. Whether this building was, like Lanfranc's at Canterbury, a free-standing house or part of the monastery, and the dates of its existence, are unknown.[53] Nor is it known whether it provided only for elderly monks or included members of the community. However, this record does introduce in Dorset, in the Latin form, the word later to appear in the English language as 'almshouse'.

Next, in 1406 a chaplain named William Dodill had given and endowed a 'messuage' in Sherborne 'for the perpetual hospitality of the poor'. He had appointed three clerical trustees. A significant step in Sherborne's history was taken when one of those trustees died, around 1418, and the remaining two decided to appoint nineteen local men as well as the vicar of All Hallows and the two churchwardens to share their responsibility. The resulting covenant in 1419 expressed the intention to honour God and included the wider brief of supporting the poor as well as those accommodated in Dodill's almshouse. Accounts survive for eleven years from 1425, showing twelve

---

51 R. C. Hays, *Records of Early English Drama – Dorset*, (Toronto, 1999) pp. 23-25.
52 Slack, *Poverty and Policy*, p. 127.
53 Fowler, *Mediaeval Sherborne*, p. 232.

residents (seven men and five women) in Dodill's messuage, the location of which is no longer known.[54]

The early part of the fifteenth century was a turbulent time in Sherborne's history. The townspeople had traditionally worshipped in the nave of the abbey church. However, discord had begun to develop between the people and the monks. As a result parishioners attended services in a small chapel, All Hallows, attached to the west end of the abbey while the monks used the abbey itself. Things eventually reached crisis point when the monks narrowed the door connecting All Hallows with the Abbey, where all baptisms still took place. In consequence the townspeople erected their own baptismal font in their chapel. A suit in the bishop's court brought a judgement intending reconciliation but quarrels continued until, allegedly, in 1436 townsmen rebelled and sent a flaming arrow into the roof of the Abbey Church causing much destruction. Parishioners had to contribute to its re-building although, at that time, All Hallows became an independent parish church.[55] Against this background, plans for a new community almshouse in Sherborne had been developing.

The Foundation

The Almshouse was, more correctly, a re-foundation in 1437 of Dodill's earlier almshouse in which a significant management group, numbering twenty-four, had overseen the almshouse business. This inspired combination of old and new trustees, clergy and churchwardens had brought together the 'old school' with links to the 1406 foundation, the parish church and a strong body of lay people. The feoffees had managed the land holdings and passed the profits to the vicar and churchwardens to maintain the almshouse and almsfolk. The group had appointed new feoffees, as necessary, and each had sworn an oath committing themselves to the terms of the covenant.[56] Almost twenty years later, this strong group was still in place to develop plans for new almshouse premises.

The new almshouse was dedicated to St John the Baptist and St John the Evangelist. It was formally established under a royal licence that was granted in July 1437 by Henry VI and named five founders. These were Robert Neville, Bishop of Sarum; Sir Humphrey Stafford, knight, lord of Hooke; Margaret Goffe, widow, Lady of Langton Long Blandford; John Fauntleroy, gentleman; and John Baret, gentleman. There was strong community support for this project, including a substantial financial contribution raised by house-to-house collection.

The almshouse was to be under the control of twenty brethren, who were to elect annually one of themselves as Master and to choose a new brother soon after each vacancy arose. The king's licence incorporated this group, enabling them to act as a body in legal matters and to acquire and hold land to a certain value.[57] Thus the brethren of Sherborne Almshouse became a more powerful group than the old

54 Fowler, *Mediaeval Sherborne*, p. 232.
55 Hays, *Early English Drama*, pp. 23-25.
56 Fowler, *Mediaeval Sherborne*, pp. 232-237.
57 Fowler, *Mediaeval Sherborne*, pp. 238-242.

one had been. This was rather different from the many fifteenth-century almshouses which 'were founded in towns by citizens and burgesses, who put them under the government of municipal corporations, city companies, or local lay feoffees'.[58] Mediaeval and Tudor boroughs were incorporated 'with a commonality of burgesses, aldermen or freemen… privileged groups…which held themselves responsible to the community at large'.[59] The almshouse management body at Sherborne was itself a corporation. Since Sherborne was not a borough there was no municipal corporation and the brethren were thus the most important secular body in the town.

Funding for the almshouse building at Sherborne came from three sources. Collectively, the founders endowed it with £40, a property in Sherborne and gifts of timber for the building. In addition, the wife of one founder gave a further £5. The town collection raised £41 13s.10d. Donations ranged from 4d. to 20s., with two exceptional payments of 40s. and 100s., or £2 and £5 respectively. Friends living outside Sherborne also made contributions. Altogether over £80 was raised for the building fund.[60]

Sherborne Almshouse benefited from a 'Fraternity of the House', a religious guild which had been established by 1443-4.[61] Guilds were often related to craft trades, comprising members of those trades and providing almshouses for the benefit of people belonging to those trades.[62] The guild at Sherborne seems to have been formed entirely on a religious basis and had as members both men and women. Quoting from early almshouse account rolls, Fowler noted that John and Margaret Branche gave £5 in 1476-7 'to be admitted as participants in the prayers of the brotherhood of the almshouse', only one of several examples which include donors living some distance from the town.[63] Initial contributions from the guild undoubtedly went to the building fund, but membership continued possibly until the last quarter of the sixteenth century, somehow surviving the Dissolution. Jasper Fridlock, master of the almshouse, recorded in his accounts for 1591 a donation by Elizabeth Byshoppe, recent widow of Laurence Byshoppe, formerly Master of the Almshouse, Churchwarden and Governor of the School. Elizabeth gave five shillings 'to be prayed for whilst she leveth in this world'.[64] Such donations would have contributed to the upkeep of the almshouse, if only in respect of the chapel.

The building
The almshouse is to be found in Half Moon Street, close to the Abbey. The inventory taken by the Royal Commission on Historical Monuments in 1952 described it as

58 Orme and Webster, *The English Hospital*, p. 142.
59 J. West, *Town Records*, (Chichester, 1983) p. 166.
60 Fowler, *Mediaeval Sherborne*, p. 240.
61 Fowler, *Mediaeval Sherborne*, p. 244.
62 R. M. Clay, *The Mediaeval Hospitals of England*, (London, 1909) p. 18.
63 Fowler, *Mediaeval Sherborne*, pp. 244-245, 357.
64 Fowler, *Mediaeval Sherborne*, pp. 244-245, 357; DHC: D/SHA/D124.

An unusually complete example of a 15th-century almshouse on a normal plan following that of the monastic infirmary; the chancel forms the chapel and the nave the hall of the establishment, the latter commonly containing the cubicles of the inmates.[65]

Thus Sherborne Almshouse was built in the church-like form of a mediaeval hospital hall with an open entry to a chapel at the east end, a plan sometimes used in earlier almshouses.[66] As was customary, funding was initially spent on constructing the chapel, completed in 1442, and the almshouse accommodation followed afterwards. With donors mindful of the teaching of the Catholic Church that they should ensure their place in heaven, the building of the chapel was of supreme importance so that they could be remembered in the prayers of the beneficiaries.[67]

A plan of Sherborne Almshouse shows the living accommodation to have been on two floors with access to the upper floor by an external staircase. The foundation deed had decreed that

every of the said sixteen poor men and women ... shall have always ... a bed and a bed place by himself and that the men harbour of a night by themselves, and that there be a reasonable and sufficient closure between them.[68]

Gender segregation was not unusual and at Sherborne the two floors facilitated this. Privacy had also become important by the fifteenth century and individual sleeping quarters in the almshouse were cubicles formed by wooden partitions.[69] A gallery on the upper floor enabled the residents accommodated there to participate in services without going downstairs.[70]

Until the residential part of the building at Sherborne was completed in 1448 Dodill's almshouse continued to care for its residents. Richard Rochell, who had kept Dodill's accounts, closed them in 1437 and immediately continued with keeping the *interim* accounts for the new building.[71] He was also to become the first master of the new almshouse.[72]

The original parts of the building are still in use today and little changed, although the accommodation has been enlarged sympathetically by nineteenth-century extensions. Opening onto Trendle Street, the original main entrance to the chapel remains with its pointed arch flanked by niches, believed to have once held

---

65 Royal Commission on Historical Monuments, *An Inventory of the Historical Monuments in the County of Dorset: West Dorset*. (London, 1952) Vol. I, p. 212.
66 Clay, *Mediaeval Hospitals*, p. 114.
67 Bailey, *Almshouses*, p. 25.
68 Fowler, *Mediaeval Sherborne*, pp. 256-257.
69 Orme and Webster, *The English Hospital*, pp. 89, 91; Fowler, *Mediaeval Sherborne*, p. 256.
70 Howson, *Social and Architectural History*, p. 83.
71 Fowler, *Mediaeval Sherborne*, pp. 232-234.
72 Fowler, *Mediaeval Sherborne*, pp. 238-239.

statuettes of St John the Baptist and St John the Evangelist. This was the main entrance until the improvements of 1866.[73] The new entrance is in an attractive courtyard facing east along Half Moon Street.

The design of the almshouse closely resembled that of a bedehouse, like Chichele's, at Higham Ferrars in Northamptonshire. Founded in 1425, that too had an infirmary hall, sub-divided by wooden partitions and opening into a chapel at the east end. Unlike Sherborne Almshouse it had no upper floor. Amongst other rules, residents of Chichele's were to stand in the doorways of their cubicles to take part in evensong each day. This building survives, although no longer used for its original purpose.[74]

Sherborne almshouse continued in its original form until the nineteenth century. Having initially housed sixteen residents, then eighteen with the help of two sixteenth-century benefactions, by 1851 the almshouse had increased the number to twenty-four without any apparent increase in residential accommodation other than possible use of a neighbouring cottage.[75] In December 1850 the brethren had decided to appoint a committee to examine the state of the buildings and to report on the management of the house and the diet and clothing of the almspeople. Mr. W. Short of Sherborne was to make a ground plan of the building.[76] More than a decade later, when the kitchen block was 'seriously dilapidated' significant private benevolence secured the expansion of the almshouse.[77] James Short of Sherborne bequeathed £3,814 14s. on his death in 1865. A year later, William Naish Allford, a serving brother of the almshouse, gave several nearby houses in the year of his death. Together these legacies enabled a major extension, increasing sleeping and living accommodation and providing a new kitchen, office facilities, a boardroom, a new bell turret to replace the former bell canopy and a cloistered courtyard with a new entrance door on the east side.[78] The number of residents then increased to twenty-seven.

With contrasting fortune, in nearby Yeovil in Somerset, Woborne's Almshouse for twelve poor people was founded by letters patent in 1477 and it too was licensed to acquire land to a certain value. It was also supported by a religious fraternity and had similar expectations of its residents. However, its founders failed to establish a management group as robust as that at Sherborne. The *custos*, or guardian, and two wardens were to meet annually with 'five or seven of the most honest and discrete men of the parish of Yeovil' to elect a new custos and wardens and to consider the accounts of the resigning custos. Any almshouse vacancies were also filled at this meeting.

---

73 C. H. Mayo, *An Historic Guide to the Almshouse of St John the Baptist and St John the Evangelist, Sherborne*, (Oxford, 1933) p. 72; National Monuments Record: *Images of England*, No. 103816 (1950), URL: www.imagesofengland.org.uk Accessed 15 November 2012; W. B. Wildman, *A Short History of Sherborne from 705 AD*, (Sherborne, 1902) p. 178.
74 Bailey, *Almshouses*, p. 95; Howson, *Social and Architectural History*, p. 79.
75 1851 Census, Sherborne, HO 107: Piece: 1859; Folio: 285; Pages: 33-34.
76 DHC: D/SHA/D4.
77 Hutchins, *The History and Antiquities*, p. 296.
78 Mayo, *An Historic Guide to the Almshouse*, p. 72.

The early nineteenth-century Charity Commissioners found several anomalies in the appointments of custos and wardens, variable numbers of vacancies due to the system of annual admission and concerns about administration of the estate that could not be confirmed because records had not survived.[79] By mid-century the building was dilapidated and was replaced elsewhere in the town in 1860. Sherborne's secure foundation established it on a more continuous and enduring basis as will be seen in the records.

The early years of Sherborne Almshouse

The first records transcribed from the Sherborne Register detail the arrangements for the management of the almshouse. The building was ready for business in 1448.[80] The doors would have opened under the management of the twenty brethren stipulated in the licence of Henry VI and the first residents would have included the survivors of Dodill's almshouse who had been maintained there until the new accommodation was ready. A perpetual chaplain, John Carpenter, had also been appointed. The founders had laid down statutes for the governance of the almshouse and had appointed the requisite number of brethren, listing their names, and identifying also the first almshouse residents. Of the first master and brethren of the almshouse at least four had been feoffees in Dodill's almshouse in 1419, providing some continuity.[81] All brethren were to be resident in the town when they were elected and, on the death of one of them, another should be elected within four weeks.[82] On accepting the position, a new brother had to swear an oath promising to serve the Almshouse faithfully and not to disclose its affairs to others.[83] After the Reformation, when the Acts of Supremacy of 1534 and 1559 were in force, as people taking public office the brethren had also to swear allegiance to the monarch as head of the Church of England. Two later Acts similarly demanded additional oaths. The Test Act of 1672 required allegiance and supremacy and effectively barred Catholics from public office and in 1695, in the reign of William III, the Act of Association required an oath vowing to protect the King's person and government.[84] Failure of any individual to take these oaths meant his election as a brother would be rescinded. This happened with Robert Avoke in 1712 who then later complied.[85] Arrangements were made to assist with an allowance to any of the brethren who might become impoverished for

---

79 J. Wade (ed), *An Account of Public Charities in England and Wales*, (London, 1828) pp. 717-721. URL: http://books.google.co.uk/books?id=7hooAQAAMAAJ&pg=PA718&lpg=PA718&dq=yeovil+almshouses+okeford&source=bl&ots=HlG5m8Uo65&sig=uYqS6Vmt_Aayn6sMcEo2oG7n37g&hl=en&sa=X&ei=l65dUZO6LeGq4ASVqoGYBQ&ved=oCDUQ6AEwAQ#v=onepage&q=yeovil%20almshouses%20okeford&f=false Accessed 15 April 2013. Thanks to June Palmer for this reference.
80 Mayo, *An Historic Guide to the Almshouse*, p. 63.
81 Fowler, *Mediaeval Sherborne*, p. 235.
82 DHC: D/SHA/D24.
83 DHC: D/SHA/D24.
84 M. Herber, *Ancestral Trails*, (Stroud, 2004) p. 530.
85 DHC: D/SHA/D24.

age or health-related reasons and also to help their widows, should it be necessary. In making decisions agreement was to be reached by majority vote and, in the event of no majority, the matter was to be decided by the 'most worthy' brethren.

Later decisions or orders made by the brethren further delineated their behaviour. The records, featuring in the transcription, detail how brethren were to be summoned to meetings. Failure to justify non-attendance would incur a fine or, on default, dismissal. The seating arrangement at meetings was also determined, as were the protocols for raising issues at meetings and the order in which brethren might contribute to debate. Unacceptable conduct at meetings was outlined and penalties defined. In 1602, rules were laid down as to the handling of money on behalf of the almshouse and in 1603 it was decreed that any brother chosen as master who refused to take office would have to pay a fine to the 'poor of this house'. Failure to pay that, or any other fine, would mean expulsion. The rules were adjusted at board meetings as need arose. A recent study of 131 English almshouses, excluding Sherborne, found rules for brethren or trustees in only ten.[86]

The brethren were responsible for appointing the successive chaplains to care for the souls of the almspeople and a housewife to care for their physical needs. In the absence of the master and brethren, who were never resident in the almshouse, responsibility for the behaviour of residents was given to one of their number, chosen by them, and known as the 'prior'. The brethren had the power to dismiss, or in the case of the prior demote, any appointee who was unsatisfactory.

The effects of the Reformation and Dissolution

One of the results of this religious disruption was the sudden loss of the greater proportion of the country's hospitals and almshouses with religious-based or ecclesiastical foundations. Sherborne Almshouse survived for several possible reasons. It was considered to have been founded by the King, due to Henry VI's licence; it was managed by a large body of lay people; and its foundation had been strongly supported by the townspeople and their financial contribution.

After the Dissolution Sir John Horsey, a former steward of the monastery, bought Sherborne Abbey, known as St Mary's Church, in the 1530s. He in turn sold it to the townspeople in 1540 and the 'people's church', All Hallows, was then demolished. Sir John did well out of the Dissolution and managed to appropriate the revenue from landholdings, known as the prebend, which had previously been used to support the abbot and others, including the vicar. With the loss of this funding, the parish found it impossible to appoint clergy of consequence, who might have been more influential in the community, possibly leaving more power with the churchwardens than they would have had otherwise.[87] The Chantries Act of 1547 brought another threat to the almshouse and its chapel, in which the almspeople had been required

86 A. Blaydon, 'Almshouse Rules and Regulations for Trustees and Almspeople with particular reference to Surrey', Chapter 9, in N. Goose, H. Caffrey and A. Langley, (eds), *New Perspectives in British Almshouse History, 1400-1914* (provisional title), (forthcoming 2014).
87 Hays, *Early English Drama*, p. 24; Fowler, *Mediaeval Sherborne*, pp. 318-325.

to pray for the souls of the founders. However, after a visit by the Commissioners a Chantry Certificate was issued and the almshouse was allowed to survive.[88] Another event, significant for the town, was to happen around this time.

The Free Grammar School
Like the almshouse, the grammar school was licensed by the monarch in 1550 after 'the humble petition of the inhabitants'. To be known as 'The Free Grammar School of King Edward the Sixth' it was to follow the Sherborne Almshouse pattern of appointing twenty 'men of discretion and integrity' as governors who were to constitute a new and distinct corporation, separate to that of the almshouse.[89] There were now two corporations in the town, together requiring forty of the chief inhabitants to manage their affairs and, in a small town, potentially in competition with each other for the most suitable candidates. In reality, many individuals became members of both corporations which worked very closely together.

Administration of the Almshouse
From 1451, masters kept annual accounts or week books throughout the centuries. These survive, almost without exception, into the twentieth century at the Dorset History Centre with later records being held at the almshouse. In the early years, inventories of the almshouse were sometimes attached to these documents, particularly during the periods 1470-1506 and 1580-1599.[90] In the latter group, reference was made to the almspeople's 'chambers' and their contents.[91]

Most of the ongoing maintenance of building and residents came from income from land and property acquired by purchase, inheritance and investment. In 1448, the brethren of Sherborne Almshouse had been further licensed to acquire land accruing annually to a maximum of £33 6s. 8d. This enabled the acquisition of a considerable amount of property in and around Sherborne by 1454, almost doubling the rental income.[92] One of the transcribed records describes this property which included thirty-nine messuages or dwelling houses with outbuildings and land belonging to them; two tofts or homesteads and almost sixty acres of land of various kinds, all 'granted, demised…and confirmed…to have and to hold' to the master and brethren. Previous occupiers are named and the land was valued at £5 3s. 3d.[93]

An ongoing, if spasmodic, form of income came from the brethren themselves. On election, they committed themselves to a contribution of £5, which could be paid annually in instalments of one mark (13s. 4d.). Completion of payment was recorded

88   E. A. Fry, 'Dorset Chantries' Pt. 2, *Dorset Natural History and Antiquarian Field Club Proceedings*, (1907) Vol. XXVIII, pp. 12-25.
89   Fowler, *Mediaeval Sherborne*, p. 345.
90   DHC: D/SHA/A.
91   For example: DHC: D/SHA/A128, 1582-3; DHC: D/SHA/A141.
92   Fowler, *Mediaeval Sherborne*, p. 159.
93   DHC: D/SHA/D25.

in accounts.[94] Any fines incurred by brethren went towards maintenance of the house. The almshouse also received many bequests. In 1589, for example, Peter Game, a brother of the almshouse, and William Masters of Sherborne each gave £50 to fund respectively, in perpetuity, a place for one poor man and one poor woman in the almshouse, thereby increasing the number of residents. In 1610, William Wood, one time schoolmaster at the Free Grammar School, enfeoffed, or gave, land and premises to provide for the ongoing maintenance of 'two, three or four' almspeople.[95] Gifts and re-investment continued to expand the portfolio and its management comprised much of the regular business of the almshouse.

Until the end of the sixteenth century the brethren seem to have been content with the accounts and other individual official documents as a record of the business of the almshouse. Then, in 1591 the first registry books were purchased for both the almshouse and the school. According to Fowler, early entries recording meetings are in the same hand.[96] The separate master's account of 1610-11 makes reference to an accountant, who had remained in office for a second year and submitted only a draft, the reason being that this had been a time of pestilence in Sherborne and the audit had not taken place until January 1612.[97] Hutchins records mortality in the town being 299 during May to October 1611, with burials for the rest of the year not being more than eight in any one month, but the burial entries in the parish register suggest that the almspeople were not affected.[98]

Sherborne Almshouse encountered several periods of financial difficulty. The town would not have been alone in suffering hardship during the Civil War and that it did so is indicated in notes concerning admissions to the almshouse on 6 September 1647. Three new entrants were chosen on that date, two men and a woman. Joan Ponde, a widow, was financed by William Woods' gift for the perpetual funding of a place for one woman. It was recorded in the admissions register that she was to have a room which had been vacant for some years. Its former occupant, Mary Callow had been admitted in 1633 but there is no indication of when Mary died. The entry for one of the men listed his possessions, as was usual, but the other, Peter Freeman, was admitted

> upon the death of a poor man who died long since and in regard that the
> provisions for the maintenance of the poor people have been extraordinary dear
> and the rents abated by reason of the late wars none was chosen until this time.

The impact on Sherborne had been such that rents for properties must have been reduced or excused for a time to alleviate poverty of their tenants. The ensuing deficit in almshouse revenue was made good, or at least improved, by keeping two places vacant for some time rather than, or as well as, reducing funding for

94 Fowler, *Mediaeval Sherborne*, p. 245.
95 DHC: D/SHA/D24.
96 Fowler, *Mediaeval Sherborne*, pp. 251, 251n.
97 DHC: D/SHA/A181.
98 Hutchins, *The History and Antiquities*, p. 209: DHC: PE/SH/RE 1/1.

almspeople's maintenance. It was also noted in the entry that Peter Freeman brought 20s. in money, which may have favoured his selection. Less information has been found about the difficulty in 1788, when money for the maintenance of the almspeople was inadequate and funds from two other charities, Burt's estate and Foster's School Charity, were diverted to make up the deficit.[99]

In the nineteenth century it became standard to record in the admissions register the ages of new entrants to the almshouse, and of those whose places they took. An occasional slip of paper between folios shows that the descendants of Peter Game, who had provided one place for a man in perpetuity, put forward three names for the brethren's consideration when the place became vacant. George Penny, Henry Roberts and Barter Chaffey were proposed in August 1843, George Penny, aged 78, being selected. Barter Chaffey, aged 69, was selected in December of the same year but Henry Roberts had to wait until 1847 before he was admitted at the age of 71. Not all candidates were re-offered for selection, perhaps having died before the place next became vacant.

Both the admissions list for the almspeople and the list of elected brethren end in the 1860s before the expansion of the almshouse was completed. Spanning, as they do, almost three hundred years, these registers contain several hundred names of Sherborne residents.

Almshouse relationship with Church, School and Town

With numbers of brethren also being governors of the school, the almshouse did not operate in isolation. How far its involvement extended into the community has not yet been fully researched but the Almshouse Register provides preliminary information, supported by other sources.

Church

From its inception Sherborne Almshouse had links with the church. Consistently clergymen, including but not always vicars of Sherborne, were numbered amongst the brethren at least until the nineteenth century.[100] The first master was also a churchwarden and initial research has found other churchwardens also acting as brethren.

Chaplains to the almshouse were appointed by the brethren. The position in the earlier years was filled by former clerics of the monastery and, from 1563-73, by headmasters of the School. After a gap until 1599 with no record of the chaplain, it became the custom for the vicar of Sherborne to assume that responsibility.[101]

School

The school and the almshouse lie in close proximity. From the school foundation in 1550 to the end of the sixteenth century, at least fourteen men were members of the

---

99 DHC: D/SHA/D2.
100 DHC: D/SHA/D24.
101 Fowler, Mediaeval Sherborne, p. 246.

boards of both institutions; at least four of those were also, or had been, churchwardens; and another thirteen had been both school governors and churchwardens.[102] Primary sources, either in themselves or linked with each other, confirm that the practice of holding office in both institutions continued.[103] Fowler suggests that the board meetings of the two institutions would follow one another without members 'even leaving their seats'.[104] This may explain how the accounts for the school for the period 1723-1802 and a plan of the school appear in the almshouse collection at the Dorset History Centre.[105] Clearly the storage of these school records at the almshouse was no error, for a loose note found in one of the almshouse books records that a school minute book had been taken from the almshouse 'for the purpose of writing up the record'.[106] Tenure of the two roles by individuals continued into the nineteenth century, the appointment of Peter Batson being an example. Mr Batson, a Sherborne attorney, was elected as a brother of the almshouse in 1789 and appointed as a governor of the school the following year. He continued to serve in both capacities until his death in 1845, at the age of 98, and within that period had served as master of the almshouse three times.[107] Not until 1869 did the constitution of the school change, reducing the number of governors and ending the close connection with the almshouse.[108]

Town

By the 1550s Sherborne was a thriving market centre. Until 1564 the profits from the regular fairs and markets had gone to the church but in that year Bishop Jewel leased them to Hugh Meer, the collector of his rents, and his sons for three lives. Meer, described as 'gent' in 1577-8, was a governor of the school and brother of the almshouse. When he died in 1582 the lease for the fairs and markets passed to the governors and brethren to be administered by them for the benefit of the town rather than for either of the institutions. This meant that both brethren and governors assumed wider responsibilities within the town, the profits from the markets being used for paving the streets, or nursing and burying those affected by pestilence in the town, for example.[109]

With its already long experience of administering bequests of land and safeguarding sums of money, it is perhaps not surprising that the almshouse became the focus for managing many legacies intended to be used for the benefit of the poor in Sherborne. Wildmans' record of a 'printed tablet in the boardroom' recording

---

102 Compilation of data from: Almshouse Registers DHC: D/SHA/D24, DHC: S.235: A1/1 and Fowler, *Mediaeval Sherborne.*
103 DHC: D/SHA/D28; DHC: D/SHA/D24.
104 Fowler, *Mediaeval Sherborne*, p. 346.
105 DHC: D/SHA/A1108.
106 DHC: D/SHA/D2.
107 DHC: D/SHA/D24; information from Rachell Hassall.
108 A. B. Gourlay, *A History of Sherborne School*, (Sherborne, 1971) p. 160.
109 Fowler, *Mediaeval Sherborne*, pp. 358, 366, 403-404.

bequests included £10 given in 1589 by Sir John Horsey 'out of the prebend of Sherborne for the remainder of his term to be employed "in stock to set on work" and to maintain the poor'.[110] In the same year, 'William Knoyle, gent, left £46.13s.4d. to be employed in loans' and a century later, in 1689, 'David Llewellen gave £10 to remain in stock for ever to be employed for the benefit of the poor.' The boardroom list also stated that in 1624 John Foster, a brother of the almshouse and governor of the school, bequeathed £200 to the master and brethren 'for the benefit of the poor as stock for ever, to be used as the master and brethren shall decide'. The intention in his will was that the money should be lent 'upon good security to the poor inhabitants of the town of Sherborne and so to be continued as a stock forever or used for their benefit as the brethren think fit'.[111] Details of some of these bequests are recorded in the Almshouse Register. The brethren decided that the gifts of Sir John Horsey and William Knoyle together would be called the "Town Stock" to be used to help the poor of the town.[112] This stock then became the focus for other similar bequests.

The writings of one of the brethren, John Toogood, in the eighteenth century refer to 'the many charities united in one trust for the benefit of its [Sherborne's] poor inhabitants'. He confirms that the gifts of Horsey and Knoyle in 1589 'were called the Town Stock and are continued in the accounts of the treasurer'. However, this level of organisation had not been in place from the beginning and confusion about ownership of funds had arisen in 1607. A decision was made in December of that year that the master of the almshouse and the warden of the school should meet on

> holidays, to examine and reduce an inventory of all monies of the Almshouse, School and Town [stock] to their proper places, that it may appear which is indebted the one to the other.[113]

It was not until many years later in 1672 that a sub-master responsible for the charities administered by the almshouse started to present reports regularly in the almshouse accounts, recording how the charitable funds were managed. This sub-master often went on to become master within a few years.[114]

Within this 'trust', the brethren managed a wide range of charitable bequests, the deployment of some of the funds having been made quite specific by the donors. In 1629 Agnes Boughton gave lands to provide revenue 'for binding poor children as apprentices'. In 1687 Dorothy Eastmont left £50 to be invested in order to buy 'linen changes for poor wives and widows of Sherborne'. In 1720 Robert Avoake, a brother and governor, left property to provide the means to buy 'bread for the poor

---

110 The 'prebend' referred to property or land providing tithes from which the stipend of Anglican clergy were paid. Sir John Horsey had acquired church land at the time of the Dissolution.

111 Wildman, *A Short History of Sherborne*, pp.180-182; DHC: D/SHA/D24.

112 DHC: D/SHA/SC809.

113 Fowler, *Mediaeval Sherborne*, p. 346; DHC: D/SHA/D1.

114 DHC: D/SHA/A.

of Sherborne'. The Reverend Charles Toogood, also a brother, left £200 in 1821 'to be invested in the public funds to provide great coats for old men in Sherborne, as the master and brethren shall direct'. Twenty years later his widow, Susannah Toogood, left property to educate and clothe a poor Sherborne girl.[115]

Managing these many charities and fulfilling the wishes of the donors could not have been an easy task. Some money was intended to be lent to certain poor townspeople on security but Toogood noted that there was reason to believe part of the donations had been lost at times because 'sureties', or guarantors, had been unable to repay the money. In addition, he said that some of the poor people had been unable to arrange security for a loan and so the money had lain idle in a chest at the almshouse.[116] A further source confirms that some were not 'careful or inclinable to repay it when borrowed and…a great part of the stock often remains useless in the chest'.[117]

In 1684 a legacy of a different nature was that of Dr Nathaniel Highmore, a brother of the almshouse and governor of the school. He left to the masters of the almshouse £50 'towards the erecting of a workhouse to set the poor to work, if they [the brethren] shall go about such a work', suggesting that the masters might decide otherwise. From before the late-sixteenth century, towns had been experimenting with different responses to poverty and by the time of the economic depression of the 1620s towns in certain parts of the country were addressing social welfare. One such area lay within a triangle formed by Gloucester, Plymouth and Southampton, which included both Sherborne and Dorchester. Charitable donors had established workhouses in Plymouth and Southampton. In Dorchester, local philanthropist John White also established one, together with a municipal storehouse to provide food and fuel for the poor. Some workhouse establishments were incorporated in attempts to secure their survival. Without this safeguard, others failed. Elsewhere, some parish vestries also set up workhouses.[118] Dr Highmore's intention was, therefore, not a new idea. He may have believed that the almshouse corporation would ensure the future of his workhouse but it is not certain that it was ever built.

By 1723 legislation sanctioned, but did not enforce, the establishment of parish workhouses.[119] These were intended as a deterrent and a place of last resort. Further legislation in 1782 had recognised that the parish was too small a unit to administer the Poor Laws successfully and advocated that parishes form into groups or unions approximately the size of the county divisions known as 'hundreds'.[120] These unions were empowered to establish common poor houses, intended only for those truly

---

115 Wildman, *A Short History of Sherborne*, 181-2.
116 DHC: D.170/1.
117 DHC: D/SHA/SC809.
118 Slack, *Poverty and Policy*, pp. 149-153.
119 The Settlement Act: *An Act for Amending the Laws relating to the Settlement, Employment and Relief of the Poor,* otherwise known as the Workhouse Test Act, 1723.
120 *The Act for the Better Relief and Employment of the Poor,* 1782.

unable to work and including the old and infirm.[121] The 1802 map of Sherborne shows the "Parish Workhouse", the name suggesting that it was not attributed to Dr Highmore but had been set up by the parish.

It was not until 1834 that the Poor Law Amendment Act established Poor Law Unions, requiring each to establish a workhouse. Entry was to be the only form of relief to the able-bodied and their families. Out-relief was to be available only for the elderly and infirm and when this became insufficient they were to be admitted to the workhouse. The new regime was much more harsh than that in the old poorhouses and fear of the workhouse continued well into the twentieth century. Even long after the last closure in the 1940s older people resisted entry into residential care in a building known to have been a workhouse.[122] In Sherborne the Union Workhouse was completed by 1840 – work was still outstanding in 1839 and repairs required in 1840, when one Hannah Taylor, of Holwell, was resident.[123] As civic responsibility for the poor increased the brethren of the almshouse continued to administer the private philanthropy entrusted to them, probably reaching out to the respectable poor who were not receiving public assistance.

The 1851 census identifies in Sherborne eighty-two people over the age of sixty, of whom twenty-six women and thirty-one men, were accommodated in either the almshouse or the workhouse. Twenty-four (29%) were almspeople, eight (31%) of all accommodated women and sixteen (51%) of accommodated men. Elsewhere evidence from nine English counties has shown almshouse provision in the nineteenth century to have more commonly favoured women.[124] The reverse was true in Sherborne. Did Sherborne residents who were selected as almspeople appreciate their good fortune?

The People of the Almshouse

The Brethren
The long-running list of brethren recorded in the Almshouse Register shows that the majority remained in office until they died. They would have been some of the leading citizens in the town. Dr Nathaniel Highmore, an almshouse brother for thirty years from 1654 and one of the benefactors mentioned in the Almshouse Register, was also governor of the school as well as being a justice of the peace, active in church affairs and a renowned surgeon. William Willmott, a silk manufacturer owning silk mills in

121 P. Higginbotham, *The Workhouse Encyclopedia*, (Stroud, 2012) pp. 209-210.

122 Higginbotham, *The Workhouse Encyclopedia* pp. 210-213; L. Lewis, *A Requiem for Workhouses*, (Faversham, 2006) Ch. 19, unpaginated. Although Higginbotham states that workhouses carried on into he 1930s, Lewis, said to have been the last surviving workhouse master, described just such an institution operating in Faversham, Kent in 1948.

123 DHC: D1479/3; DHC: PE/HOW/OV/5/2/24.

124 N. Goose and S. Basten, 'Almshouse residency in nineteenth century England', *Family and Community History*, (2009) Vol. XII, 2, p. 69-70.

and around Sherborne, was a brother of the almshouse, a governor of the school and had been a Guardian of the Poor under the Old Poor Law for some years before his death in 1787. From the late-seventeenth century all new brethren had been afforded a title in the records. Esquires, the rank below a knight, and gentlemen, a courtesy title for those of good family, had been mentioned from the late-sixteenth century but from the late-seventeenth century all new brethren without a higher of professional title were recorded as 'Mr'.

Unless they were clergymen or doctors the occupations of brethren are rarely mentioned in the almshouse records and have to be sought elsewhere. A preliminary search of miscellaneous sources has revealed a number of occupations, although few have been found before the eighteenth century. Reflecting the cloth industry of the area several of the earlier brethren were mercers, or traders in textiles, with the occasional clothier. There were also a number of apothecaries throughout the years. By the nineteenth century, if not before, the brethren appear to have been men of substance. For example, Samuel Pretor, elected in 1821, was a banker and tenant of Sherborne House. A later brother, Robert Willmott, elected in 1851, also occupied Sherborne House. Described as a silk throwster, he was the third generation of the Willmott silk manufacturing family. His father, Thomas, and grandfather, William, had preceded him as both silk manufacturers and brethren of the almshouse. There were also several solicitors or attorneys, such as Peter Batson and his partner, George Warry, whose office was in Cheap Street, and a number of doctors or surgeons. At least two nineteenth-century brethren, Edward Benthall and J. F. Falwasser were Justices of the Peace and it is likely that many of the brethren held other offices within the town.

Some surnames are repeated, sometimes in fairly quick succession, in the list of elections and occasionally relationships to other or former brethren are stated It is likely that tracing repeated surnames and researching inter-marriage between Sherborne's leading families would find a network of extended kin relationships between brethren. Indeed, Sherborne parish registers show that Carew Harvey Mildmay, an almshouse brother from 1719 to 1757, was the son-in-law of John Eastmont, a brother from 1651 until his death in the early 1720s. Carew Mildmay and his wife, Dorothy also known as Martha, had five children baptised in Sherborne Abbey.[125]

Despite the probability of close relationships between the brethren, the almshouse board meetings were not always free from strife. In the registry book containing orders and resolutions for 1756-1813 an early page for 1757 has had almost two thirds of the record physically cut out and removed. An attached note tells us that during the meeting the Reverend Peter Smith, recently master,

> did in an arbitrary manner cut out a part of this page, because it contained an order that was disagreeable to him, and he was afterwards expelled this house.

125 Janet Cumner kindly provided this information from her own research.

There is nothing in the document to indicate what had so angered the clergyman that he committed this act of vandalism. The remaining part of the page concerned records that for some years the income from the almshouse estate had been insufficient for the number of residents accommodated and an enquiry was to be made.[126]

That incident is not mentioned in the contemporary account by John Toogood, although he graphically describes another board meeting in that year, 1757. He records the brethren as

> a motley mixture of different complexions, of jarring interests, of secret or open animosities, not without much mulish nonsense often in loud and flaming fervent disputing and differing in trifles, negligent and inattentive to the more essential parts of the trust.

He complained that there were often declarations about what is 'wrong' and what is 'right' but that there were 'seldom any proper measures taken either to prevent the wrong or to execute the right'. Another complaint was that the brethren seated either side of him at a meeting were 'one in haste to go to his own concerns and another to his dinner'.[127] It must be rare to have such an eye-witness account of the internal affairs of an almshouse!

The notes made by John Toogood also include details of a very direct involvement of the almshouse with the town in 1757. He begins by recording the suffering of townspeople due to the high price of food, particularly of corn for making bread. There had been news of riots 'from all parts'. Sherborne's bread riot was triggered by Toogood's brother William, a local farmer and former master of the almshouse. He had sold wheat at a high price (14s. 10d. a bushel) to a miller and had that very morning, April 30th, travelled with his servant to deliver it and to guard against interception.

This action gave rise to 'much ill nature and falsity, not by the poor only, but by the rich men also of this place'. As a result, 'many of our idle and insolent poor men and women assembled' in the market and then moved to a local mill where they appropriated several bags of flour and shared them between themselves. A threatening letter was sent indirectly to William Toogood. Although the letter was destroyed before it reached him, the content became known.

Rioting in the town had not happened in living memory but there was fear that neighbouring parishes might join in the unrest. A meeting of brethren was called. It seemed 'there was no time to be lost' and that 'it was proper to crush this evil in the bud'. A course of action was agreed. John Toogood and a colleague were to take a survey of 'all the most necessitous families in the town'. The brethren raised a subscription of £100 and the Justice of the Peace and some of the most prominent

---

126 DHC: D/SHA/D2.
127 DHC: D.170/1.

citizens were to parade through the town, before the next market day, accompanied by the town crier. The town crier would explain the plan to provide poor families with a sufficient weekly allowance of wheat until harvest, at a cost to each family of eight shillings a bushel. Inhabitants were warned that any threat, rioting or disorder would incur committal to prison. The money raised by subscription enabled the brethren to buy sixty bushels of wheat where they could, some at ten and some at twelve shillings, and deliver it weekly as promised. Peace was successfully restored.[128] No record of this event has yet been found in the records of meetings of the brethren but the Sherborne Castle Estate Accounts for Michaelmas 1757 mention £1 4s. 0d. in expenses for a riot in the town.[129]

The year 1830 saw a public event involving most of the town's population, either as participants or as observers. The occasion was Sherborne's celebration of the accession to the throne of William IV. A local newspaper reported proceedings. A procession through the town stopped at various places for the reading of the proclamation. Leading the procession were local officials, such as constables, overseers and surveyors of the highways, followed by Anglican and nonconformist church dignitaries and representatives of friendly societies. Then came children in receipt of charity; a band; military and naval representatives; staff and pupils of the King's School and members of Lodges, such as Freemasons. Almshouse brethren were not mentioned. However, trumpeters preceded a carriage carrying Thomas Fooks, the Steward of the Liberty, who was to read the proclamation. He was almost certainly Thomas Fooks, senior, who had been a brother of the almshouse since 1800 and was to become master in 1831. He was accompanied by four others, including Peter Batson, already mentioned as both brother of the almshouse and governor of the school, and Dr Pew, a brother of the almshouse from 1806 until his death in 1834. Whether Mr Batson, aged 83, and Dr Pew were selected to accompany Mr Fooks because they were brethren, because they held other positions in the town or because they were too aged or infirm to walk is not known. The celebration was followed by a dinner at the town hall for the more important participants; a separate dinner at the Swan Inn for tradesmen; and beer on a ticket-only basis in the market place for the 'humbler classes'. It is unlikely that the almspeople would have attended the celebration in the market place but they would almost certainly have witnessed the procession as it left the abbey into Half Moon Street, just outside the entrance to the almshouse.[130]

128 DHC: D.170/1.
129 Sherborne Castle Archives: SHR/CD1: for details of a subsequent riot in 1831 see: J. Fripp, 'The Sherborne Riots of 1831: Causes, Characters and Consequences', *Proceedings of the Dorset Natural History and Archaeological Society*, (2006) Vol. CXXVII, pp. 21-30. Several brethren were involved co-incidentally, Thomas Fooks (attorney) and Edward Turner (surgeon) were among those whose windows were damaged. Two other brethren tried separately to quell the riot, the Reverend John Parons (recently appointed acting magistrate) ineffectually and Thomas Wilmott (silk manufacturer) successfully.
130 'Proclamation of King William IV in Sherborne', *The Sherborne Mercury*, 26 July 1830. Thanks to Brian Miller for this reference.

The Almspeople

The records of Sherborne Almshouse may be unique in including an unbroken, detailed nominal list of almshouse residents, as they were admitted, from 1582 to 1866.[131] As in the record of elections of brethren, the admissions register shows the re-occurrence of certain surnames with occasional reference to relationships. Again, further research would probably show a network of family relationships and raise the, perhaps unanswerable, question of whether preference was given to certain families.

A recent study of 131 almshouses, mainly in Surrey but including variable amounts of evidence from twenty-two other counties, found only nine almshouses (6.7%) keeping a register, some relating to almspeople, the others to punishments.[132] At Sherborne, where new entrants were required to bring their moveable goods into the house, the register recorded their possessions until the mid-eighteenth century. This provides an insight into clothing, household goods and, occasionally, tools in use at the time.[133] A few newcomers brought money in the early years. Occasionally relatives made donations which suggests they were fulfilling their obligations as kin, either from a sense of family responsibility or as expected by the Poor Relief Act of 1601. One person, Anne Selby in 1667, 'yields up in the hands of the master and brethren her rights in her house and garden at Horsecastle well to buy her a bed and other necessaryes'. It is unclear how this donation would translate into money and whether it would be of any significance to the almshouse. However, over the years there are also records of people being too poor to bring anything with them. The admissions register continues to 1866. Although it contains less detail towards the end of that period, in the early-nineteenth century it begins to note ages on entry and death.

There is only one reference in the admissions register to the former occupation of an almsperson. William Jervis, admitted in 1594 had been a cardmaker or maker of cards for carding wool in the cloth trade.[134] Some male occupations can be deduced from tools taken into the almshouse. Other sources reveal that John Dier, another early resident, had been a deponent in a lawsuit in 1603/4 when 'he was eighty-eight years old and living in Sherborne almshouse'. The case concerned the removal of trees from the churchyard and John gave evidence that the wood had been used for making a stage for the Corpus Christi play in the 1570s. He had designed the costumes for the play and had been involved with other productions.[135] Tracking almshouse residents in nineteenth-century censuses prior to their admission shows them to have been employed in skilled and unskilled occupations. Many had been agricultural labourers

---

131 DHC: D/SHA/D24.
132 Blaydon, 'Almshouse Rules' in Goose *et al.* (forthcoming 2014) Ch. 9.
133 A. Clark, 'Almspeople and their possessions: gleanings from an admissions register, Sherborne, 1582-1866', in Goose *et al.* (forthcoming 2014), Ch. 12.
134 Wrightson, *Earthly Neccessities*, p. 310.
135 Hays, *Early English Drama*, pp. 36, 360.

and some of the women laundresses, some had been cordwainers, tailors, carpenters or woodsmen. Others reflected local industry, stone masons and female silk workers, for example. Some had been masters of their trades.[136] It is likely that this range of occupations had changed little over time.

In the early years, almshouse living conditions would have been spartan. A study of Dorset inventories indicated a limited range of furniture in use in the 1590s, mainly tables, stools, chairs and bedsteads.[137] Reference to 'beds' in the admissions register indicates only mattresses. These were filled with straw, dust (left after threshing grain), flock or feathers, the varying quality perhaps telling something about their owners. Although four men, admitted in the 1590s, brought bedsteads with them on admission no such item was recorded in their rooms when an inventory was taken in 1598.[138] Early accounts show floors to have been covered with rushes or straw, sometimes plaited into mats.[139]

Religious duties featured strongly in the lives of earlier almspeople. In the days of the foundation they were to pray five times each day, by 'tell[ing] over their beads four times' when and wherever they chose and, for the fifth time, they would be summoned by the bell to hear Mass in the chapel and pray together. Instead of grace at mealtimes, they were required to say 'one Pater Noster and one Ave Maria' before and two of each after every meal.[140] Although the number and pattern of prayers altered with changing times, chapel services continued to be a prominent part of their lives. In 1862 the master and brethren re-issued the rules of the house

> to promote the welfare of its inmates and particularly their due preparation
> for the hour of death, and for the day of Judgement, according to the pious
> intention of the founder.[141]

The almspeople were to attend chapel services twice daily, first thing in the morning and again in the evening. They were also to continue to attend 'the public worship of Almighty God' in the Abbey Church, 'going and returning two and two in good order, according to the custom of this house'.[142]

The peer-elected Prior was to inform the master if any almsperson was in breach of any of the house rules, which were read to the almspeople once each month. Penalties for failure to attend 'to worship Almighty God' or to comply with the other rules were harsh. For a first offence, the guilty person would forfeit the 'next day's

---

136 Thanks to Brian Miller for providing information from the censuses.
137 R. Machin, *Probate Inventories and Manorial Exerpts of Chetnole, Leigh and Yetminster,* (Bristol, 1976) pp. 5-6.
138 D/SHA/A158.
139 Fowler, *Mediaeval Sherborne,* p. 256.
140 Fowler, *Mediaeval Sherborne,* pp. 243-244.
141 Sherborne Almshouse Rules 1862, displayed in the almshouse.
142 J. Hutchins, *The Annals and Iconography of Dorsetshire and Dorset Worthies,* Extra Illustrated Edition, (London and Bridport, 1904) Vol. XI, pp. 144-145.

ordinary allowance of diet' and would have to remain in the almshouse during that day. A second offence would mean expulsion and appointment of another person to take up the vacated place in the house.[143]

 Early accounts reveal expenses for the maintenance of the almspeople, including food, clothing and shoes, candles, shoe mending, beer, payment to the barber and burial costs.[144] In 1763, the master and brethren agreed that every poor man in the house should have a new gown since 'the condition of their clothing is such that they cannot appear decent into Church to be worn on Sundays only'.[145] One imagines the old gowns would continue to be worn during the week. Burials of almspeople took place in Sherbourne and until the end of the 1640s, they were identified as such in the parish register with the words *elemosinarius*, meaning 'almsman', and its feminine form *elemosinaria*.[146] From the 1650s, English was used in the parish registers and almspeople continued to be identified by the words 'in Almshouse'.

 The almshouse regime was strict and on entry each almsperson had to swear on oath to comply with the rules. Apart from the religious obligations other rules related to daily activities in the almshouse, such as arrangements for meals. Anti-social behaviour in the form of profane cursing, swearing, drunkenness or 'promoting strife or debate' would not be tolerated. Residents were able to come and go in the town but nobody was allowed to enter or leave the almshouse after the door was closed at the usual time in the evening, which varied in summer and winter. Nor was any resident allowed to beg or to work for recompense in any form but had to 'live by the alms of this house'. They were also to be respectful towards the prior, whose responsibility it was to report transgressions to the master and brethren.[147] For those willing and able to keep the rules there would be care and security for the rest of their lives.

 Blaydon's study of alsmhouses in Surrey, but with additional data from twenty-one further English counties helps to put the Sherborne rules in context. Regulations for almspeople's behaviour included religious commitments in 47% of the 131 almshouses where rules were found. 'Stealing and begging, scolding and brawling…blaspheming [and] insobriety' all incurred fines or expulsion in 66% of the almshouses and 23% had rules about locking the doors at night. Swearing on oath to keep the rules was not uncommon.[148] The Sherborne regime included all of these rules.

 A few residents left the almshouse voluntarily, although reasons were only sometimes recorded. One fortunate person left because he had received an inheritance and no longer required charity, probably a very rare occurrence. Over

143 Hutchins, *The Annals and Iconography*, pp. 144-145.
144 Fowler, *Mediaeval Sherborne*, p. 249; Mayo, *An Historic Guide to the Almshouse*, (1st edn., Oxford, 1926) p. 48.
145 DHC: D/SHA/D2.
146 DHC: PE/SH/RE/1/1.
147 Hutchins, *The Annals and Iconography*, pp. 144-145.
148 Blaydon, 'Almshouse Rules' in Goose *et al.* (forthcoming 2014) Ch. 9.

the centuries almspeople committed various offences which incurred sanctions and there were a number of expulsions, for reasons found in various sources. In 1596 Katherine Symonds, the new wife of John Symonds, was admitted to the almshouse, with the consent of her husband. For a misdemeanour a year later she was allowed only one meal, bread and water, each day for three days, to be delivered to her room by the Prior and so excluding her from the communal meals of the house. A second offence would be punished by six days of the same treatment and a third offence would mean expulsion.[149] Katherine died in the almshouse in 1616. In 1641 Steven Toogood had often been admonished for drunkenness and other misdemeanours but refused to conform and was finally expelled. In 1702 John Coward met the same fate after not obeying orders and subjecting the master and brethren to 'sawcy and abusive language'. Jane Stickland's offences in 1855 were drunkenness and leaving the almshouse after the door was closed and, a year later, Isaac Baker was admonished for working in a garden.[150] Instant dismissal was rarely used. Even in 1611, when John Hixe, perpetrator of earlier misdemeanours, had entered a house infested by plague and tried to bring goods from there to the almshouse, his instant dismissal was accompanied by an 'allowance of diet and firewood'.[151]

Two instances suggested that the almshouse was not willing, or perhaps not equipped, to deal with some aspects of ill-health. Margery Pond had been 'turned out for lunacy' in 1679 and in 1743 John Rapson, who was then the prior, was 'turned out for indisposition'.[152] However, Fowler found among the week books of the masters an instance of the housewife sharing the bed of an almswoman 'who was too feeble and ill to be left alone' and, on another occasion, 'special mutton broth' was made for another almswoman who was sick.[153]

The rules at Sherborne Almshouse changed little over the years, although the religious requirements were relaxed to some extent in accordance with changes in the church. The rule regarding the wearing of uniform continued unchanged for longer. From the foundation until at least the 1590s, this was a white gown with 'a mitre on the right breast in token that the chief founder was the Bishop of Salisbury, and on the left a shield with the arms of St George [the English flag]'.[154] At a later (unknown) date the livery gowns were changed to the more practical colours of dark blue for the men and red for the women. The men wore black hats and the women black poke bonnets outside the house, the women wearing white caps indoors. The mitre was still represented but on the buttons of the gowns.[155]

Earlier almshouses often required their residents to wear a uniform or a badge. These identified the wearer as a recipient of the founder's beneficence but were also

149   Mayo, *An Historic Guide to the Almshouse*, p. 49.
150   DHC: D/SHA/D24; DHC: D/SHA/D1-4.
151   DHC: D/SHA/D1.
152   DHC: D/SHA/D24; DHC: D/SHA/D1-4.
153   Fowler, *Mediaeval Sherborne*, p. 251.
154   Mayo, *An Historic Guide to the Almshouse*, (1st edn., 1926) p. 48.
155   Mayo *An Historic Guide to the Almshouse*, (1st edn., 1926) pp. 48-49.

a form of control since they made it difficult for almspeople to beg in the street or misbehave in other ways without notice.[156] Endowed charities of the seventeenth century continued this practice and badging the poor to identify them as eligible for poor relief was also, in some places, a feature of the old poor law system.[157] In Winchester, almsmen at St Cross still wear the livery, black gowns with a badge in the shape of a cross and a trencher hat for those under the old foundation; and a mulberry gown with a silver cardinal's badge and a mulberry hat for those under the later foundation.[158] Almspeople at Ryves Almshouses, Blandford, founded in 1682, wore a badge showing a greyhound, the family crest of the founder; purple was the colour of gowns at Doughty's Hospital in Norwich, founded 1687.[159]

In their distinctive uniform Sherborne almspeople would have been easily identified in the streets. In 1905, sixteen residents wearing their hats and gowns took part in a town pageant, held in the castle grounds to celebrate the history of the town.[160] They continued to wear the livery until 1968, when they asked that it be discontinued.[161]

The significance of the Sherborne Almshouse Register

The Hospital of St John the Baptist and St John the Evangelist has its roots in the late mediaeval period when religious beliefs encouraged those with wealth to secure their souls in the after-life through charitable bequests during their earthly lives. While this was a major factor in the foundation of Sherborne Almshouse, considerable funding was also derived from the local population. The almshouse was constructed by local people with local stone quarried by local people. It was also managed by local people and accommodated only local people. From its beginning it was a community almshouse and, by the end of the period covered by the records in the Almshouse Register, it had housed more than eight hundred Sherborne residents.

It is, perhaps, a measure of the diligence of the almshouse brethren that they copied into one volume the important foundation and endowment documents, at the same time making them readily available for themselves and preserving the originals. That this dedication continued throughout the centuries is evident through the addition of details of benefactions and the updating of the registers of elected brethren and admissions of almspeople. Had the brethren not collated these individual election and admission entries from their minutes into the separate registers within

156 Orme and Webster, *The English Hospital*, p. 99.
157 Hindle, *On the Parish*, pp. 233-237.
158 Bailey, *Almshouses*, p. 25; *The Hospital of St Cross and Almshouse of Noble Poverty*, URL: http://stcrosshospital.co.uk/the-brothers/ Accessed 21 November, 2012.
159 Goose and Moden, *Doughty's Hospital*, p. 31; B. G. Cox, *The Book of Blandford Forum*, (Buckingham, 1983) p. 33.
160 C. P. Gooden, *The Story of Sherborne Pageant*, (Sherborne, 1906) p. 24.
161 J. H. P. Gibb, *The Almshouse of SS. John, Sherborne*, (Guide Book, 1990) p. 3.

the volume access to this nominal information as a whole, if noticed, would be tedious and time consuming.

It is unusual to find biographical details of so many members of discrete populations, like the brethren and almspeople, in one place and over such a long period of time. These populations form two distinct groups of Sherborne inhabitants – the 'worthy' members of the community who, over the centuries, filled prominent positions in the town and 'the poorer sort' who were considered eligible recipients for private charitable support. In addition to these main groups of people the Almshouse Register contains, in the grant of lands in 1454 and the surveys of the 1580s, names of occupants of Sherborne properties, which will be of local interest.

The first main group, the brethren, numbered almost one hundred before 1863, many individuals having held their positions for much of their adult lives. The fact that the almshouse was established as a corporation at its foundation, yet Sherborne was never to be incorporated as a borough, left the brethren in a powerful position in the town. Benefactors entrusted them to improve the lives of the poorer inhabitants who formed the second group. Importantly for historians, the transcribed records indicate that the almshouse became a conduit for charitable bequests to the poor of the town and the brethren established a 'town stock' for the purpose, normally the preserve of the parish or the municipal corporation. Had the brethren not considered it important to record bequests in the Register, this important function of the almshouse would have been buried in the archive. The originals of these transcribed records, and the many to which they are cross-referenced, would provide a wealth of primary sources for studying the contribution of private philanthropy to the 'economy of welfare' in a small market town. Who were the brethren, were they inter-related and what other roles did they play within the community?

The second group, the recipients of charity, can be considered as three sub-groups. The almspeople were victims of life-cycle poverty due to age; a number of younger adults were either employed or were capable of being employed but needed assistance to that end; and several children or young people were in need of education to enable them to escape the cycle of poverty. These younger people are unexpected in almshouse records and, although fewer in number, are not without interest. However, the almshouse admission data provide a very large discrete sub-group with greater possibilities for research. Could nominal linkage with other records identify relationships? Did some families supply successive almshouse residents? Since the approximate date of death is given for most almspeople when their successor was admitted, was there any change in average duration of stay over time? What could we learn about exclusions, or from the possessions listed for new entrants? Could this long run of data add to what is already known about almshouse populations?

More generally, could Sherborne records reveal whether the almshouse chest was the only means of distributing private philanthropy within the town or did the school corporation have a similar function, perhaps with a different focus and reaching different people? Did the community role of the almshouse change over time with developing poor law legislation?

The Sherborne Almshouse Register has raised a number of research questions that are beyond the scope of this introduction. The survival of this particular document is key to future research and our understanding of charitable relief within Sherborne, the southwest and nationally. That the almshouse itself has survived to this day owes much to the secure basis on which it was founded. The establishment and maintenance of such a large management body provided continuity in its governance. Its strong financial footing enabled it to maintain its building and its residents through difficult times and the brethren's commitment to their responsibilities and attention to detail have ensured the almost complete survival of their records. Their unintended legacy is an archive of records, represented by the Sherborne Almshouse Register, to interest academic, family and local historians alike.

THE TEXT

The Sherborne Almshouse Register is one of a number of large registry books purchased by the brethren from the late sixteenth century onwards. This register differs from the others in the series. Instead of recording decisions and events as they happened, it draws together a collection of manuscripts relating to the foundation and administration of the house by gathering copies of some of the most significant documents into one volume.

Editorial Method

The transcribed records have not been presented in the *ad hoc* order in which they appear in the volume, but have been grouped under headings to present them in a more meaningful way in terms of content and sequence. To avoid repetition, two copies of oaths for the brethren have been omitted from the transcription. In essence they are little different from those described below.

The registry book has no contemporary foliation and the folios have been very lightly numbered in pencil. The inclusion of these numbers below, and in the transcription, indicates the position of each record in the volume. Blank folios were left between each section, presumably acknowledging that this was a working document to be extended by future administrators. Eleven folios have become detached from the volume and are presently housed with it. Some of these loose folios are sections of records, parts of which remain bound in the volume. The loose folios have been identified alphabetically on each side so that they can be read in the correct sequence. These folios sometimes stand alone, bearing complete records that have become detached from the volume. Folio letters and numbers in combination indicate that separated sections of records have been linked in date sequence to the transcription. There is some loss of text where these loose folios are frayed at the edges, but for the most part they and the remainder of the volume are in good condition.

To facilitate ease of use the manuscript has been transcribed into modern English. Those passages and sections in Latin have been translated, with the original in round brackets where the meaning may be obscure or of interest. Square brackets have been used to include insertions, annotations by a later scribe and marginalia. A verbatim transcription has been placed with the manuscript at the Dorset History Centre.

Forenames and place names have been modernised where they can be identified. Surnames have been left in their original forms and variants of a surname have been indexed under the most common occurrence or the most likely modern spelling. Dates have been modernised and all numbers are given in Arabic characters.

As far as possible the word order and original language of the text have been retained. Spurious capital letters have been removed and punctuation modernised throughout. However, in some circumstances, even with the introduction of punctuation, the text is still not easily accessible to the modern reader. In these passages some words have been changed and the syntax altered. The following description of individual records includes comment on hands, style and content.

Description of the Records

The Sherborne Almshouse Register is a collection of twenty-eight gatherings of paper folios all with the same mid-sixteenth century watermark. It is bound in vellum, contemporary with the gatherings and measures 43cm x 29cm x 6cm. The volume bears no title, as such, but on the front cover in a barely legible italic hand is written

> Names of the Governors and the Poor in the Almshouse – also the oath for the
> master and brethren of the house and of the governors of the school, for the
> upper and under master and for the poor men and women and housewife.

A twentieth-century annotation to the outer cover reads "book 2" which is repeated in the inside cover. The spine is annotated "24", apparently in the same ink as the inscription on the front of the cover.

The faint description of the contents on the front cover does not fully represent the range of the records contained within. While the lists of names of the governors and the poor could be individually called registers, the title given to the volume for the purpose of the transcription uses the term "register" in its wider sense as a book in which official records are kept.

FOUNDATION AND ADMINISTRATION

Letters Patent of Henry VI, 1437. Folio 117

This is a late eighteenth- or nineteenth-century translation in a rounded italic hand. The document licensed the founders to establish the almshouse. It assigned their duties and responsibilities in making the first appointments and listed the rules of governance they were to put in place. The letters patent also established the resulting group of twenty brethren as a charitable corporation, entitled to acquire land and property and to participate in court action as necessary. This comprehensive document provided royal authority that enabled the founders to proceed with the construction and management of the almshouse.

The Founders' Statutes. Folios 118-19

This is a late eighteenth- or nineteenth-century transcription in the same rounded italic hand as the copy of the letters patent. The record is a partial copy of the foundation deed of 10 January 1437. The first two paragraphs of the originals were omitted from this copy, possibly because they reiterated details of the founders already reproduced in the copy of the letter patent described above. This extract of the foundation deed starts with the third paragraph of the original and lists the founders by first name only. Then follows a condensed version of the next four paragraphs of the original deed. As a result, only the first person named on the three lists of original brethren, almsmen and almswomen is recorded in this copy. The medieval obligations of the chaplain and almspeople to pray for the souls of the founders and others are also ignored.

The remainder of the dcument follows the same sequence as the foundation deed. It details arrangements for election of master, brethren and almspeople, the rules for the ongoing management of the house, its business and the routine of daily life for the almspeople.

Statutes and Ordinances, 1590-1613. Folios 125-6

This document is written in contemporary secretary hand, the same hand as compiled the 1589 survey, a large section of bequests and the terrier which follow below. As such it forms part of the original scheme for the Register.

The record represents a revision of the arrangements for the governance of the almshouse, the management of its business and rules for the almspeople previously laid down in the founders' statutes. Oaths for the brethren and the almspeople, together with the housewife, are recorded at the beginning. The oath for the brethren is followed by the oath of supremacy, recognising the monarch as head of the Church of England as well as of the realm. This additional oath was required of all holders of public office in the time of Henry VIII and Elizabeth I. Any brother refusing to recognise the supremacy of the monarch would be disqualified from office: the names of the brethren who took the oath in 1590 are recorded.

The oath for the housewife is the same as that for the almspeople, since she lived with them in the almshouse. They all swore on entry to obey the rules of the house and to be of good behaviour. The wording changed little over the centuries.

The remainder of the document clarifies rules for the behaviour of brethren and details the conduct of their meetings with penalties for default. Those failing to comply faced a fine or expulsion. This period, at the turn of the sixteenth century, appears to have been one of review and reorganisation of the administration of the almshouse.

ENDOWMENTS AND BEQUESTS

This section was compiled in several distinct hands. Broadly these are secretary hands for those entries from the 1580s to the 1640s and italic hands thereafter. The frequent changes of hand give the strong impression that much of this section was compiled close to the events and actions which the document records.

Founders and Benefactors. Folio 4

This record copy dates the foundation of the almshouse as 1448, 1454 having been crossed out. However, the copied text states the date to have been the sixteenth year of the reign of Henry VI (1437). Another copy of the original document is to be found, loose, at the back of the first volume of the series, the 'Register of assemblies of Master and Brethren of the Almshouse, 1590-1756'.[1] That version too gives the date 1448 in numerals, while the text gives the regnal year for 1437. It is likely that both copies were made more than a century after the foundation. There may have been confusion about the date of foundation (1437); the date of completion of the almshouse and the licence to acquire further land (both 1448); and the date when the almshouse land and property holdings were surveyed in 1454.

The text concerns the founders' endowment of the almshouse, the Sherborne house-to-house collection with names of donors and amounts given, and details other benefactors. The gift of Elizabeth Latimer was land given to Dodill's Almshouse in 1408 and passed in 1437 to the new almshouse.[2] In other documents this property is known sometimes as "the Beer Hacket land" and sometimes as "Subtrowe". It was a significant contribution which provided continuity between the old and the new almshouses and was to remain part of the property portfolio for centuries to come.

Bequests, 1589-c.1610. Loose folio A and folio 5.

The first part of this record is found on the loose folio A, which was originally positioned between the bound folios marked 4 and 5 in the volume. This document was compiled in the same secretary hand as the Statutes and Ordinances and forms part of the original scheme for the volume.

The bequest of William Masters in 1589 matched that of Peter Game which is listed in the record entitled 'Founders and Benefactors', above. Peter Game funded one place in the almshouse for a man and William Masters did the same for a woman. Together these bequests increased the occupancy to thirteen men and five women.

Sir John Horsey's provision, of the same year, was of great significance to the town. His gift of £10 annually was to come from the prebend, or tithes from church

1 DHC: D/SHA/D1.
2 DHC: D/SHA/CH104-113.

land that he had acquired after the reformation, and was due to revert to the Crown in a number of years. The gift was therefore time-limited but in the meantime the funds could be invested to provide income. Sir John's will stipulated that the brethren were to create a Town Stock of funds to benefit the poor of the town and to facilitate work for those who were able-bodied.

Sir John predeceased his wife, and on her demise the prebend passed, along with the executorship of Sir John's will, to a relative, Sir Raufe Horsey.[3] He seems to have uncovered some irregularity in the use of the funds already paid to the almshouse, the money having contributed to the maintenance of the poor in the almshouse rather than the poor of the town. Taking the view that this had been done unwittingly, he determined that this should be corrected with repayments being made in instalments to fulfil Sir John's intentions, which Sir Rauffe reiterated to ensure there was no doubt.

The importance of this bequest was two-fold. Firstly, it designated the almshouse corporation as trustee of the new charity. The brethren had been managing funds for over a century and their business was relieving the poor. Secondly, this appears to be the first mention of a town stock in Sherborne to combat poverty in the general population. The long-running almshouse accounts show that this stock was to be a feature of local poor relief for centuries to come. Two further bequests follow in this document.

Disposition of Mr Wynniffs gift. Folio 6.

This next document consists of ten entries made over five years between 1629 and 1633 in several contemporary secretary hands. It provides an account of when, how, why and to whom the bequest was disbursed.

Gift of William Knoyle, c. 1678. Loose folio C verso.

Originally this gift was recorded on one of the folios which have become detached from their position between folios 5 and 6 in the volume. The entry in an italic hand was a further bequest intended to fund, in perpetuity, loans to poor deserving residents.

Bequests, 1589-1673. Folio 7- 8.

This section contains entries by several different scribes in secretary and italic hands. It summarises some of the gifts, already mentioned, which formed the foundation of the town stock. Then follow a number of further bequests to be added to the stock for the benefit of poor townspeople. Some recipients are named, together with the amount received and, occasionally, an occupation is noted. Of particular interest is Dr Highmore's will of 1684 which, amongst other charitable bequests, gave money to fund the erection of a workhouse in the town.

---

3 Fowler, (1951) p. 320.

LAND AND TENEMENTS OF THE ALMSHOUSE

This group comprises three records. The first lists the property acquired by 1454, following the second licence of 1448 authorising the brethren to increase the land held by the almshouse. The remaining documents are surveys of land held by the almshouse in the late sixteenth century. After the upheaval related to land holding following the Reformation, and with ongoing changes in legislation, it would have been important for the brethren to have ready access to the details of lands held by the almshouse in order to face any legal challenge.

A grant of land and tenements, 1454. Loose folios B recto – C recto.

These loose sheets were originally bound between folios 5 and 6 in the volume and constitute this complete document. Compiled in the same secretary hand as the following survey, the record consists of a grant, or ffeofment, which was a legal device to allow a donor, or feoffor, to transfer the use of land to a recipient or feoffee. The document details lands and tenements which had been acquired by the almshouse by 1454, only six years after a second licence had authorised further such expenditure. Properties in Sherborne are identified by some indication of location, sometimes a street name or a tithing, and by the names of former occupiers of neighbouring properties.

Surveys, 1581 and 1589. Folios 28-29 and 30-33.

These surveys are written in contemporary secretary hand updated throughout with annotations shortly afterwards by a second hand. Both surveys record admissions of tenants to various properties, with some description of land or buildings and their location. They are rich in names of local people, sometimes giving details of family relationships.

Terrier of property of the Free Grammar School. Folio 122.

This document is in Latin in the volume, written in contemporary secretary hand, the same hand as compiled the 1589 survey and a large section of the bequests. Here, it has been translated into English. School documents are occasionally found amongst almshouse documents.

Summons, 1631. Attached to folio 4.

This is a standard printed summons form with details relevant to the case added by hand at the Exchequer. It is annotated in a contemporary italic hand with notes relating to tenure and land occupancy of land acquired by "an obit and other suspicious uses".

It is likely that this summons was issued under the 1601 Charitable Uses Act (43 Eliz. I c.4) designed to redress the misuse of land, goods or money previously given for charitable uses. Effectively it enabled the state to have supervision over private charity by appointing commissions to enquire into the use of charitable bequests.[4]

OATHS

Oaths for the brethren, school governors, school master, almspeople and housewife. Folio 123.

The text dates from the late seventeenth or early eighteenth century and is in round italic hand, possibly about 1743 since the unrelated memoranda which follow are in a similar hand.

The oath for the master and brethren is little different from that of the sixteenth century. At various times legislation required brethren to take additional oaths, such as the Oath of Supremacy, mentioned above, and the Oath of Association after 1695, to which reference will be found in the record 'Elections of Brethren', below.[5]

The oath for the governors of the school is much shorter than that for the brethren because it includes no detailed reference to property but otherwise the wording is similar. The schoolmaster's oath requires him to educate his charges in manners as well as learning in accordance with rules laid down by the governors.

Finally, entry to the almshouse as a resident was dependent on willingness to swear to obey the rules. Two copies of the oath for the almspeople appear in the volume, the other, like the oath for the brethren, being found in the 'Statutes and Ordinances'. The housewife was usually appointed from outside but lived in the almshouse and was therefore obliged to take the same oath as the almspeople. There is no oath for the prior of the almshouse since he was appointed from amongst the almspeople and would have taken the oath on entry.

THE BRETHREN AND THE ALMSPEOPLE

Elections of Brethren (1582-1863). Folios 144-153

This section starts in the same secretary hand as the statutes, ordinances, surveys and other documents that were brought together by the original scribe. It was periodically updated by later scribes, usually close to the events recorded, with minor variations in style.

---

4 Tate, W. E. (1983) *The Parish Chest*, Chichester, Phillimore and Co. Ltd., p. 110.
5 DHC: D/SHA/D24, Register of Brethren, 6 April 1699.

Effectively a register, it begins with a remembrance of former brethren. Seemingly the compiler of this list retrieved the names from the earlier documents, since all brethren named in those documents are included.

A few brethren, not previously named in any of the documents, appear in the early years of the register up to 1613 as they vacated their position, usually through death. They would have been elected before these records were started and may appear in other almshouse documents not included in this volume. Perusal of the almost complete run of masters' accounts to 1582, listed in the Dorset History Centre catalogue, reveals that this remembrance is not complete.[6] From 1582, the register has been compiled, from time to time, from the entries recording the election of brethren which can be found scattered throughout the minutes of meetings of the masters and brethren.[7] The name of the brother whose place each new entrant was assuming is usually given, often with his reason for leaving. In cases of expulsion more detail can sometimes be found in the minutes.

Further elections beyond 1863 can be found as scattered individual entries in later volumes in the series.[8]

Almshouse Admissions, 1582-1866. Folio 181, loose folios D-K, followed by G-U, then folios 182-205.

This final record has been the most badly affected by the detachment of folios from the binding. The eight folios, marked D-K, were originally bound together between folios 181 recto and 182 verso. At the time of the compilation the scribes left the verso of several folios blank and returned to complete them with later entries. While the order of entries is apparent from the context the original order of binding can not now be established.

Folios 181 and 182 form part of two distinct gatherings. Folio 181 recto is blank and the entries on folio 181 verso continue on folio 182 and subsequent folios in chronological order, continuing the sequence from the detached folios. It may be tentatively suggested that the detached folios separated from the volume by 1660 or 1661 and that, if they became detached over a period of years, this would account for the peculiar order of entry. The starting date of each folio is shown below in chronological order:

5 May 1582	John Chepman	Folio D verso
25 April 1586	Uppon a view had at	H verso
28 March 1591	Thomas Riall	F recto
23 January 1597	Ambrose Chetmyll	G recto
20 March 1602	William Maunfell	G verso

6 DHC: D/SHA/A, Catalogue of Masters' Accounts.
7 DHC: D/SHA/D1-4.
8 DHC: D/SHA/D6, 1876-1894; D/SHA/D7, 1895-1910.

7 October 1610	Robart Manfeld	D recto
27 April 1617	At this day Giles Stone	I recto
9 November 1624	This day Bryant Dewe	F verso
15 October 1627	[*manuscript torn*] man into this house	J recto
	Blank page on the back of J	J verso
January 1633	The said day Mary Callowe	K recto
6 April 1636	The said day William Chafin	K verso
3 June 1640	This day Thomas Callow	E recto
23 October 1643	At this day Anne Justins	E verso
1 March 1648	This day Robert Harvy	H recto
18 April 1657	This day John Trew	I verso

Like the elections of brethren, this admissions register was part of the original scheme for the volume. At times it was regularly updated with some new annotations at the time of entry and at other times it was extended in batches over several years.

Details of new entrants to the almshouse were copied from admission entries intermingled with the minutes of the brethren's meetings.[9] Initially detailed records of the possessions they took into the house are recorded, continuing to the 1760s. Latterly almspeople's ages on both admission and death are noted. Almost every entry records the swearing of the oath. The names of the former occupants of the rooms are given in most entries, often with the reason for vacating the room which, in most cases, was death. For most almspeople it is possible to calculate the duration of their residence at the almshouse, which for some exceeded twenty years. As with the brethren, the decision to punish or expel an almsperson would be recorded in the minutes, where sometimes more detail than appears in this document can be found.

For both brethren and almspeople, the terminology of the appointment varies. An individual would be 'elected' as a brother or 'chosen' as an almsperson. However, in both documents, the wording of their admission - in either 'the room of' or 'the place of' another - is interchangeable and indicates that their appointment would fill a vacancy, rather than a room. The brethren were never resident in the almshouse.

9 DHC: D/SHA/D1-4.

1. The Founders' Statutes (pp. 3–7). The first residents are named (for full list see Appendix), the brethren's powers under the King's letters patent are recorded and rules set for election of brethren, appointment of the Master and admission of almspeople.

2. *The Hospital of St John the Baptist and St John the Evangelist, Sherborne, c. 1803. Note the height of the chimneys, later reduced, and the housing on the ridge of the roof for the bell which summoned brethren to meetings in the boardroom (p. 8).*

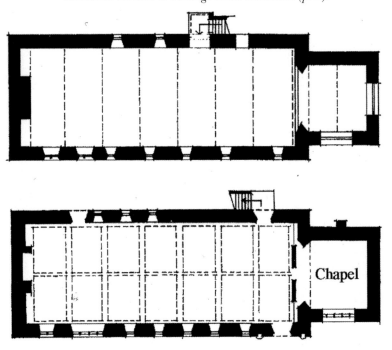

3. *Plan of the Almshouse and Chapel, showing outside staircase to upper floor.*

4. Founders and Benefactors (pp. 11–13). This first page records details of the founders and what they contributed to the foundation of the Almshouse, followed by a list of other benefactors and their donations.

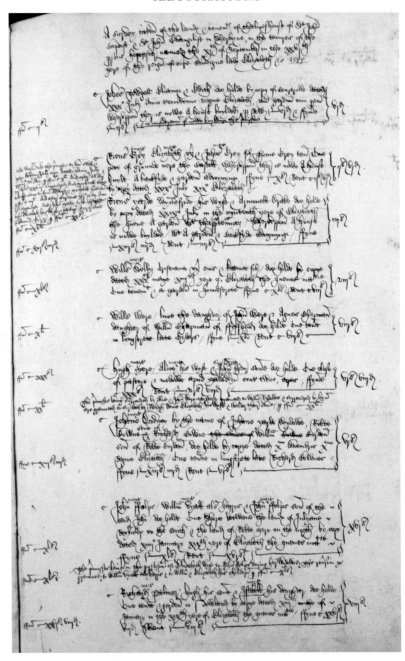

5. *A survey of property held by the Almshouse in 1589 (pp. 30–7). Names of occupiers and their present or former neighbours are given to identify location. Occasionally street names are given, or names of other local identifiable features.*

6. *The Almshouse hall. The hall was also the Nave or ante-room of the chapel. Note the bell rope looped to the side of the chapel screen and the display of pewter ware on the left. Each piece bears an Almshouse stamp.*

7. *One of two Almshouse chests. This one is located in the hall, the original in the boardroom. The original chest, or coffer, is described on page 6. These chests would have been used to store documents and/or money.*

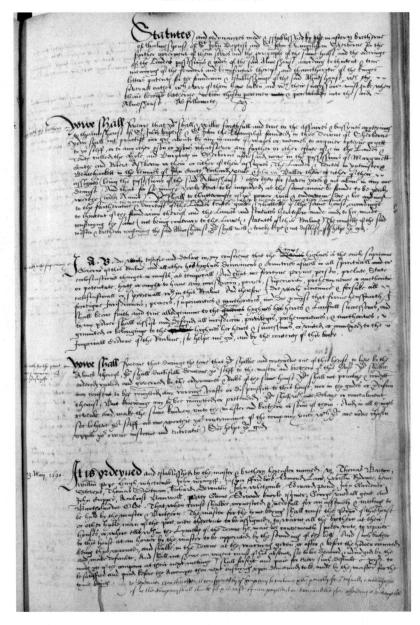

8. Statutes and Ordinances of the Master and Brethren, 1590–1613 (pp. 7–11).
The document sets out how the Almshouse should be governed. This first page shows
the oaths the brethren and almspeople needed to swear at that time, before taking
up office or residence. Subsequent pages tell us how the prior summoned brethren
to meetings and gives the rules for the conduct of those meetings and for handling
money related to charities.

9. Dr. Nathaniel Highmore, surgeon. Almshouse Brother, 1654–1685. Governor of School, 1654–1685. He bequeathed money to the Brethren to build a workhouse in the town.

10. Mr. Simon Pretor, banker. Almshouse Brother, 1761–1765. Governor of School, 1762 –.

11. Mr. William Willmott, silk throwster. Almshouse Brother, 1769–1789. Governor of School, 1769–.

12. Mr. Peter Batson, attorney. Almshouse Brother, 1790–1845. Governor of School, 1790 1845.

13. Almshouse and chapel in the snow, showing proximity to the Abbey.

14. Print of the Almshouse, looking down Trendle Street.

15. (left) View from the chapel looking through the screen into the hall. Note the pewter display in the hall on the right and the gallery above, which allowed residents with rooms on the first floor to participate in chapel services without descending the outside stairs.

16. (below) Mr. George Gristock Caines, an almsman and prior of the almshouse, seated in the hall. He was "a Game's man", admitted on the recommendation of the descendants of Peter Game, an early Brother and benefactor (pp. 12, 41, 43). Mr. Caines died in 1905.

17. The Sherborne triptych, seen through the chapel screen.

Christ casting out the Devil
Inset: Curing of
Bartimeus

Raising of Lazarus

Raising of widow's son
Inset: Raising of
Jairus' daughter

18. The Sherborne triptych, featuring the raising of Lazarus and several of Christ's other miracles. On the back of the folding panels are paintings of four saints. It has been dated c. 1480 but the artist is unknown. There is no known record of how the triptych came to be in the possession of the Almshouse. As a religious icon it was probably hidden to escape the Reformation, since the Almshouse was visited by the Chantry Commissioners in the mid-sixteenth century (pp. xxviii–xxix).

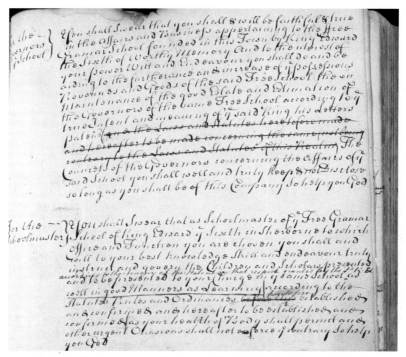

19. *Oaths for the Governors of Sherborne King's School and for the Schoolmaster.*
These oaths are found with the almshouse oaths, since — until the mid-nineteenth
century — many brethren became Governors when, or soon after, they became
Brethren.

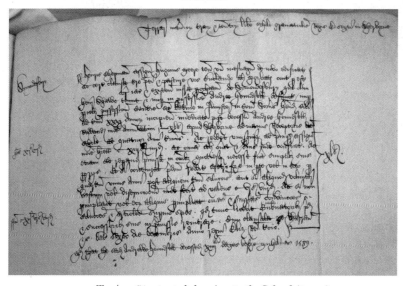

20. *Terrier of property belonging to the School (p. 37).*

21. (above) Portrait of an almswoman wearing
the uniform for women. The red cloak was worn
outdoors. The white cotton cap was worn indoors
and covered with the poke bonnet when she went
out. Her dress beneath the cloak was black. This
painting hangs in the Almshouse hall.

22. (right) The mitre badge, symbolic of the main
founder, the Bishop of Salisbury. This emblem
was worn on the right breast of the original
white woollen gowns and these silver badges were
worn on the men's coats until the livery was
discontinued at the residents' request in 1968.

23. *The oath for the almspeople and the housewife. One of the almsmen was elected as prior by the residents of the almshouse. As one of the almspeople, he had already taken this oath on entry to the house.*

24. *The rules of the Almshouse in 1862. From this date all new entrants to the almshouse swore to obey this version of the rules, which had changed little over time. Note the salutary reminder of impending death and the order to go to and from church two by two. These rules are, today, displayed on a board on the first floor landing.*

25. *Almsmen returning two by two from the Abbey, according to the almshouse rules.*

26. *Almswomen arriving back at the almshouse, two by two, after attending church.*

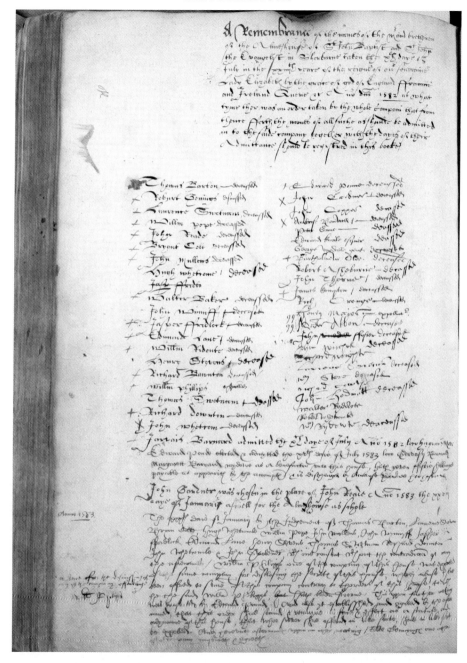

27. *The beginning of the register of brethren (p. 41). It begins with a 'remembrance' of former brethren (see appendix for others not mentioned). The remainder of the document records admissions, resignations, deaths and expulsions of brethren till 1863.*

28. (left) Almsmen in discussion in the hall.

29. (below) Almsmen in the almshouse cloister courtyard.

ILLUSTRATIONS

30. A page from the almshouse admissions register (pp. 62–134). The fourth
entry records George Watts's admission in the place of John Coward, who was
expelled for saucy and abusive language to the master and brethren and for not
obeying the rules of the house.

31. Almswomen with the Matron, formerly known as the Housewife, 1905.

32. Almsmen, 1905. Note the silver mitre badges on their coats.

33. *Another page from the admissions register, showing a variety of possessions brought into the almshouse by new residents.*

Inmates of Sherborne Almshouse for the year 1893.

34. *Almspeople in the almshouse cloister courtyard, 1893. Note the indoor uniform of the women.*

35. *Sherborne pageant of the history of the town, 1905. The almshouse is represented by the facsimile of the triptych behind and the participation of almspeolpe on the right and left. The pageant was held in the grounds of Sherborne Castle.*

36. The back of the Almshouse from the Abbey precincts, showing some of the nineteenth-century extension.

37. The original almshouse building as it is today. Note the reduced chimney stacks and the local stone. The uprights of the railings outside the old entrance each has a finial moulded like a bishop's mitre to represent the main founder, the Bishop of Salisbury.

38. *The original entrance door-way, showing a niche on either side. It is thought that statuettes of St. John the Baptist and St. John the Evangelist, to whom the Almshouse was dedicated, occupied these niches, possibly until the Reformation.*

39. *Nineteenth-century additions to the Almshouse. The original chapel is on the left, but the bell tower above the original part of the almshouse was replaced. The upper part of the extension on the right accommodates the current boardroom and further building of the same date can be seen in the centre behind the attractive cloister.*

40. The courtyard garden at the rear of the Almshouse.

Transcription of the Sherborne Almshouse Register

FRONT COVER

Names of the governors and the poor in the Almshouse. The oaths for the master and
brethren of the house and of the governors of the school, the upper and under
master and for the poor men and women and the housewife.

FOUNDATION AND ADMINISTRATION

Letters Patent of Henry VI, 1437. Folio 117.

Henry by the Grace of God King of England and France and Lord of Ireland to all to
whom these present letters shall come greeting. Know ye that of our special grace
and favour we have granted and licence given for us and for our heirs as much
as in us lies to our Venerable Father Robert Nevil Bishop of Salisbury, Humphrey
Stafford knight, Margaret Gogh, John Fauntleroy and John Barret that they four
three or two of them to the Honour of God, and of his Saints John the Baptist and
John the Evangelist may begin make, found, unite and establish a certain perpetual
Almshouse consisting of twenty brethren and twelve poor weak and impotent men
and also of four poor weak and impotent women which said poor men and women
may be for ever obliged to pray for our health as long as we live and for the health
of the brethren of the house and their benefactors as long as they shall live and
also for our soul and for the souls of our ancestors and of the said brethren and
benefactors after we or they shall depart this life and for the souls of all faithful
persons departed this life, and likewise consisting of a perpetual chaplain whose
office shall ever be to pray for the health and for the souls of the persons above
named at Sherborne in the county of Dorset according to the appointment of
them: bishop Humphrey, Margaret, John and John four, three or two of them.
And that the same Almshouse shall forever consist of the said brethren of the said
house and of the same poor weak and impotent men and women and also of the
said chaplain as chaplain of the said house, and that the brethren of the said house
and their successors may make and choose from their body a master from year to
year as often as shall be expected and for the advantage and honour of the said
house and if one or more brethren happen to die that they who survive and their

successors may elect and make other brethren of other persons to the number of the said twenty brethren and also may remove and expel the said master from his said office and the said poor men and women from the said house, and may always make and choose another master from their number and other poor men and women to the number of the said sixteen poor men and women, agreeable to the ordinance of them Bishop, Humphrey, Margaret, John and John four, three or two of them and also when the said house shall be begun, made, founded, united and established the master and brethren of the said house and their successors shall be called master and brethren of the Almshouse of St John Baptist and St John the Evangelist of Sherborne and the chaplain of the said house shall be likewise called the perpetual chaplain of St John Baptist and St John the Evangelist of Sherborne and likewise that the said master and brethren and their successors shall by the name of the master and brethren of St John Baptist and St John the Evangelist in Sherborne and the said chaplain and his successors shall by the name of perpetual chaplain of St John Baptist and St John the Evangelist of Sherborne be deemed capable of obtaining and receiving lands, tenements, rents and other possessions whatsoever to be held to them and their successors for ever. And that the said master and brethren and their successors and the said chaplain and his successors may sue and be sued in any courts or places whatever appertaining to us and our heirs and in all other courts and places belonging to any other persons within our Kingdom of England according to the laws and customs of our said realm, and in all other lawful respect may act in the same manner as others his majesty's liege subjects, and also that the said master and brethren and their successors may have for ever a common seal and that the master and brethren of the said house and their successors may meet in a lawful and honest manner, and statutes and ordinances for the well governing of the said house as necessity shall require and as often as there shall be occasion may lawfully and with impunity make without any let, molestation or impediment of us or our heirs our justices, sheriffs or any other our officers, and that the chaplain of the said house who shall hereafter celebrate divine service for the health of our bodies and the salvation of our souls in the form before recited shall be named assigned and deputed immediately after the founding of the said house by the master of that said house for the time being and that when the chaplain shall in any manner depart from his duty the master of the said house for the time being shall at all times hereafter name, assign and depute other chaplains of the said house to perform on their parts all and singular the premises as before recited. We have also farther granted out of our more especial favour that after the said house shall have been made and founded the said master and brethren and their successors may acquire lands, tenements, rents and other possessions whatever which are now held of us by others in socage or burgage to the value of forty marks per annum to be held to them and their successors for the support of the house for ever the statute for restraining grants of lands and tenements in mortmain or any other statute and ordinances made to the contrary notwithstanding provided that such acquisitions may be found by inquisitions thereof duly taken and to be returned in our Court of Chancery to be in no sort detrimental to us or our heirs. In witness whereof we have granted these our letters patent Teste, etc, at Westminster the eleventh day of July in the fifteenth year of our reign [1437].

A Copy of the Founders' Statutes. Folios 118-119.

Know ye, us the said Bishop, Humphrey, Margaret, John and John to the worship of God and of the said saints of St John Baptist and St John Evangelist by authority and virtue of the said letters patent, begin, make, found, gather and establish one Almshouse everlasting in Sherborne aforesaid of twenty brethren; of twelve poor, feeble and impotent men of four poor, feeble and impotent women and of a priest perpetual. And that John Brunyng parson of the Green etc. be the said twenty brothers. Also that William Gore etc. be the said twelve poor, feeble and impotent men also that Agnes Knyghtesse etc. be the said poor women also that John Carpenter priest be the said priest perpetual.

Also that the master of the said house that first shall be chose next after this present foundation and the said brethren and all their successors for evermore and also that the said priest and his successors shall be called named and have capacity and be persons habiles [i.e. competent] to purchase, plead and be impleaded, and all other authority and thing have, make, enjoy, receive and do as our said sovereign lord the King by his said letters patent hath called, named and given ability, power and authority to them and to their successors.

Also that the said brethren or their successors a master among themselves within twelve days next after the date of this present foundation choose and make and at the feast of the nativity of St John Baptist or within four days after then following that the said brothers or their successors put down and depose the said master and another master among themselves choose and make and so from year to year for ever more at the said feast or within four days then next following that the said brothers or their successors the master for the time being put down and depose and a new master among themselves choose and make and that also the said brothers and their successors for ever have power and authority to depose and put down the master of the said house for the time being at what other time that they shall seem fit, expedient and necessary for the good of the said house and another master among them within ten days then next following choose.

And also if any of the masters or brothers or poor men or women die then the surviving brethren of the said house and their successors another master and other brothers to the number of the said twenty and other poor men and women to the number of said sixteen men and women shall choose and make provided always that the brothers that shall be chose into the said house be dwelling in the said town of Sherborne when they are chosen and also that they be chosen within four weeks after the death of the said brethren and that the said poor men and women be chosen and made within eight days of the death of every of them provided also that the said poor people shall be chose out of such men and women as have been continual householders in the said town of Sherborne, if any such may be had, and if not then they may be chosen of other men and women dwelling within the said town.

Also if the said brothers and their successors may not agree in their elections or in making statutes or orders for the good rule of the said house if then most voices shall be preferred and if they shall be equal in voices, then the voices of that side that shall be most worthy men shall be preferred.

Also if any of the said poor men and women debate with any of their fellows or else obeys not all the rules and orders and statutes of the said house or otherwise misbehaving himself then it shall be lawful for the master and brethren of the said house him or her to put out of the said house and another within eight days in their place to elect or choose.

Also if the said priest or his successors shall not observe the statutes that now are and hereafter maybe made concerning his office that then it may be lawful for the said master and brethren him to depose and another to choose another within fifteen days and if the priest be disseised off or quits the said office then the said master and brethren shall choose another within fifteen days after every of the said avoidances.

Also that the said sixteen poor men and women and their successors for the time being shall always choose amongst themselves a governor which shall be called the prior of St John's House, which prior shall have the governance of the said sixteen poor men and women in the absence of the said master and brethren and if the master and brethren do not approve of the person so chosen that it shall be then lawful for them to depose him and command the poor men and women to choose another.

Also that there shall be a woman in the said house who for the time being shall buy, order, make, fetch in and dress the victuals of the said sixteen poor men and women and serve them according to the order of the master of the said house for the time being and that she shall be called the housewife of St John's House and that she shall wash the said poor men and women and make their beds etc. as the master shall direct and that she shall be satisfied for the same by the master of the said house. Also if any of the said brothers shall by misfortune come to poverty he and every of them during his life or lives shall receive 20*d.* per week out of the profit of the estate during his or their lives if the master and brethren of the house think fit and if any of the widows of the said brethren who were wives at the time they were made brethren be also poor that then every such widow shall have every week during her life 10*d.* for her sustenance to be paid by the master every Saturday if it shall seem to the said master and brethren necessary and needful.

Also that the said sixteen poor men and women shall forever have during their lives being in the said house every week 10*s.* to be laid out in meat and drink for their sustenance by the master of the said house, and also that the said poor men and women shall have eight marks [£5 6*s.* 8*d.*] per annum which shall be laid out by the master of the said house for cloaks linen and woollen hose and shoes and other necessaries.

Also that every of the said poor men and women shall have yearly at Christmas a new gown and a new hood of white woollen cloth with the bishop's mitre set before on the right breast of every of the gowns in token that the chief founder of the said house is and was bishop of Salisbury and also on the left breast of the said gowns there shall be an escutcheon of the arms of St George made in the same form as the young men of the town of Sherborne in time past have used provided that the said gowns and hoods shall be paid for with the said eight marks.

Also it shall so happen that livelihood competent to fulfil the said payment of 10*s.* every week shall be purchased by any of the masters and brethren then of the said house in time to come for the sustenance of the said sixteen poor men and women that then the said sixteen poor men and women shall eat their meals together in the said house and that they shall have every fasting day one meal and every other day two meals competent and reasonable and that they shall daily eat their first meal at eleven o' the clock in the forenoon and the second meal they shall eat after St John's evensong the which afterwards in this present foundation is written and over that they shall have at three o' the clock in the summer times a reasonable drinking after the orders of the master of the said house.

Also every of the said poor men and women shall have a bed and bed place by themselves in the said house according to the order of the master of the said house for the time being and that the men harbour by themselves and that there be sufficient closure between them.

Also that the said housewife shall eat and drink in the manner that is ordained for the sustenance of the said sixteen poor men and women and over that the said housewife every quarter that she shall be in the said office shall receive 20*d.* and more if needful and also at every Christmas shall have a new gown and hood as the master shall think fit.

Also to the end that no default or failure be made in the said payments if the revenues of the lands etc. that shall be purchased by the master and brethren of the said house shall more than suffice for the said payments and if the said revenues shall be insufficient for such payments that then the said poor unfortunate brethren and their poor widows and also the said sixteen poor men and women shall have a proportionable share of money out of the revenue according to the payments before mentioned, provided that the said bedding and bed places and the salary and clothing of the said housewife be bought and paid for out of the said revenues.

Also that the said poor men and women shall always have fuel sufficient if such may be had on the lands that shall be purchased by the master and brethren without doing waste on the same lands.

Also that every of the said poor men and women when they shall come into the said house shall bring thither all their moveable goods which they may use at their discretion except when they fall sick or are likely to die at which times they shall have no power to bequeath them to any person except the master and brethren of the said house and that to the use of the same house.

Also that if hereafter the said master and brethren shall obtain sufficient revenues to fulfil all the said payments that then none of the said poor men and women shall afterwards ask alms in the town of Sherborne or any other place and if any of them do then the master and brethren shall do well to put out of the said house such person asking alms and other in his or their stead to choose.

Also that every Master shall at the feast of St John Baptist or within two days after and also at every other time when required by the brethren of the said house having two days warning shall account to the said brethren how and in what manner he hath occupied and disposed him in the said office during the time he hath held it and if during the time of his office it be found upon his account that he hath made any increase that then he shall deliver up unto his brethren the said increase with all such goods belonging to the said house as may come into his hands by virtue of his office, which goods and evidences of the said house (except things in daily use) shall be put into a strong and mighty coffer, bound with iron, standing in a treasure house within the said house, the which coffer shall have five diverse locks and five diverse keys and shall be locked with the said five keys of the which one key shall be delivered to the master of the said house and the other four keys shall be delivered to four other brothers as the house shall agree to, so that the said coffer be not opened but by the assent of the majority of the brethren provided that the master and the four men that shall have the four keys shall be present as often as the said coffer shall be opened.
Also that every brother of the said house who shall be hereafter chosen by their brethren shall pay at his coming into the profit of the said house a certain good as he for the time shall reasonably bear after the advice and assent of the master and brethren.

Also that the said brethren and poor men and women, priest and housewife when they shall first come to the said house shall be sworn on a book that every of them to the utmost of his or her power shall make, do, obey, perform all the said statutes, ordinances and rules and all other statutes, ordinances and rules that in time to come shall be made established and ordained by the master and brethren of the said house and also all other things make do and obey as shall seem to them necessary and expedient for the good governance of the said house.

Statutes and Ordinances of Master and Brethren 1590-1613. Folios 125-126.

Statutes and Ordinances made and established by the master and brethren of the Almshouse of St John the Baptist and St John the Evangelist in Sherborne for the further government of themselves and the poor people of the same house, and the ordering of the lands, possessions and goods of the said Almshouse according to the intent and true meaning of the founders and benefactors thereof, and the authority of the King's letters patent for the foundation and establishing of the said Almshouse, with the several oaths which every of them have taken, and which their successors must take when they become brethren, or been chosen poor men and poor women into the said Almshouse As follows, viz:

The oath of the brethren: You shall swear that you shall and will be faithful and true in the affairs and business appertaining to the Almshouse of St John the Baptist and St John the Evangelist founded in the town of Sherborne. You shall not practise nor go about by any manner of way or means, to acquire obtain or get to your self, or to any other person or persons whatsoever any further or other estate of and in the lands and tenements called the Hyle, and Burports in Sherborne aforesaid, now in the possession of Margaret Couthe and Robert Ashborne or their or either of their assigns, the lands and tenements in Yetminster and Beer Hackett in the tenures of John Couth, Richard Veale and John Baller their or either of their assigns (being the possessions of the said Almshouse) other than for seven years and not above in any one demise. And that for so much yearly rent to be improved as the same may be found to be yearly worth (communibus annis). You shall to the utmost of your power, wit and endeavour do and be aiding to the furtherance and the maintenance of the good estate and estimation of the master and brethren of the same and their successors and increase of the lands, tenements, goods and chattels of the same house, according to the intent of the foundation thereof and the laws and statutes heretofore made and to be made concerning the same (not being contrary to the laws and statutes of this realm). The counsels of the said master and brethren concerning the said Almshouse, you shall well and truly keep and not disclose. So help you God.

The oath to the Supremacy: I A. B. do utterly, testify and declare in my conscience that the ~~Queen's~~ King's highness is the only supreme ~~sovereign~~ governor of this realm, and all other his highness dominions and countries, as well in all spiritual or ecclesiastical things or causes, as temporal, and that no foreign prince, person, prelate, state or potentate, has or ought to have any jurisdiction, power, superiority, pre-eminence or authority, ecclesiastical or spiritual within this realm. And therefore I do utterly renounce and forsake all foreign jurisdictions, powers, superiorities, and authorities, and do promise that from henceforth I shall bear faith and true allegiance to the ~~Queen's~~ King's highness his heirs and lawful successors, and to my power shall assist and defend all jurisdiction, privileges, pre-eminence's, and authorities, granted or belonging to the ~~Queen's~~ King's highness his heirs and successors, or united or annexed to the imperial crown of the realm, so help me God, and by the contents of this book.

The oath for the poor men and women and the housewife: you shall swear that during the time that you shall be and continue one of this house to live by the alms thereof, you shall dutifully demean yourself to the master and brethren of this house. You shall be ordered, ruled and governed by the ordinances and rules of the same house, you shall not practice and commit nor consent to be committed any wrong, waste or disprofit to this house, nor in the goods or provision thereof, but knowing any to be committed or pretended you shall without delay or concealment, reveal and make the same known to the master and brethren or some of them. And in all things so behave yourself as one worthy of your continuance of the company to which you are now chosen upon your own instance and entreaty, So help you God.

13 May 1590. It is ordained and established by the master and brethren hereafter named: Thomas Barton, William Pope, Hugh Whetcombe, John Wynnyff, Jasper Fridlock, Edmond Lane, William Rydowte, Henry Stevens, Thomas Swetnam, Richard Downton, John Whetcombe, Edward Pond, John Gardener, John Cupper, Ambrose Banwell, Peter Game, Edward Knoyle esquire, George Uvedale gentleman and Bartholomew Olde, that when cause shall be ministered and needful for an assembly and meeting to be had by the master and brethren: the master for the time being shall cause the prior of this house or other able man of the poor men thereunto to be assigned, to warn all the brethren at their houses, or elsewhere within the limits of the town who may be conveniently spoken to, to repair to this house at an hour by the master to be appointed by the sounding of the bell. And such brother being thus warned, and shall be in the town at the warning given, or after and before the hour occurred and make default, and shall not show an urgent cause of his absence, so to be deemed and adjudged by the most part of the company at their next meeting, shall forfeit and pay for every such default 12*d.* to be satisfied and paid before the account then next ensuing upon demand to be made by the master for the time being.

20 September 1700. This order is confirmed by the company to continue and the penalty for the default is to be disposed of as the company shall think fit and in case of non-payment on demand the person offending is to be expelled.

Item that the master and brethren being assembled: the master and steward of this house for the time being shall take their place amidst the table and the master shall require every brother then present to take their place according to the length of his being a brother of this house, excepting to the gentlemen which are and shall be of this house, their place according to their worthiness as the master shall also appoint.

Item that after the table is set, the master or steward for the time being, by the master's appointment shall propound to the company the cause of their assembly, beginning upon some one cause first which being moved, any one brother, (taking leave of the master and brethren with his hat or cap put off) may speak to it. And if the cause thus propounded shall grow to a question the master shall require the youngest brother to speak first his mind and consent, the rest giving way without disturbance, and so every brother in his degree, and the master last. And what shall be ordered and consented by the most part, shall stand and be allowed, firm and stable. And if the voices be equal, the voices of the most ancient brethren are to stand and be allowed.

Item if any brother shall have any matter to be moved for the wellbeing and good of this house, he shall first deliver the same to the master or steward of this house, to be delivered over to the company by them as aforesaid. Or as it shall come to his mind in any such present assembly as abovesaid taking then leave of the master and brethren being set at the table with his hat or cap put off, shall and may move the same, which being received and shall grow into a question shall be determined as in the article last before recited.

Item if any brother or brethren of this house upon any matter or cause are against each other, or upon any cause for the wellbeing of this house, shall in any such assembly fall into any indecent speech or high words and shall not give over upon the motion of the master or steward for the time being. He and they for offending shall pay for every such offence such fine and fines as on him, or them, shall be imposed by the major part of the company then present. And if he or they shall wilfully refuse to pay such fine or fines, or shall refuse to be ordered by the major part of this company, or shall disclose and make known from out of this house, to any other person or persons whatsoever, any matter, thing or cause, that may or shall be prejudicial to this house, or thereby to bring the name of any brother of this house in question, for and concerning any cause of this house, that then such brother or brethren so offending and being adjudged by the most part of this company worthy of expulsion, shall be expelled and lose his place in this house for ever.

9 August 1602. Item it is this day ordered and agreed by the consent of the assembly of John Wynchell master, Thomas Barton, Hugh Whetcombe, Edmond Lane, Henry Stevens, Thomas Swetnam, John Cupper, Peter Game, Edward Knoyle esquire, George Uvedall gentleman, Robert Ashborne, John Thorne, Walter Albyn, John Foster and Richard Wright, that whereas various sums of money, that are already given to the use of the Almshouse, to be employed to sundry godly and charitable uses part whereof are already received, and do remain in the hands of some of the brethren of this house and part hereafter are to be received: it is now fully consented that if any of the brethren of this house shall not answer and pay, all such sums of money and goods as shall remain in his hands upon any arrears of account or otherwise be certainly known to rest in his hands due to be employed by this corporation. That the company shall admonish him in a friendly manner three times, at reasonable days to be set, to bring in the same sums. At which third time, if any refuse or fail to pay the same the party so offending is forthwith to be expelled out of this society and present course to be taken by course of law to recover the same. And such stocks and sums of money shall be employed by the consent of the major part of the brethren and not otherwise. And afterwards to this consents, John Wynnyff.

19 April 1613. Item it is this day ordered agreed and established by the consent of Lawrence Swetnam master, John Wynnyff, Henry Stevens, Robert Ashborne, John Wynchell, Walter Albyn, John Foster, Richard Couthe, William Sterr, Walter Rydowte, Robert Whetcombe, William Rydowte, Joseph Forrest and Richard Foster, according to former motions in this behalf made and agreed upon. That if any brother of this house shall be chosen to be master of this house to execute that office for one whole year and shall refuse the same, shall forfeit and pay for a fine to the use of the poor of this house 40s. and to be paid within one month. And if any such brother shall refuse to pay such fine, or any other fine imposed or to be imposed upon him for any offence or contempt to be by him committed shall be deemed adjudged and taken as no brother of this house. And that it shall be lawful to the said master and brethren and their successors to elect and choose another inhabitant of this town to be a brother in his place, as though he were for good cause expelled or dead.

19 April 1613. Item it is ordered, agreed and established by consent aforesaid that for avoiding of many inconveniences which by late experience, is found that the affairs of this house have been much hindered in the good purposes intended by the master and some brethren by the absence of some other brethren departed to dwell far remote from this town as in any reasonable time they can not be called hither to attend and bear office according to the statute, rules and ordinances established in and by the founders and foundation of this house and to which they are sworn. It is therefore now ordered, according to former purposes agreed upon

herein, that every such brother of this house that is departed from this town with his family, and now resident and dwelling above three miles from this town (being made to understand this order) and shall not return within one year from the feast of the Nativity of St John Baptist now next ensuing and make his continuance and abode here in this town or parish or within three miles of this town, or shall refuse to take upon him and execute the office of master of this house, being there unto lawfully elected and chosen, and notice thereof given at his house and place of abode, shall be deemed adjudged and taken no longer to be a brother of this house. And that it shall be lawful to and for the said master and brethren and their successors or the major part of them, to elect and choose one other inhabitant of this town to be a brother in his place as though he were for good cause expelled from the society of this company or dead. And that if any brother now of this house or shall be hereafter chosen to be a brother of this house, shall depart this town to be resident and dwelling from this town above three miles as aforesaid, and shall so continue above one whole year from the day of such his departure shall likewise be deemed adjudged and taken to be no longer a brother of this house, and that it shall be lawful to and for the said master and brethren and their successors to elect and choose another inhabitant of this town, to be a brother in his place as though he were for good cause expelled or dead. The like orders as these two last, for the school are so agreed

ENDOWMENTS AND BEQUESTS

Founders and Benefactors. Folio 4.

Memorandum that the Almshouse of St John Baptist and St John the Evangelist was founded 10 January 1448.

The names of the founders and benefactors of the same house:

Robert Neveile, then Bishop of Sarum who procured the licence of mortmain.

Sir Humphrey Stafford, lord of Hooke, who gave £10 and nine oaks of timber towards the building.

Margaret Goffe, widow, lady of Langton Long Blandford who gave one messuage called the Julyan on the green in Sherborne.

John Faunteleroy, gentleman, dwelling at the marsh now called Fauntleroys Mershe gave £20 and eighty loads of timber towards building the house and his wife gave £5.

John Baret, gentleman, dwelling in Sherborne in Lodburne street £5.
John Browning, clerk, parson of the Green gave £5.
John Gothill, clerk, gave £5.
John Therlewin, clerk, gave £5.
Roger Lyffdon and his wife gave £5.
John Scriveine and his wife gave £5.
John Knaplock and his wife gave £5.
John ~~Walis~~ Wyleis and his wife gave £5.
John Dene and his wife gave £5.
John Keylway and his wife gave £5.
Thomas Donne and his wife gave £5.
John Spacard and his wife gave £5.
John Giet and his wife gave £5.
Stephen Leymon and his wife gave £5.
Thomas Doget and his wife gave £5.
Thomas Sparow and his wife gave £5.
Richard Deveas and his wife gave £5.
John Grening and his wife gave £5.
Richard Heckis and his wife gave £5.
Walter Weston and his wife gave £5.
Richard Rochell, the first master of the Almshouse, and his wife gave £5.
John Barvote and his wife gave £5.
William Smith junior and his wife gave £5.
William Moris of Compton and his wife gave £6 13*s.* 4*d.*
Thomas Worffe and his wife gave £5.
John Gilbert of Camyll and his wife gave £20 towards purchasing the land and to be a brother of the house.

Elizabeth Latimer, widow, gave this house the lands that are in Yetminster, Spittell and Beer Hackett.

Peter Game has given into this house for the maintenance of one poor man for ever according to the intent and meaning of an indenture dated the 1 June 1589 the counterpart of which remains in this house £50.

Sir John Horsey knight deceased gave to this house £10 yearly during the term that he, the said Sir John Horsey, had held the prebend of Sherborne. The payment began from the death of the said Sir John Horsey at £10 per annum.

Memorandum that Mistress Jane Serger gave to the poor of this house 40*s.* by the year to be paid for ten years 40*s.* per annum.

Memorandum that Mr John Chetmill senior lately deceased and a brother of this
    house by his will gave 40*s.* to this Almshouse to be disposed of by the master and
    brethren as they shall think fit, and it was paid to John Whetcombe, master, 13
    April 1640 by John Chetmill junior.

Bequests 1589-1610. Loose folio A and folio 5.

William Masters 1589
William Masters of Sherborne, being so moved in good zeal of the relief of the decayed
    householders and inhabitants of this town, to be relieved in this Almshouse,
    following the charitable and laudable example of the founders and benefactors
    of this same house, has this Easter eve 1589 freely given and delivered into this
    house the full sum of £50. One poor woman, as of his free alms and gift, being now
    presented by him and received into this house, shall have and enjoy the benefit of
    the same during her life. And after her death another poor woman will be selected
    from time to time for ever. This charitable deed of the said William Masters, the
    master and brethren of this house, now presently assembled, do most thankfully
    accept; and according to the foundation of this house to be registered amongst
    the records of the acts and deeds of the founders and other benefactors. The
    poor people here are to make continual commemoration of him by giving thanks
    to God in their prayers. This was done in the presence of Mr Cowper now master
    of the house, Thomas Barton, Brian Cole, John Moleyns, Hugh Whetcombe, John
    Wynnyff, Jasper Fridlock, Edmond Lane, Henry Stevens, Thomas Swetnam, John
    Whetcombe, Edward Ponde, John Gardener, Ambrose Banwell, Peter Game,
    Edward Knoyle esquire and George Uvedall gentleman.

Sir John Horsey
The right worshipful Sir John Horsey by his last will and testament bearing date 9 April
    1589 gave to this house in manner and form following: where as I am possessed
    of the prebend of Sherborne and of all and singular tithes, oblations, pensions,
    profits, commodities and emoluments whatsoever to the said prebend belonging
    or appertaining with the appurtenance for the term of thirty years of which twenty
    six years or there abouts are yet to come of the demise of our sovereign Lady the
    Queen's majesty by her letters patent under her great seal of England dated the 13
    June 1574, I do by these presents devise and bequeath the same lease and the term
    to my beloved wife. Nevertheless my mind, intent and purpose is, and I do devise
    will and appoint that the master and brethren of the Almshouse of Sherborne shall
    have out of the said prebend one annual or yearly rent of £10 to be paid by my
    said wife her executors or assigns to have and to hold the same annuity or yearly
    rent for and during so many years of the said term of twenty six years as shall be
    to come next ensuing after my death at the feast of St John Baptist, St Michael
    the Archangel, Christmas and the Annunciation of our Lady by even and equal

portions to be paid <u>upon this condition</u> trust and confidence that they the said master and brethren by the direction of my executor shall employ the same in stock to set on work and maintain the poor of the town of Sherborne aforesaid, with a clause of distress by 28 days after the quarter being last demanded. For default of distress then to retain the said prebend, the tithes and profits to their own use until they be [*illegible word*] paid or tendered the averages of the said rents and no longer.

Sir John Horsey died the 26 July 1589 and made Sir Raffe Horsey his executor and the first quarterly payment began at Christmas following.

Sir Raufe Horsey

According to the intent and gift of the said Sir John Horsey, and for the due and true execution of the trust placed by him in the said master and brethren, Sir Raufe Horsey executor of the last will and testament of the said Sir John Horsey, by his writing under his hand and seal has authorised the said master and brethren to do and perform in the premises as follows. I Sir Raufe Horsey of Clifton in the County of Dorset executor of the last will and testament of Sir John Horsey deceased do consent ordain and allow that the master and brethren of the Almshouse of St John Baptist and St John Evangelist in Sherborne in the said county of Dorset, do demand and receive of George Uvedall, gentleman, so much of the sum of £25 remaining in his hands with the obligations taken in the name of me the said Sir Raufe Horsey of the several persons to whom the residue of the said £25 is delivered (being part of the annuity of £10 received), devised and bequeathed to the said master and brethren to the use and purpose declared by the said Sir John Horsey by his last will and testament.

I do further ordain, consent and allow the said master and brethren and their successors, or the more part of them, to deliver such sums of money as they have already received and shall hereafter receive by virtue of the said last will, to the most sufficient persons, inhabitants of the said town of Sherborne, (being men of handy craft, science, trade or mystery) that will undertake the same in a proportionable manner, that the poor inhabitants of the same town that can labour, may be set on work and maintained, according to the true intent and meaning of Sir John Horsey by his last will expressed.

To that end the said sums of money shall and may continue in stock for ever for the purpose before mentioned. I the said Sir Raufe Horsey do further consent ordain and allow the said master and brethren and their successors, or the more part of them, to take security of the person and persons to whom they shall deliver any such sum or sums of money, to be bound to the said master and brethren and their successors in double the sum by obligation with two or more sufficient sureties (if cause require) to repay the said sum and sums of money to the said master and brethren and their successors in the feast day of the Holy Trinity [*Sunday after*

Pentecost] or within [blank] days after the same feast. Provided always that none of the brethren nor their successors nor any of them shall be sureties for any of the said parties to whom any part of the said money shall be lent or delivered. Provided also that the said master and brethren have received some part of the said annuity for certain years now past, not knowing otherwise but that the same appertained to the proper use of the said Almshouse, and not for the purpose or use above mentioned. The same money by means of the Late Deare years were spent and employed in the sustenance and relief of the poor of the said Almshouse, the meaning of me the said Sir Raufe Horsey is, that the said master and brethren shall not otherwise be compelled to pay the same, but by an yearly payment in sort as their ability shall afford. In witness whereof I the said Sir Raufe Horsey to this deed my seal have put, 24 October 1597

The gift of Charles Broke esquire, October 1612.
Memorandum that George Rowkley servant of the right worshipful Charles Broke esquire deceased did deliver to the master of the Almshouse of Sherborne, 18 October 1612 as the gift of Charles Broke £10 to be employed for any uses of the said town that the master and brethren of the Almshouse shall think most fit and convenient, to be continued in perpetuity. And this was entered in the presence of Laurence Swetnam master, John Wynnyff, Henry Stevens, Walter Albyn, John Foster, Robert Whetcombe, William Rydowte, Thomas Compton gentleman, Richard Foster, Richard Couth and William Sterr.

The gift of William Woode gentleman, 20 October 1609.
The gift of William Woode gentleman, master of art in the university of Oxford, late deceased, and for diverse years past schoolmaster of the Free Grammar School of King Edward the Sixth in Sherborne in the County of Dorset, by his writing under his hand and seal 20 October 1609, out of his godly zeal and love to the poor of the said town of Sherborne and the poor people, inhabitants of the City of Hereford, and for the more increase of the revenues, lands and tenements of the Almshouse of St John Baptist and St John the Evangelist in Sherborne. For the maintenance of two: three or four poor people with the other alms people there, as the master and brethren of the said Almshouse and their successors shall think convenient, and as the profit of the premises, according the maintenance and allowance of the other almsmen and almswomen proportionably will keep, relieve and maintain and that the said poor inhabitants of the City of Hereford might be assured of £10 by the year did by his writing grant Laurence Swetnam and John Cupper diverse messuages, lands and tenements in Hermitage in the County of Dorset, to have and to hold to the said Laurence Swetnam and John Cupper or their heirs and assigns to these uses and intents following:
1. The messuages, etc, lately the inheritance of Thomas Sherwyn, and lately in the tenure of Richard Lane, that were granted to the use of William Wood and Agnes his wife for term of their lives. Afterwards to the use of John Foster and his

assigns for term of his life. After their decease to the use of Richard Cupper son of the said John Cupper during his life, and after his decease to the use of the said Laurence Swetnam and John Cupper and their heirs forever.

2. The two closes called Upper Newporte and Nether Newporte, and all other premises to the use of the said William Wood and Agnes for term of their lives and after their decease, to the use of the said John Foster for term of his life. After his decease to the use of the said Lawrence Swetnam and John Cupper their heirs and assigns for ever, yielding and paying to the said William Wood his heirs and assigns 1 *d.* upon demand at Michaelmas [29 September] yearly with warranty against the said William Wood and his heirs.

After the end of the estate of William Wood (and licences obtained from the immediate lords of whom the premises are held) the said Laurence Swetnam and John Cupper by learned counsel, shall convey and assign the remainder of the premises to the master and brethren of the said Almshouse. In default of such a licence, by like advice, to such person and persons and their heirs, as to the said William Woodd, Laurence Swetnam, John Foster and John Cupper, or the survivor or survivors of them shall seem convenient, for the relief, sustenance and continual maintenance of the said two, three or four poor people, and that the said premises by the advice of learned counsel, shall be by Lawrence Swetnam and John Cupper and their heirs charged and made liable to the yearly payment of £10 of lawful money of England for ever for and towards the relief of the poor people and inhabitants of the city of Hereford in the county of Herefordshire. The payment is to begin immediately after the decease of William Wood, Agnes his wife and John Foster and the £10 is to be conveyed to such persons and in such manner and form as by the counsel, learned in the law, of the said Lawrence Swetnam and John Cupper and their heirs as shall be reasonably and lawfully thought fit.

The said Lawrence Swetnam and John Cupper by one other deed dated the 20 December 1610 conveyed all the premises to Edward Knoyle esquire, George Uvedall gentleman, John Wynnyff, Henry Stevens, Robert Ashborne, Richard Wright, Walter Rydoutt, William Sterr, John Wynchell, Richard Couthe, John Hodynott, Walter Albyn, Peter Game, Robert Whetcombe, Joseph Forrest, William Rydowte and Thomas Compton gentleman, and their heirs.

Mistress Agnes Wood wife of William Wood, deceased, by her deed 1 September 1608; gave and granted to Robert Whetcombe and Walter Albyn all the lands mentioned in the grant of William Wood [above], with livery and seisin executed by Walter Glover her attorney, 3 September 1608.

A note of how the lands came to the master, sergeant Hanam or his father John Hanam and how the said lands came to Mr William Wood before they were conveyed to the Almshouse:

1. 14 July 1592. Thomas Hanam sergeant at law by a bargain and sale granted to Thomas Sherwyn of Forston and his heirs all that messuage, etc, lately in the tenure of Richard Lame.

2. 2 July 1592. Thomas Hanam did bargain and sell to John Fryer and his heirs all the tenements, etc, then or lately in the tenure of Richard Chick. And afterwards a release was made from Sir John Hanam, son and heir of the said Thomas Hanam with a release from Penelope wife of Thomas Hanam in her widowhood.

3. 2 July 1592. Thomas Hanam did bargain and sell to William Myntern and his heirs, a meadow and pasture containing 12 acres in the tenure of John Peter alias Poynter, acknowledged by the said Thomas Hanam and his wife Penelope. The property being leased by Thomas Hanam 10 April 1577 to John Peter, Richard his son and Constance daughter of Richard for the term of their lives.

4. 20 April 1577. Lease by Thomas Hanam and Penelope his wife to Richard Chick of one tenement, etc, for life with remainder to Agnes his wife and Timothy Chick for their lives. Rent 23s. heriot the best beast.

5. 7 October 1595. Bargain and sale, from Thomas Sherin and John his son to Robert Lovelace and his heirs of all that messuage and tenement, etc, in the tenure of Richard Lane with two other deeds lending the uses of the premises for the livelihood and maintenance of Thomas Sherin for his life, and afterwards to the use of John Sherin and his heirs.

6. 31 March 1597. Robert Lovelace by a bargain and sale granted the premises in the tenure of Richard Lane, to William Wood, gentleman, and his heirs with a covenant that within ten years, he and all persons pretending any interest shall further act, etc. [*Contemporary note*] Query: what Thomas Sherin and John Sherin have done.

7. 2 January 1606. John Fryer, Agnes his wife and Timothy Chicke, bargained and sold to William Wood and Agnes his wife and their heirs certain closes in Hermitage formerly in the tenure of Richard Chick, with a covenant for further assurance within one year upon request, with related obligations.

8. 25 March 1606. The same parties bargained and sold to William Wood and Agnes his wife and their heirs a messuage and tenement, etc, with a covenant that they were, within ten years, to make further assurance upon request with a bond of this date to perform covenants. With a fine from Robert Lovelace, Joan his wife, John Fryer, Agnes his wife and Timothy Chick to make good both the two last recited deeds.

9. 20 January 1605. William Mynterne and Constance his wife a bargain and sale granted to Henry Mintern and his heirs certain meadow and pasture in Hermitage containing by estimation twelve acres, with a covenant at all times upon reasonable request to make further assurance.

10. 20 September 1605. William Mynterne and Constance and Henry Mynterne and Anne his wife bargained and sold the said twelve acres of meadow and pasture to William Wood and Agnes his wife, and the heirs of William Wood with a covenant to make further assurance within one year upon request, with a

bond of William and Henry of £280 and a bond of William to Henry to perform covenants and a fine by all four parties to make good the grant to William Wood and his wife.

Bequests to Almshouse, 1589-1673. Folios 7- 8.

Sir John Horsey's will, 9 April 1589.
£10 annually to the master and brethren of the Almshouse of Sherborne for certain years. Upon this condition, trust and confidence that they, by the direction of my executor, (which was Sir Rauff Horsey, knight) should employ the same in stock and set it to work to maintain the poor of Sherborne.

Mr William Knoyll's will.
£46.13s 4d. to be employed in loans to young occupiers in Sherborne of good conversation and disposition to remain and endure as a perpetuity for ever.

Mr John Foster's will, 21 December 1628.
Imprimis, I do give and bequeath to the master and brethren of the Almshouse of St John the Baptist and St John the Evangelist in Sherborne and to their successors the sum of £200 of lawful money to be paid within one year and six months after my death. To be used by the master and brethren, their successors and my executors either lent yearly, upon good security, to the poor inhabitants of Sherborne and so to be continued as a stock forever or to be lent, ordered, employed or bestowed for the best benefit of the poor inhabitants as to the said master and brethren, or the greater part of them, together with my executors their assigns shall be thought best as well for the preservation of the stock as for the continual benefit of the poor.

Mr Nicholas Winniffe's will.
The other fourth part of the profits of the leases shall be by them paid to the master and brethren of the Almshouse of St John Baptist and St John the Evangelist in Sherborne to set poor artificers of the town to work for their better maintenance according to the discretion of the master and brethren.

The will of Mr Robert Eaves, late minister of Hermitage, 24 March 1639.
I give to the master and brethren of the Almshouse of St John the Baptist and St John the Evangelist in Sherborne and to their successors £100 of lawful English money. To be paid within one year after my death in trust to be employed by them in purchasing some land, the yearly profit and benefit of which shall remain and be paid to the vicar of the parish of Hermitage and to his successors there for his and their better maintenance for ever.
This will was proved in the Arches by George Fox the elder his executor.

Mr Eastmont's gift, 26 October 1668.

Mr John Eastmont, formerly a member of the company, by his will gave £100 to the master and brethren of this house in manner and form following: I give and bequeath to the master and brethren of the Almshouse of Sherborne and to their successors for ever £100 of lawful English money to be paid to them within two years after my death. It is to be used by Master and Brethren to the best advantage as they shall think fit: the yearly increase or proceed shall be employed for buying of such necessary garments for the poor people in Sherborne that are not maintained by the Almshouse as my executor shall think fit and appoint during his life time at Michaelmas yearly. After my executor's decease it shall be distributed as the master and brethren and their successors shall think fit for ever. Mr Eastmont died 4 March 1668.

18 January 1670. The said £100 was paid into the Almshouse by Mr John Eastmont the testator's son and executor 18 January 1670 in the presence of John Whatcombe the elder, James Wallis, William Sansom, William Thornton, John Whetcombe junior, Thomas Foyle, George Cunington, Robert Avoake, Hugh Hodges junior, William Martin, and Valentine Smith, master.

1 May 1673. Mr Hugh Hodges the elder by his will gave £40 to the master and brethren of this house in manner and form following: I give to the master and brethren of the Almshouse of Sherborne £40 to be distributed by them with the consent of my executors to such poor artificers of Sherborne as they and my executors shall think fit.

5 August 1673. The said £40 was paid into the Almshouse by Hugh Hodges esq. the said testator's son and executor in the presence of John Whetcombe the elder, James Wallis, William Sansom, Thomas Sansom, John Durnford, William Thornton, Thomas Foyle, George Conington, Robert Avoke master, Hugh Hodges esquire, William Martin, Valentine Smith, Mr John Eastmont and John Fisher. The persons to whom the £40 was distributed are as follows:

	£	s.	d.
William Hodges		03	00
William Blake		02	00
George Bishop		01	00
Thomas Michell		01	00
Robert Hider		01	00
William West		01	00
Jasper Walter		01	00
John Stichen		01	00
Roger Mandfeild		01	00
William Gent senior		00	10

	£	s.	d.
Jacob Thorneton		01	00
Richard Chant smith		01	00
Edward Michell		01	00
Walter Hancocke		01	00
John Upshall		00	10
Robert Foster		01	00
John Glyde smith		01	00
Christopher Osmond		01	00
William Eddings		01	00
John Pike		01	00
James Jeffery		01	00
Samuel Piddle		01	00
Edward Justins		00	10
Thomas Hayward		01	00
John Scott		01	00
George Easley		00	10
William Brittaine		01	00
William Michell weaver		00	10
John Dober senior		00	10
Robert Justins		01	00
Phillip Warr		00	10
Thomas Matthew		00	10
Richard Chant buttonmaker		01	00
Thomas Whellier		01	00
John Gulliford		00	10
Hercules Hodges		01	00
Robert Talbot		00	10
Thomas Ridout		01	00
Humfrey Penney		01	00
George Holis		00	10
John Penney mason		00	10
William Hopkins		01	00
John Hamblin tailor		00	10
John Ryall		00	10

Memorandum: 27 December 1682. Mrs Dorothy Eastmont of Sherborne, widow, the administrator of Elizabeth Eastmont, spinster, her late daughter, deceased, gave and delivered to the master and brethren of this house and to their successors for ever the sum of £100 of lawful English money to be either let out on security at interest by the said master and brethren and their successors or laid out in land as they shall think fit. The yearly increase and profit of any land to be paid to the vicar of the parish Church of Sherborne for the time being by half yearly payments. The said Elizabeth Eastmont often declared in her life time that it was her intention and desire that so much of her money should be bestowed to such a charitable use after her death. The £100 was paid to Mr Robert Wyer, submaster.

Memorandum: 15 December 1686. The said Mrs Dorothy Eastmont gave and bequeathed to the master and brethren of the Almshouse of St John the Baptist and St John the Evangelist in Sherborne and their successors the sum of £50 lawful English money to be either invested in lands or let out on security at interest as they shall think fit. The yearly profits to be paid to the vicar of the parish church of Sherborne by half yearly payments (that is to say) at Michaelmas and Lady Day in equal portions. Then she gave and bequeathed to the master and brethren and their successors a further sum of £50 to be either invested in lands, or let out on security at interest, as they shall think fit, the yearly profit and increase to be bestowed yearly at Lady Day in linen changes for poor old wives and widows of the inhabitants of Sherborne. My wish is that these sums shall be paid within one year after my decease. The said sum was paid in by Mr Francis Eastmont and by Mrs Martha Eastmont, executors of Mrs Dorothy Eastmont, the 27 December 1687, and are put into the school chest.

Memorandum: 4 March 1684. Dr Nathaniel Highman of Sherborne did devise by his last will and testament, which afterwards was proved in the Prerogative Court of Canterbury, by Richard Highmore clerk and George Parry esquire the 7 December 1695 in manner following: after the Decease of my wife I do give to the masters of the Almshouse in Sherborne the sum of £50 to be employed towards the erecting of a workhouse to set the poor to work, if they shall go about such work, to be paid by my executor. Died 20 March 1684.

And there is a clause in the same will to this effect following that I give to my cousin Sir John Burbidge £5 per annum for six years towards his maintenance in the university, if he stays there so long, to be raised out of the rents of my houses in the borough of Newland in Sherborne by my Executors and paid by them. After the expiry of that six years, or when he leaves the university, then I give that £5 per annum to such poor boys as shall be sent from the Free Grammar School in Sherborne by the choice of the governors of the school and the master with my executors to the university for the same term of six years, if he shall continue there so long, and so from time to time during the term of seventy six years.

Memorandum: 23 February 1730. Mr John Ellis was nominated by the governors to receive the £5 per annum pursuant to Dr Highmore's will from the 25 March 1730.

Memorandum: 14 April 1733. The above named Mr John Ellis left the university and it is agreed that Benjamin Wilding, son of the Reverend Mr Wilding, shall have the £5 per annum pursuant to Dr Highmore's will from the 25 March last past.

Memorandum: 3 April 1739. The term of six years has expired during which the above mentioned Benjamin Wilding was to receive the £5 yearly pursuant to the said Dr Highmore's will it is agreed that Samuel Stavely, son of Mr Joseph Stavely of Emmanuel College in Cambridge, shall have the said £5 from the 25 March now last past.

Memorandum: 27 December 1742. The term of six years has expired during which the above mentioned Samuel Stavely received the £5 yearly pursuant to Dr Highmore's will it is agreed that Charles Yetman, son of Mr Charles Yetman of Emmanuel College in Cambridge, shall have the said yearly £5 from the 25 March last past.

Memorandum: 27 December 1748. The term of six years is expired during which the above mentioned Charles Yetman received the £5 yearly pursuant to Dr Highmore's will it is agreed that Samuel Berjew, son of the Reverend Mr John Berjew deceased of Corpus Christi in Oxford, shall have the said yearly sum of £5 from the 25 March next coming.

Memorandum: 4 November 1751. The term of six years is expired during which the above mentioned Samuel Berjew received the £5 yearly pursuant to Dr Highmore's will. It is agreed that John Ridout, son of George Ridout of Sherborne of Corpus Christi College, Oxford, shall have the yearly sum of £5 from the 25 March last past.

8 June 1753. The above mentioned John Ridout has left the university and has vacated the grant given by Dr Highmore. It is agreed and ordered that John Shuttleworth, son of the Reverend Mr Digby Shuttleworth, of Exeter College, Oxford, shall have and receive the said £5 yearly commencing from Lady Day last.

Memorandum: the before mentioned John Shuttleworth has left the university and has vacated the grant given by Dr Highmore. It is agreed and ordered that [*blank*] Langdon, of Oriell College, Oxford, son of the Reverend Mr Langdon of Mudford, shall have and receive the said £5 yearly from the 25 March 1757.

Mr Wynniff's money disposed. Folio 6.

14 July 1629. Received the sum of £65 11s. 0d. from Mr John Chetmill which is the first money received out of the dividend granted and given by Nicholas Wyniffe to this town of Sherborne due before the feast of St John the Baptist last past.

The same day of the said sum of £65 11s. 0d. was delivered to Mr Richard Cooth the sum of £10 0s. 0d. to be employed and bestowed according to the intention of the donor.

The same day also taken out the sum of £6 0s. 0d. which was allotted to Mr Chetmill for his pains and charges for the profiting of that business for ten years or thereabouts.

28 November 1629. There being received upon the whole revenue £262 4s. 6d. £95 13s. 8d. The dividend to this town amounts to £65 11s. 0d. £23 18s. 5d. delivered up by Mr Chetmill this day into the chest.

The same day delivered to Mr Cooth towards the binding of apprentices £10.

8 June 1630. Delivered to Richard Speede for the binding of apprentices £10 2s. 0d.

Received 18 June 1630 the whole dividend £191 4s. 5d. The dividend thereof to this town amounts to £47 16s. 10d. which was received by Mr Chetmill in London and was on 20 July 1630 left by him in this house.

20 July 1630. This day 20s. paid to Mr Chetmill for his attendance about these receipts in London these two last half years.

The same day £20 was lent to Mr Beakar.

16 November 1630. On this day a fourth part of the dividend money was withdrawn by Mr John Chetmell in London out of the gift of Nicholas Winefe for half a year ended at Michaelmas the sum of £27 12s. 6½d. The said sum of £27 12s. 6½d. was paid by Mr John Chetmell to this house 11 January 1630.

11 January 1630. On this day £47 was taken out of the stock to be given to poor artificers in this house according to the will.

21 January 1630. Taken out to be distributed in the town to poor artificers £9 0s. 0d.

31 May 1631. This day from Mr Chetmill delivered £29 3s. 3d. of Mr Wynniffe's gift due at Our Lady Day [25 March]. Whereof 20s. was paid to him for his attendance this last year.

19 July 1631. The same day the sum of £10 1s. 1d. was taken out of Mr Winniff's money and delivered to Mr Richard Coothe to be employed according to the intent of the donor.

4 June 1632. Mr John Chetmill the elder brought in £24 15s., one quarter of the dividend of the gift of Mr Nicholas Winiffe at the account for the last six months ending at Lady Day, taken the 11 May 1632 at which time Mr Chetmill was allowed 20s.

19 September 1632. Delivered to Mr R Couth for ~~bringing~~ binding apprentices £4.
> To William Reade, a fisher, delivered by Mr R Whetcombe 20s.
> To William Banusen, a butcher, delivered by Richard Speede 20s.

17 July 1633. Delivered into the house by John Chetmill the elder of Mr Winniffe's gift for the last half year ended at Lady Day £20 2s. 4d. of which 20s. is given to George Morgan 10s. to William Pond, and £7 taken out to bind apprentices to Henry Durnford.

Gift of William Knoyle of Sherborne 1678 or thereabouts. Loose folio C verso.

Item I give and bequeath unto the master and the brethren of...Almshouse of St John Baptist and St John the Evangelist in Sherborne aforesaid and to their successors to be employed in a loan to the occupiers in Sherborne aforesaid of good conversation and...the sum of £46 13s. 4d. which is to be paid and now remaining in the hands of...Godden of Sherborne aforesaid as appears by two obligations...which employment of the said £46 13s. 4d. after the same received...by the order and discretion of William Couth, Laurence Swetnam, Thomas Swetnam, Bryan Cole and John Wynniffe the elder delivered charged and committed to the said master and brethren of the Almshouse aforesaid to be ordered according to this my intent to remain and endure as a perpetuity for ever.

LANDS AND TENEMENTS OF THE ALMSHOUSE

A copy of a grant of certain land and tenements given to this Almshouse ~~at the erection thereof~~ with the bounds as they were 9 April 1454. Loose folios B recto – C recto.

To all faithful Christians to whom these presents shall come William Combe, John Downton of Folke and William Coulard send greeting in our lord God. Know ye that we (the King's licence to that end obtained) have granted, demised and by these presents confirmed to William Smyth master of the Almshouse of St John Baptist and St John Evangelist of Sherborne and to the brethren of the same house thirty nine messuages, two tofts, one colverhouse, thirty-nine and a half acres of land, nineteen acres and one rood of meadow and one acre of alders with their appurtenances in Sherborne, Beer Hackett and Caundle Marsh.

The messuages:
> 1. One messuage is situated in the town of Sherborne in the tithing of Houndstreet between the tenement lately held by Roger Guldene to the east and the tenement lately held by William Youngs to the west.

2. Another messuage in Sherborne, in Longstreet, between the tenement of the Abbot of Sherborne to the east and the tenement lately held by Richard Rochell to the west.

3. Another messuage in Sherborne, in the liberty of Newland, between the tenement lately held by John Sharp to the west and the tenement lately held by Richard Mucheld nearby to the east.

4. Another messuage in Sherborne in the liberty of Newland, between the tenement lately held by John Boore and the tenement lately held by John Kayle.

5. Another messuage in Sherborne, in the liberty of Newland, between the tenement lately held by John Sparow to the west and the land lately held bye Ivo Fitz-Warreine, knight, to the east.

6. Another messuage in Sherborne in Longstreet in the tithing of Eastbury between the tenement lately held by John Carters to the east and the tenement lately held by John Sparow to the west.

7. Another tenement in Sherborne in Longstreet in the tithing of Eastbury between the tenement lately held by John Draper, to the east and the tenement lately held by William Gauler to the west.

8-9. Two messuages in Sherborne in the tithing of Eastbury in a street called Lodborne between the tenement that William Milward lately held as a tenant of the bishop of Salisbury to the north part and a garden that Walter Winter lately held of the Bishop to the south.

10-11. Two messuages in Sherborne between the tenement of the Abbot of Sherborne near the Bow to the west and the tenement lately held by John Thirlewind near the pillory to the east.

12. Another messuage in Sherborne, in the liberty of Newland, between a tenement lately held by John Sterkerton to the east and the tenement lately held by Hugh Dunpayne to the west.

13. Another messuage in Sherborne, in the liberty of Newland, between the tenement lately held by Walter Kervers to the west and the tenement lately held by Thomas Draper of Camell to the east.

14. Another messuage in Sherborne, in the liberty of Newland, between the tenement lately held by John Ford to the east and the tenement lately held by John Newton to the west.

15. Another messuage in Sherborne, in the liberty of Castletown, between the garden lately held by John Corneys on one side and the cottage of the Bishop of Salisbury that was tenanted by Nicholas Peny on the other side.

16. Another messuage in Sherborne, in the liberty of Newland, in the market place near the pillory.

17. Another messuage in Sherborne, in Houndstreet tithing, between the tenement lately held by Agnes Bores on one side and the cottage of the Bishop of Salisbury that was tenanted by Nicholas Peny on the other side.

18-19. Two messuages in Sherborne, in the liberty of Newland, between the tenement of the Bishop of Salisbury to the west and the tenement lately held by John

Barret in which John Pupelpen lately dwelt to the east.

20-24. Five messuages are situated together in Sherborne, in Houndstreet tithing, between the tenement lately held by Edmund Gildon and afterward by Henry Panters to the east and the wall of the parish churchyard of Sherborne to the west.

25. Another messuage in Sherborne in Longstreet, within the tithing of Eastbury, between the tenement lately held by Thomas Wyffing to the west and the tenement lately held by Robert Langyere to the east.

26. Another messuage in Sherborne on the east side of Westbury street between a tenement of the Bishop of Salisbury on one side and the cottage lately held by John Fitz of the other side.

27. Another messuage in Sherborne in Abbots Fee tithing between the tenement lately held by John Sturtons in which Robert Glover lately dwelt to the south and the tenement lately held by Alice Swettiforde in which Thomas Helier now dwells to the north.

28. Another messuage in Sherborne upon the Green between the tenement lately held by Alice Cote to the east and a tenement of the Abbot of Sherborne near Abbey Lane to the west.

29. Another messuage in Sherborne at the shambles between the tenement lately held by John Ilberte to the north and the tenement of the Abbot of Sherborne to the south.

30. Another messuage in Sherborne at the corner of the lane that leads to the Abbey.

31-32. Two messuages in Sherborne, in Castletown liberty, between Sherborne Castle to the east and the tenement lately held by Silvester Everard to the west.

33-35. Three messuages in Sherborne, in Houndstreet, between the tenement lately held by John Leveden to the north and the tenement lately held by John Ilberd to the south.

36. Another messuage is called the Julyans Inn and is situated in Sherborne between the tenement of the Parson of the Green of Sherborne called the Georges Inn to the north and the street that leads from the Green to Sherborne Castle to the south.

37. Another messuage is called Bridporte Place and is situated in Sherborne in Westbury street.

38. Another messuage in Sherborne between the tenement lately held by John Mucheldever on one side and the Bally near the Churchyard on the other side.

39. Another messuage in Sherborne, in Newland liberty, between the tenement lately held by William Hawkins to the west and tenement lately held by Thomas Gyldon to the east.

The two tofts are situated in Sherborne in Longstreet between the tenement of the Abbot of Sherborne to the east and the tenement lately held by Richard Rochell to the west.

The Colverhouse is situated in Sherborne in the croft near Otters Lane and two and a half acres of the thirty-nine and a half acres of land lie in Sherborne within the liberty of Newland between the tenement lately held by Robert Sharpe to the west and the tenement lately held by Richard Mucheldever to the east.

Half an acre lies in Sherborne within the liberty of Newland between the tenement lately held by John Bort on the one side and the tenement lately held by John Kayle on the other side.

Half an acre lies in the liberty of Newland between the tenement lately held by Roger Gilden on one side and the tenement held by Henry Chapleyne on the other side
One acre lies in the north field of Sherborne near to Woburne Wood.
Two acres lie in the west field of Sherborne the heads of which acres extend them selves on the pasture called Lenthay.
Four acres lie in the furlong called Stoke.
Three acres lie in the croft near Otters Lane.
Two acres lie in Oldlande.
Five acres lie in the croft called Cadenham.
One acre lies in the furlong called Decombe.
Two acres lie in the furlong called Clanneveyle.
One acre lies near Sewelake.
One acre lies on Riggeway.
Two acres lie near old Quarre.
Seven and a half acres lie in Gyldenlond.
Two acres lie in Py furlong.
One and a half acres lie in Standsmore furlong.
One acre lies near Woburne.
Nine and a half acres of meadow of the nineteen acres and one rood of meadow are called Subtrowe and lie in Beer Hackett between the meadow Cadenhamsmead to the east and the bridge called Bowedbrigge to the west.
One acre meadow lies at Caundle Marsh in a certain meadow called Attemede between the meadow once held by Henry Cooke and the meadow once held by Martin of Sherborne.
Four acres lie in a meadow called Cadenhamsmead.
Three roods of meadow lie at Sherborne in Boldmeade.
Two acres of meadow lie at Sherborne in West Moor.
Two acres of meadow lie at Sherborne in Pynteldirne.
The acre of alders lies in Sherborne in Westbury street.

[*Entries in margin:*] The yearly value of the lands: £5 3*s.* 3*d.* The date of this deed is 7 February 1454.

Survey of Lands and Tenements belonging to the Almshouse, 1581. Folios 28-29.

A Survey taken of the lands and tenements belonging unto the Almshouse of St John
the Baptist and St John the Evangelist in Sherborne 1581.

Tenants by indenture:

The parishioners of Sherborne hold of the Almshouse by an indenture dated 18
January 1529 certain cottages where the Church House now stands for the term
of eighty-one years with a covenant for a further grant of eighty-one years of the
premises to be made to the parishioners immediately upon the expiry of the first
eighty-one years, as appears on the counterpart of the grant, for the yearly rent of
26s. 8d.

Yetminster. The assigns of William Meer hold of the Almshouse by an indenture dated
21 December 1538 one tenement with appurtenances called Davidshold for the
term of sixty-one years from Christmas day for the yearly rent of £4. [*Annotated:* this
is ended at Christmas 1599 and granted as after appears. Note that there is a rent
payable on the premises to the bishop of Salisbury of 6s. 10d. And that there is a
rent of 18d. paid to the tenants of the premises by one Shertey.]
[*Annotated:* Now in the tenure of Hugh Whetcombe.]

The assigns of Roger Engelbert hold of the Almshouse one messuage situated at the
Abbylanes end in Sherborne aforesaid by indenture dated 20 August 1535 for the
term of sixty years beginning at Michaelmas for the yearly rent of 16s.
[*Annotated:* This lease is ended and the property is now granted to Robert Ashbornes
for eighty-one years if Jane his wife, George his son, Frances and Jane his daughters
so long shall live, together with the woodbarton. Entry fine £40 and rent as above.]

John Baller holds by an indenture dated 4 July 1532 for the term of his life one close
of pasture lying in Beer Hackett within the hundred of Sherborne commonly called
Subtrow. The yearly rent is 20s. Robert and William his sons hold the same jointly
with their father for the term of their lives by the same deed and for the same rent.

Beer Hackett. Two closes of meadow lying by the river containing (by estimation)
twelve acres are granted by a deed dated 4 October 1558 to John Baller for term
of his life with the remainder to Robert and William his sons for the term of their
lives. Rent 20s. to be paid quarterly. Entry fine £7.
[*Annotated:* Now in the tenure of Richard Duffett.]

The assigns of Sir William Courtney, clerk, hold by an indenture dated the 24 June
1545 one tenement with appurtenances lying within the tithing of Westbury in

Sherborne for 60 years for the yearly rent of 10s.
[*Annotated:* Note: John Wey now holds the same by a grant]

Hugh Meer and Alice his wife hold one tenement granted to the said Hugh Meer, Alice his wife and William their son for the term of their lives, or the longest living, by an indenture dated 9 May 1540 for the yearly rent of 20s. [*Annotated:* Once they had all died, the premises were granted to William and John Bysshopp sons of Jerome Bysshopp of Ilchester by the agreement of Henry their brother, for the same rent.
[*Annotated:* Now in the tenure of Jasper Fridlock.]

The assigns of John Drewer hold one burgage or messuage set within the borough of Newland in Sherborne by an indenture dated 21 March 1564 for the term of 41 years from 24 June for the yearly rent of 20s.
[*Annotated:* The premises at the end of the term are granted to John Busshride for [*blank*], if he and his children so long live, for the fine [*blank*], heriot [*blank*] and rent as above.]

The assigns of John Sterre hold five closes of meadow and pasture called Redlandes with their appurtenances lying within the parish of St James in Shaftesbury within the Liberty of Alchester, one close of pasture called the cliffs lying in Shaftesbury and also a garden in Shaftesbury in the parish of St Laurence formerly in the tenure of Henry Boucher by an indenture dated the 1 June 1566 for the term of 41 years to start after the expiry of a lease held by Walter Percy or his assigns (which lease expired the [blank] day of [blank] in the [blank] year of the Queen's reign. The yearly rent is 27s. 6d.

John Harvy holds one tenement with appurtenances within the tithing of Abbots Fee in Sherborne called the Julyan for the term of [blank] years. The estate was not granted in his lifetime and was afterwards granted to Walter his son for 20s. rent, entry fine £3 waived in consideration of the repairs to be done by the tenant, which were previously done by the master and brethren.

Nicholas Jones holds one parcel of ground adjoining the west part of Nicholas' tenement upon the Green, containing by estimation one yard, upon part of which he built a stable by an agreement dated the 20 September 1578. The term is sixty years from the 8 June 1571 if Nicholas, Robert his son or Anne his daughter live so long. Annual rent 1s. 4d.

William Couth holds by an indenture dated 24 September 1566 all of the farm called the Hyle with all the houses and buildings and one close of pasture called the Colverhaye containing by estimation twelve acres, one close of meadow and pasture called the Hyle Meade containing by estimation five acres, one close of pasture called Deepe Lease containing by estimation six acres, one close of meadow and pasture called Hylehame containing by estimation three roods, one acre of meadow lying in a close belonging to James Toogood at Four Pitts and forty acres of arable with common of pasture for 160 sheep and eight rother beasts in Lenthay and in the common fields of Sherborne. For the term of sixty years from 25 March last past for the yearly rent of 56s. 8d.

[*Annotated*: To set two oaks, two ashes or two elms yearly. To do suit of court as often as it is kept. The master to take pigeons at his discretion twice each year.]

The same William Couth holds one messuage in the market place near the conduit which he inhabits together with one piece of ground, twenty five feet long and two feet broad, lying to the east of the messuage within the house of the bishop of Salisbury. The house was recently built by William Couth who also holds a stable and curtilage in a street called Lodburne by an indenture dated 20 June 1559 for sixty-one years from the previous 25 March for the yearly rent of for the said messuage, stable and curtilage 24s. 8d. and for the ground within the tenement of the Bishop of Salisbury 12d.

[*Annotated*: The premises in the market place are now in the possession of Robert Whetcombe, assigned to him by John Couth son of William Couth by a deed dated 26 January 1603. The tenement in Lotborne is assigned to Jasper Gillett alias Skynner.]

Robert Asheburne holds by an indenture dated the 1 July 1574 a messuage and a toft called Byrporte in Sherborne, a curtilage and a close of pasture lying next to Otter Lane containing three acres, a close of pasture called Cadnam containing five acres, a close on the east side of Okemill containing by estimation one acre and all the arable land, meadow, moor and pasture belonging to the property for the term of thirty-four years for the yearly rent of 53s. 4d.

Richard Spurryar holds by an indenture dated 20 December 1579 a messuage or tenement with appurtenances near the churchyard of Sherborne for the term of ninety-nine years if the said Richard Spurrier, Agnes his wife and Henry his son, or any one of them, so long shall live, for the yearly rent of 14s. 4d.

[*Annotated*: afterwards Agnes being dead and Richard and Henry surrendering their estates, the premises were granted to the same Richard, Henry and Elizabeth wife of Henry for term of their lives by a deed dated [*blank*] in the [*blank*] year of Queen Elizabeth's reign. Entry fine £5, rent as above.]

Survey of Lands and Tenements, 1589. Folios 30-33.

A survey taken of the lands and tenements of the Almshouse of St John Baptist and St John Evangelist in Sherborne, in the tenures of the persons hereafter named 10 September 1589.

John Towgood, Eleanor and Edith hold by copy of court roll dated 30 July 1571 one garden with appurtenances where a house has been built. Rent of 6*d*., entry fine 2*s*. and in consideration of the newly-built premises.

Richard Grey, Elizabeth his wife and John Grey the son of Thomas Grey hold one piece of ground near the Castle, where a house has been built, a backside and garden adjoining. Entry fine 10*s*., rent 2*s*. 6*d*. by copy of court roll dated 29 July 1577.
[*Annotated:* Richard, Elizabeth and John are dead. Robert Wason took the premises to himself and Mary Devenishe by copy dated 31 July 1592 for the entry fine of £10 and at the court held 12 April 1596 surrendered it to Michael Baggi who became tenant with Edward and Michael his sons for the entry fine of £4, and at the court held 16 May 1598 he surrendered it to John Mewe to hold with Elizabeth his wife and Philipp Tyzer son of Edmund Tyzer for the entry fine of 20*s*.]

Richard Yarde, Winifred his wife and Amonell Drake do hold by copy dated 29 July 1577 a garden with appurtenances upon which a house is now built with a garden and backside adjoining, fine 13*s*. 4*d*., rent 4*s*.

William Selby, Cristiana his wife and Katherine his daughter hold by copy dated 30 May 1572 one tenement and a garden in Houndstrete, fine 40*s*., rent 8*s*.

William Were, Lucy the daughter of John Were and Agnes Chapman daughter of William Chapman of Fifehead hold one tenement in Longstreet, late O—, fine £4, rent 8*s*.

Hugh Mere, Alice his wife and John their son hold one close of pasture and meadow beside Mawdlyn [*Magdalene at Castleton*] containing two acres, fine 30*s*., rent 6*s*. 8*d*.
[*Annotated:* The premises being surrendered by Alice and John were afterward granted to William Rydowte and surrendered by him are granted to Sir Walter Raleigh, Dame Elizabeth his wife and Walter their son for the entry fine of £20.]

Joan Dudney by her previous name of Joan Yarde, widow, Robert Downe son of Richard Downe, William Durden son of Robert Durden hold by a copy of court roll dated 10 December 1567 one tenement in Longstreet formerly held by Richard Downes. Entry fine 13*s*. 4*d*., rent 6*s*.

John Felps, John Felps his son and William Vyall alias Harrys hold a shop, between the lands of Julian Reynolds to the south and the land of Robert Mere to the north, by a copy of court roll dated 14 January 1577. Entry fine 40*s*., rent 16*s*.

[*Annotated:* the premises were in the possession of Elizabeth wife to John Felps during her widowhood. The reversion is granted to William Vyall alias Harris and to William and Elizabeth his children, fine 40*s.*]

Richard Palmer, Hugh his son and Isabel his daughter hold one tenement and garden in Newland by a copy of court roll dated 14 January 1577. Entry fine 26*s.* 8*d.*, rent 8*s.*

Richard Willesdon, Brian and Agnes his children hold one tenement in Eastbury by a copy of court roll dated 3 July 1552, entry fine 50*s.*, rent 10*s.*
[*Annotated:* The premises were surrendered by Bryan Willesdon and were granted to Cuthbert Ribby and Elizabeth and Temperance his daughters for the entry fine £15.]

John Hackwood holds one tenement with appurtenances in Longstreet by a copy of court roll dated 26 June 1563, entry fine 10*s.*, rent 8*s.*
[*Annotated:* The premises are granted to John Hackwood the son of John Hackwood, William Glyde and Henry Glide sons of John Glyde by a copy of court roll dated 15 October 1589, entry fine £6 13*s.* 4*d.*, of which £4 13*s.* 4*d.* was paid by John Glyde.]

John Oke and Thomas and Robert his sons hold one tenement in Westbury and one acre of meadow in Pryde Moor by a copy of court roll dated 31 July 1549, entry fine £4, rent 16*s.*

Julian Tynewe the wife of John Tynewe under her former name Julian Rogers, William and Joan her children hold a newly built tenement in Newland by a copy of court roll dated the 7 August 1581, entry fine 30*s.*, rent 8*s.*
[*Annotated:* besides the new building thereof, the previous being in ruins.]

Julian, widow of Thomas Towgood, now wife of Richard Lambe, and Nathaniel son of Thomas Towgood hold one tenement in Newland by a copy of court roll dated 29 July 1577, no entry fine, rent 8*s.*

Henry Taswell and Eleanor his daughter hold one tenement in Newland by a copy of court roll dated 3 July 1552, entry fine 13*s.* 4*d.*, rent 8*s.*
[*Annotated:* Robert Shackle and Eleanor Taswell took the premises by copy of court roll dated 16 April 1593 naming Eleanor, and Christopher and Jerome sons of Robert and Eleanor paying the fine of £5.]

Robert Furks and Thomas (his son) hold one close of pasture in Oborne containing half an acre and one close of meadow in Vertnam containing three rods by a copy of court roll dated 20 May 1559, fine 13*s.* 4*d.*, rent 1*s.* 4*d.*

[*Annotated:* This property was surrendered by Thomas Furks to Walter Hamond and Thomas and James his sons by a copy of court roll dated 16 April 1589, entry fine £2 10s.]

John Wynchell and Agnes his wife hold one tenement in Newland by a copy of court roll dated 3 July 1549 entry fine 5s., rent 10s.
[*Annotated:* The reversion is granted to Laurence Michell, Emma Roberts and Thomas Ladbroke son of Thomas Ladbroke for the entry fine of £10 at a court held 11 September 1584. Afterwards at a court held 5 November 1586 the property was surrendered and granted to John Gillett and two others to be named by him for 20s. over and above the fine of £10 due by Michell and Ladbroke. Afterwards at the court held 28 May 1594 the same John Gillett surrendered his estate and it was granted to John Chaplyn alias Wase son of Jane Chaplyn and two others still to be named for the entry fine of 20s. Afterwards at the court held [*blank*] the same estate was surrendered by John Chaplyn and granted to John Kippen.]

Hammett Hyde, Jane his wife and John Buysshopp son of Laurence Buysshopp hold one tenement in Cheap Street by a copy of court roll dated the 30 June 1560. Entry fine £6, rent 13s. 4d. Hammett Hyde received a licence to hold the land alone 1 March 1574.
[*Annotated:* the premises were surrendered by Hammett, Jane and John and granted to Andrew Redmy, Joan his wife and Alice the daughter of Jerome Chirchill by a copy of court roll dated 11 September 1598, entry fine £7.]

Robert Marchman, Margery Talbott and Elizabeth Burden daughter of Robert Burden hold one tenement in Longstreet by a copy of court roll dated 2 August 1569, entry fine 6s. 8d., rent 8s.

Christian the wife of Thomas Pope, Elizabeth and Mary his daughters hold one tenement in Longstreet by a copy of court roll dated the 16 October 1582. Entry fine £3 6s. 8d., rent 8s.

John Lightfote, Edith his wife and Thomas Michell hold one tenement in Houndstreet by a copy of court roll dated 10 September 1561, entry fine 10s., rent 6s. 8d.
[*Annotated:* The premises are granted to Richard Slade, Thomas and Dorothy his children by copy dated 3 December 1588, entry fine £2 6s. 8d.]

John Howper, Avice his wife and Elizabeth their daughter hold one tenement in Newland by a copy of court roll dated 9 July 1556, entry fine £6 13s. 4d., rent 10s.
[*Annotated:* the premises were surrendered by Avice and Elizabeth at a court held 12 April 1596 and granted to Henry Meer esq. for 99 years if Hugh Meer, Francis, Rose and Eleanor his children so long shall live, entry fine £20.]

John Anderson holds one tenement in the market place by a copy of court roll dated
[*blank*], entry fine [*blank*], rent 6s. 8d.
[*Annotated:* The reversion is granted to Henry Farr, Jane and Emma his daughters for
the term of their lives by a copy dated 8 November 1591, entry fine 20s., rent as
above.]

John Furks, Julian his wife, now wife of John Reynolds, and Joan their daughter now
wife of Jasper Fridlock hold one tenement in the market place by a copy of court
roll dated [*blank*], entry fine [*blank*], rent 13s. 4d.
[*Annotated:* Upon the surrender by John Reynolds and Julian, Jasper and Joan at a
court held 12 April 1596 the premises were granted to Jasper Gillett and Jasper
and [*blank*] his children. And afterwards at a court held 12 October 1601 Jasper,
the father, surrendered the same estate and Thomas Wills took it by copy of court
roll. Fine 20s.]

John Prickett, Alice his wife and John Ittery son of John Ittery hold one tenement
in Houndstreet lately held by John Jorden and one garden formerly held by John
Yardes in Houndstreet for the term of their lives by a copy of court roll dated 17
January 1586. Entry fine £5, rent for the tenement 5s. and for the garden 8d.

Brian Cole, Jerome Cole and Jervais Cole his sons hold one tenement in Lodborne by
a copy of court roll dated [*blank*], entry fine 20s., rent 8s.

John Gardener holds one close of pasture in Castletown containing half an acre by a
copy of court roll dated 30 July 1588. Entry fine £5 3s. 4d., rent 1s. 4d.
[*Annotated:* Surrendered by John Gardener and re-granted to himself and his sons
Edward and Ambrose at a court held 14 January 1590, entry fine £2. And afterwards
at a court held 28 July 1595 the same estate was surrendered and granted to John
Meer and William and Anthony his sons by copy. Entry fine 10s.]

John Thorne, Alice his wife and Julian their daughter hold one tenement in Longstreet
by copy dated 15 June 1576, Entry fine 60s., rent 20s.
[*Annotated:* the same estate was surrendered at a court held 16 April 1593 and
regranted to John Thorne, Alice his wife and Thomas their son, entry fine 6s. 8d.]

John Yarde and Anne his wife hold one tenement in Longstreet for term of their lives
by a copy of court roll dated [*blank*]. Entry fine [*blank*], rent 20s.
[*Annotated:* The premises were surrendered by John and Anne Yarde and granted to
John Thorne, Alice his wife and Thomas their son at a court held 16 April 1593,
entry fine 30s. the rent remains the same.]

Robert Gennyngs holds the parlour, cellar and chambers over the tenement in
Longstreet held by John Yarde and part of the kitchen and barton at The George at

the will of the master and brethren, but he claims that he has a lease of which there is no record. Rent 6s. 8d.

[*Annotated:* The premises are granted to Thomas Forde of Yeovil for [*blank*] years to begin at [*blank*], entry fine 100s. rent as above.]

Thomas Cammell and Nicholas his son hold by a copy of court roll for term of their lives a tenement with appurtenances in Newland, rent 6s. 8d.

[*Annotated:* the premises were surrendered by Nicholas Cammell and granted to John Michell and John and Thomas his sons at a court held 21 January 1595, entry fine £6 13s. 4d., rent as above.]

William Haywood in the right of [*blank*] his wife, daughter of John Drewer, holds one tenement in Newland, rent 8s. Hugh Michell, Robert his son [*the remainder of this entry is blank aside from the rent*] 5s.

Robert Cooke and Margery Parker his daughter, now wife of Edward Parker hold for the term of their lives one tenement and garden in Newland by a copy of court roll dated 25 April 1586, entry fine paid many years ago, rent 8s.

Robert Batten and Gervais Batten hold one tenement in Newland by a copy of court roll dated 25 April 1561, no entry fine, rent 9s.

Cristiana Myles widow of Nicholas Myles, Andrew her son and Agnes her daughter hold one tenement with appurtenances in the tithing of Abbotts Fee of the term of their lives according to the customs of the manor for the annual rent of 8s. by a copy of court roll 10 September 1568 entry fine 13s. 4d.

Thomas Lodge and John his son hold one tenement in Westbury with a garden adjoining by a copy of court roll. [*Rent*] 8s.

[*Annotated*: Upon forfeiture by John Lodge for not repairing the premises and for rent arrears over many years, for which there was no distress to be found, the property was granted to William Vyall alias Harris, and Elizabeth and Joan his daughters, inconsideration of the new building, by a copy at the court held 14 January 1600, entry fine £3.]

Avice Marshall holds one tenement in Le Trendle and a garden by a copy of court roll dated [*blank*]. Rent 8s.

[*Annotated:* the premises are granted to Laurence Michel, Agnes his wife and their first born child, entry fine [*blank*]. And afterwards at a court held 25 April 1586 it was surrendered and granted to Osmond Clothier, Edith Duffet daughter of Anthony Duffet and their first born child, entry fine 6s. 8d. and 15s.]

Thomas Lambert and his sons Edward Lambert and William Lambert hold four acres
of land and a little close with appurtenances in Knighton formerly held by William
Dowle, annual rent 20d., entry fine £8 10s. 0d. by a copy dated 10 September 1568.

William Bisshopp and John Bissopp sons of Jerome Bisshopp of Ilchester hold one
tenement and house in the market place situated between the almshouse on the
east and the lands of William Felipps on the west, for the term of their lives, entry
fine £13 6s. 8d., rent 20s.

Thomas Andrewes and his sons Christopher and Thomas hold by a copy of court
roll dated 5 August 1588 one tenement which Richard Stokes surrendered into the
hands of the master and brethren. Entry fine £5, rent 10s.

John Hull in right of [blank] his wife holds one tenement and garden in Longstreet
for the term of her life by a copy court roll dated [blank], entry fine [blank], rent 8s.

William Franklyn [the remainder of this entry is blank].

Richard Jeffreys in the right of Agnes his wife holds one tenement and garden in
Longstreet for the term of her life by a copy of court roll dated 5 April 1586.
Afterwards at a court held 14 January 1600 Agnes surrendered the property and
it was granted to the same Richard, James and Robert his sons, entry fine £3, rent
11s. Robert Ashborne paid 10s. of the entry fine on behalf of James and Robert.

Walter Albyn and [blank] hold by deed dated the [the remainder of this entry is blank].

Richard Cowthe holds [the remainder of this entry is blank].

John Minterne gentleman holds [the remainder of this entry is blank].

James Munden holds [the remainder of this entry is blank].

Walter Fryer holds a tenement, house and backside in Sherborne in Cheap Street as
assignee of [blank] by a lease made by William Knoyle gentleman deceased for the
term of [blank], rent 13s. 4d.

Laurence Michell holds a tenement and a house near the Broadstone, adjoining the
Almshouse, rent 6s. 8d.

William Lambe holds a close near the Parkgate in Sherborne, rent 4s.

William Weare, Agnes Chapman daughter of William Chapman and Lucy Weare
deceased daughter of John Weare held a tenement in Longstreet which was

surrendered and regranted to William Weare, Alice and Edith his daughters by a copy of court roll 15 March 1602, entry fine £4. The fine is to be paid 20s. at the next account and 20s. at each account for the next three years. Upon any default of payment the estate to be forfeited. Rent 8s.

Margaret Lacye the widow of John Lacye, upon surrender by Cuthbert Ribbye, and Elizabeth and Temperance his daughters, of his estate in a tenement, garden and backside in Longstreet, has taken it for the term of the lives of herself and the said Temperance, by a copy of court roll dated 15 March 1603, entry fine 40s., rent 10s.

Richard Michell has taken the reversion of Lucy his mother of her tenement in Newland, in her possession during her widowhood, for the term of his life and the life of Robert his son by a copy of court roll dated 15 March 1603, entry fine £3 6s. 8d. to be paid 13s. 4d. next Michaelmas and 13s. 4d. annually until the fine is paid. Upon any default of any payment the property will be forfeit. Rent 5s.

Edward Parker and Margery his wife, daughter of Robert Cooke deceased, surrendered a tenement in Newland to Michael Baggi and his sons Edward and Michael for the term of their lives by a copy of court roll dated 15 March 1603. Entry fine to be paid £4 in hand and 40s. 10 July next and so yearly 40s. every 10 July until that sum is paid. Upon any default of any payment the property will be forfeit. Rent 8s.

Terrier of the manors, lands and tenements of the King Edward VI Free Grammar School in Sherborne. Folio 122.

Symondsbury: Henry Chapman's lessee Hugh Meere holds one messuage with a new building and certain closes of land, meadow and pasture called Butlands alias Morbath containing by estimation [*blank*] acres lying and being within the parish of Symondsbury. The closes are sub-tenanted by Henry Shawe and were formerly in the possession of Andrew Houndsell, deceased, and previously they were held by the Chantry of St Katherine in Ilminster in Somerset. The lands are held for the term of thirty one years beginning immediately after the death of Andrew Houndsell for the annual rent of 40s. to be delivered at Sherborne into the hands of the receiver of the school at the four usual terms. The tenant owes a heriot of 13s. 4d. and all rents and services as are customary He is to make all necessary repairs as previous lease holders have at his own expense. And if it happens that the aforesaid rent is in arrears whether for part or the whole of one quarter of a year after it is due, or it happens that wilful waste or damage occurs to the property, the fine is 6s. 8d. and if the arrears are not repaid or repairs not carried out completely and all covenants, payments and articles specified within the agreement are not carried out then the Governors may dismiss the tenant and their successors may reclaim the premises. Entry fine £13 6s. 8d., 6 December 1560.

[*English*]

Memorandum that Andrew Houndsell died fourteen days before Michaelmas 1589.

Summons by HM Commissioners 1631. Attached to Folio 4.

Richard Ballmayne
Humphrey Braddon
Dorset 133

By virtue of his Majesties Commission out of his Highness Court of Exchequer to us and others in that behalf directed. These are to will and require you to make your personal appearance before us his Majesties Commissioners at the Crown in Blandford the 13th of this instant August by eight in the morning. Then and there to pay, or show sufficient cause to us why you should not pay to us his Majesties said Commissioners, or any two or more of us, such rents, arrears of rents, reliefs, and other duties as are now due to his Majesty, for or in respect of the manors, lands, tenements, or other hereditaments hereafter mentioned, and now in the possession of you, or some of your under tenants. And fail you not, as you will answer the contrary at your peril. Given under our hands and Seals the 8 August 1631.

The Queen granted to William Tupper and Robert Daw 25 February 1589 in fee farm: All those lands, tenements and hereditaments in Sherborne in the County of Dorset formerly given to the maintenance of an obit and other superstitious uses within the hospital of St John Baptist and St John the Evangelist of Sherborne amounting to 10s. per annum.

To the owners and occupiers of the premises and to the Constables of Sherborne for the discovery, delivery and return of the above lands, tenements and hereditaments.

OATHS

Oaths for the Brethren, School Governors, School Master, Almspeople and Housewife.
   Folios 179-180.

The master and brethrens oath.

You shall swear that you shall and will be faithful and true in the affairs and business
   appertaining to the Almshouse of St John the Baptist and St John the Evangelist
   founded in the town of Sherborne. You shall not practice or go about by any manner
   of ways or means to acquire obtain or get to your self, or any other person or
   persons whatsoever, any further or other estate of and in the lands and tenements
   in Yetminster and Beer Hackett and the lands and tenements called the Hile and
   Burports (being the possessions of the said Almshouse) other than for seven years,
   and not above, for any one demise and that for so much yearly rent to be improved
   as the same may be found to be yearly worth (Communibus Annis). You shall to
   the utmost of your power, wit and endeavour do and be aiding to the furtherance
   and increase of the lands, tenements, goods and chattels of the said house, the
   maintenance of the good estate and estimation of the master and brethren of the
   same and their successors according to the intent and foundation thereof ~~and the
   Laws and Statutes before made and to be made concerning the same (not being
   contrary to the Laws and Statutes of this Realm~~. The councils of the said master
   and brethren concerning the said Almshouse you shall well and truly keep and not
   disclose so help you God.

For the Governors of the School.

You shall swear that you shall and will be faithful and true in the affairs and business
   appertaining to the free grammar school founded in this town by King Edward VI
   of worthy memory and to the utmost of your power, wit and endeavour you shall
   do and be aiding to the furtherance and increase of the possessions, revenues and
   goods of the said Free School the maintenance of the good estate and estimation of
   the Governors of the same Free School according to the true intent and meaning
   of the said King his letters patent ~~and the laws and statutes heretofore made and
   hereafter to be made concerning the same (not being contrary to the laws and
   statutes of this realm)~~. The councils of the governors concerning the affairs of the
   said school you shall well and truly keep and not disclose so long as you shall be of
   this company. So help you God.

For the schoolmaster.

You shall swear that as schoolmaster of the free grammar school of King Edward VI
   in Sherborne to which office and function you are chosen you shall and will to

your best knowledge, skill and endeavour truly instruct and govern the children and scholars presented, and to be presented, to your charge in the same school, according to the tenor of the letters patent in that respect granted by the said King Edward, as well in good manners as learning according to the statutes, rules and ordinances heretofore established and confirmed, and hereafter to be established and confirmed, as your health of body shall permit and other urgent occasions shall not enforce if contrary. So help you God.

For the poor men and women and housewife.

You shall swear that during the time that you shall be and continue one of the house to live by the alms thereof. You shall dutifully demean yourself to the master and brethren of this house. You shall be ordered, ruled and governed by the ordinances and rules of the same house. You shall not practice and commit nor consent to be committed any wrong, waste or disprofit to this house, nor in the goods or provision thereof, but knowing any to be committed or pretended you shall, without delay or concealment, reveal and make the same known unto the said master and brethren or some of them. And in all things so behave your self as one worthy the continuance of the company unto which you are now chosen upon your own instance and entreaty. So help you God.

Memorandum: 10 August 1743 the Right Honourable William Lord Digby went with the warden and several of the governors of the free school in Sherborne to take a view of the ball court. He was then pleased to declare that he believed the court did belong to the said free school and was not granted to his tenants in his lease of the Abbey house.

Memorandum 6 October 1743 in the presence of Mr Abraham Forrester, Mr John Wickham senior, Mr John Cooke, Mr Henry Oke, Mr William Sampson, Mr John Wickham, junior, Mr William Toogood, Mr George Parsons, Mr Richard Wickham, Mr Thomas Samson, Mr Thomas Rodber and Mr John Pearce that whereas on the death of the late Reverend Mr James Lacy, perpetual chaplain of the Almshouse, the chaplainship thereby become vacant, we nominate and appoint the Reverend Mr Digby Shuttleworth, a member of this house, to be perpetual chaplain in his stead.

Memorandum, 19 February 1750 in the presence of Mr John Wickham senior, Mr John Cooke, Mr Henry Oke, Mr George Parsons, Revd Mr Smith, Mr Isaac Toogood, Mr John Toogood, Mr John Glover, Mr Thomas Rodber, Mr John Wickham junior, Mr William Toogood, Mr John King and Mr Benjamin Bastard - The Revd Mr Digby Shuttleworth has resigned his chaplainship to this house, and Revd Mr Sampson, the present vicar of this town, is elected chaplain in his stead.

THE BRETHREN AND ALMSPEOPLE

The Brethren. Folios 144-153.

A remembrance of the names of the masters and brethren of the Almshouse of St
John Baptist and St John the Evangelist in Sherborne taken the 10 July 1582, at
which time there was an order taken by the whole company that from that date
the names of all those admitted into the company together with the dates of their
admittance should be registered in this book.

*[names in the first column are in a single hand; names in the second column are later annotations.
Words in brackets have been added in different hands]*

Thomas Barton [deceased]
Robert Genings [dismissed]
Lawrence Swetnam [deceased]
William Pope [deceased]
John Reade [deceased]
Bryant Cole [deceased]
John Mullens [deceased]
Hugh Whetcombe [deceased]
Walter Baker [deceased]
John Winniff [deceased]
Jasper Fridlock [deceased]
Edmund Lane [deceased]
William Ridoute [deceased]
Henry Stevens [deceased]
Richard Bawnton [deceased]
William Phillips [expelled]
Thomas Swetnam [deceased]
Richard Downton [deceased]
John Whetcom [deceased]

Edward Ponnd [deceased]
John Gardner [deceased]
John Copper [deceased]
Ambrose Banwell [deceased]
Peter Game [deceased]
Edward Knoile, esquire, [deceased]
George Uvedalle, gentleman, [deceased]
Bartholmew Olde [deceased]
Robert Asheburne [deceased]
John Thorne [deceased]
James Compton [deceased]
Richard Orenge [deceased]
Henry Major [expelled]
Walter Albon [deceased]
John ~~Uvedall~~ Foster [deceased]
John Winchell [deceased]
Richard Wright
Lawrence Swetnam [deceased]
William Stere [deceased]
Richard Cowther
John Hodinott [deceased]
Walter Ryddote
Robert Whetcombe
William Rydowte [deceased]

10 July 1582. Gervais Barnard admitted in the place of Hugh Meer.

15 July 1583. Edward Ponde elected and admitted in the place of Gervais Barnard Margaret Barnard, widow, as a benefactor of this house has given 50s. payable as appears in the account, and is discharged by Ambrose Banwell her husband.

28 January 1584. John Gardner was chosen in the place of John Reade for the Almshouse as well as for the School.

30 January 1584. By the judgement of Thomas Barton, Lawrence Swetnam, Bryan Colle, Hugh Whetcome, William Pope, John Mollens, John Wynnyff, Jasper Fridlock, Edmund Lane, Henry Stevens, Thomas Swetnam, Richard Dounton, John Whetcombe and John Gardener unanimously expelled William Philipps, one of the company of this house, for disclosing the secrets of this house, whereby abuse had been offered to some of this company contrary to the orders of this house, to which he the said William Philipps, had been sworn. This upon a further meeting was consented by Edward Pound. Further it was established and agreed by the above named, that this order shall stand and remain in force and effect as a statute and ordinance of this house, that whosoever shall offend in like sort, shall in like sort be expelled. And hereunto afterwards at another meeting Robert Gennyngs, another of the company, consented and agreed.

5 May 1584. ~~William Fowke is admitted into this house upon the death of John Lightfote deceased.~~ [*Marginal note: "vacat quia alibi" i.e. removed, because this is dealt with elsewhere.*]

5 May 1584. John Cowper is chosen and admitted into the fellowship of this house upon the death of Walter Baker, deceased, and is sworn.

20 July 1584. By the consent of Thomas Barton, Robert Jennings, Lawrence Swetnam, William Pope, Brian Cole, Hugh Whetcombe, John Wynnyff, Edmund Lane, Henry Stevens, Thomas Swetnam, John Whetcombe, Edward Pond, John Molleyns and John Gardener, Alice Meere, widow, sworn as a sister of this house being present in this house. At an account, according to ancient usage of this house, being required to deliver certain books of account, court rolls and other records concerning this house in her custody she absolutely refused, with diverse contemptuous words and speeches of slander and depravation, against the brethren of this house and therefore with the full consent of all the said company, is absolutely dismissed and deprived of this company and the benefits of this house.

26 December 1584. By the consent of Lawrence Swetnam, Thomas Barton, Bryan Colle, Hugh Whetcombe, John Moleyns, John Wynnyff, Jasper Fridlock, Edmund Lane, Henry Stevens, John Whetcombe, Edward Pond, John Gardener and John Cowper present: William Phelepps, one of this company, is sequestered from the fellowship of the School for suspicion of his fidelity towards the School affairs,

for he thinks we have no authority to minister an oath put him, and for apparent occasions in this place ministered. And for his continuance in the offices he is wholly expelled 20 July 1586. William Pope and Thomas Swetnam also present.

July 1585. An order for the poor: It is agreed that if any of the poor of this house shall misdemean themselves, contrary to the ordinances of this house, for the first offence he shall have for his diet for two days only bread and water, for the second offence the like diet for one whole week and if they shall offend the third time, or refuse this diet, they are to be utterly expelled for ever.

20 July 1586. Ambrose Banwell is chosen and admitted into the fellowship of this house and of the school upon the expulsion of William Phelps. His brotherhood money is to be added to the remnants of his wife's money and is to be 6s. 8d. per annum.

It is ordered and decreed by the company present, Lawrence Swetnam master, Thomas Barton, William Pope, John Mulleyns, John Wynnyff, Edmund Lane, Henry Stevens, Thomas Swetnam, John Whetcombe, Edward Ponde, John Gardener and Ambrose Banwell, that Robert Jenyngs, one of this company, for his misdemeanours and conversation, is wholly expelled this house and company, but in respect of his poverty the said company are contented that he shall have paid by the master for the time being 34s. 8d. per annum so long as this company shall think fit.

10 July 1587. [*Marginal entry:* paid 6s. 8d. this present day] Peter Game at this day of account is chosen a brother into the fellowship of this house in the place of Robert Jenyngs.

16 January 1588. Edward Knoyle esquire at this day is chosen a brother into the fellowship of this house in the place of Lawrence Swetnam deceased.

8 April 1588. George Uvedalle, gentleman, at this day is chosen a brother into the fellowship of this house in the place of Richard Bawnton deceased.

20 August 1589. Bartholomew Olde is chosen into the company and brotherhood of the Almshouse in the place of Brian Cole, deceased.

14 May 1590. Robert Asheborne is chosen into the company and brotherhood of the Almshouse in the place of John Moleyns.

6 March [1591 *or* 1592] John Thorne is chosen into the company and brotherhood of the Almshouse in the place of William Pope.

17 December 1593. The lease for Buyshopp tenement is sealed and delivered to Henry Stevens, that he retains the counterpart sealed upon the delivery of the said lease.

4 April 1594. Memorandum that Robert Barlett alias Lodge came before the master of the said Almshouse, the steward, and John Gardener, John Hull and William Solly and surrendered into the hands of the said master and brethren the tenement with the appurtenances in the tenure of [*blank*] Prickett and all his rights and demands in the tenement in consideration of 20s. now paid. [*Presumably this entry refers to Buyshopp tenement*].

20 January 1595. James Compton esquire an inhabitant of this town is chosen a brother into this house in the place of Bartholomew Olde deceased.

17 March 1596. Memorandum that Richard Orenge an inhabitant of this town was chosen a brother of this house in the place of Edward Ponde deceased.

7 August 1598. Mr Henry Meere is chosen into this house in the place of John Whetcombe, deceased, and afterwards upon good occasions was absolutely expelled the fellowship by the master and brethren.

25 April 1599. Walter Albin is chosen into this house in the place of Ambrose Banwell and is sworn.

21 July 1600. At this day John Foster is chosen into this house in the place of John Gardener deceased, and is sworn.

13 November 1600. At this day John Winchell is chosen into this house in the place of Mr Comton and is sworn.

9 December 1601. At this day Richard Wright, gentleman, is chosen into this house in the place of Henry Meer, esquire, expelled from out of this company, and is sworn.

2 October 1603. At this day Laurence Swetnam is chosen into this house a brother in the place of Jasper Fridlock, late deceased.

19 December 1603. At this day Richard Couth is chosen into this house a brother in the place of William Rydowte, late a brother and deceased.

2 October 1604. At this day William Sterr is chosen into this house a brother in the place of Edmond Lane, deceased.

10 July 1605. At this day John Hodinot is chosen into this house a brother in the place of Thomas Barton, deceased.

7 December 1605. At this day Walter Ridowte, gentleman, is chosen a brother in the place of Richard Downgton deceased.

[*blank*] October 1606. At this day Robert Whetcombe is chosen a brother into this house in the place of Richard Orenge, deceased, and is sworn.

9 February 1606. At this day William Rydowte is chosen a brother into this house in the place of John Thorne, deceased, and is sworn.

17 September 1610. At this day Joseph Forrest is chosen a brother into this house in place of Thomas Swetnam, deceased, and is sworn.

4 January 1611. At this day Mr Thomas Compton, gentleman, is chosen a brother in the place of Hugh Whetcombe, deceased, and is sworn.

16 December 1611. At this day William Fissher is chosen a brother of this house in the place of John Cupper, deceased, and is sworn.

23 January 1612. At this day Richard Foster is chosen a brother of this house in the place of Peter Game, deceased, and is sworn.

24 April 1613. At this day Oliver Lottysham, gentleman, is chosen a brother into this house in the place of Edward Knoyle esquire, deceased, and is sworn.

5 July 1613. At This day William Poundfold is chosen a brother into this house in the place of John Hodynott, deceased, and is sworn.

14 August 1613. This day George Morgan is chosen a brother into this house in the place of Henry Stevens, deceased, and is sworn.

2 April 1616. This day John Chetmill is chosen a brother into this house in the place of Oliver Lottesham gentleman, deceased, and is sworn.

9 February 1618. This day John Jeanes is chosen a brother into this house in the place of Robert Ashborne, deceased, and is sworn.

7 April 1620. This day Richard Baunton is chosen a brother into this house in the place of William Poundfold, deceased, and is sworn.

2 June 1621. This day Jonathan Pennye is chosen a brother into this house in the place of John Winchell, deceased, and is sworn.

10 July 1621. This day Robert Hoddinot is chosen a brother into this house in the place of William Ridout, deceased, and is sworn.

29 October 1624. This day Arthur Hooper is chosen a brother into this house in the place of Walter Albon, deceased, and is sworn.

26 January 1625. This day Thomas Sterr is chosen a brother into this house being an inhabitant of this town, in the place of Lawrence Swetnam, lately deceased, and is sworn.

16 June 1626. This day Robert Saunders is chosen a brother into this house in the place of Joseph Forrest, deceased, and is sworn.

25 February 1629. At this day Josiah Couth is chosen a brother into this house in the place of George Uvedale esquire, deceased, and is sworn.

25 February 1629. This day Henry Durneford is secondly chosen a brother into this house in the place of John Foster, deceased, and is sworn.

25 February 1629. This day John Maren is thirdly chosen a brother into this house in the place of Arthur Hooper, deceased, and is sworn.

25 February 1629. This day Richard Speed is fourthly chosen a brother into this house in the place of Robert Hoddinot, deceased, and is sworn.

6 July 1629. The said day Richard Voakes is chosen a brother into this house in the place of William Fisher, deceased, and is sworn.

22 January 1630. This day William Sampson is chosen a brother into this house in the place of John Jeanes, deceased, and is sworn.

4 September 1630. This day John Chetmill the younger is chosen a brother into this house in the place of Richard Foster, deceased, and is sworn.

[*Entry crossed out and illegible*]

2 November 1630. The said day John Whetcombe is chosen a brother into this house in the place of John Wynniffe, deceased, and is sworn.

29 September 1632. Nicholas Romayne is this day chosen a brother into this company in the place of Thomas Sterr, deceased, and is sworn.

18 December 1633. The said day Richard Foster is chosen a brother into this house in the place of George Morgan, deceased, and is sworn.

11 March 1636. The said day ~~Richard Foster~~ George Swetnam, gentleman, is chosen a brother into this house in the place of William Sterr, deceased, and is sworn the 6 April 1636.

6 April 1636. The said day Mr William Lyforde, bachelor of divinity and vicar of this town, is chosen a brother into this house in the place of William Sansom, deceased, and is sworn.

31 July 1637. The said day Mr Hugh Hodges is chosen a brother into this house in the place of Richard Baunton, deceased, and was sworn 8 August 1637.

19 January 1638. This day Mr James Wallis is chosen a brother into this house in the place of George Swetnam deceased and was sworn.

22 April 1639. This day William Sansom is chosen a brother into this house in the place of Richard Wrighte, deceased, and is sworn.

13 April 1640. This day Thomas Sansom is chosen a brother into this house in the place of John Chetmill senior, deceased, and is sworn.

7 September 1640. This day William Eares is chosen a brother into this house in the place of Richard Foster, deceased, and is sworn.

2 July 1644. This day John Durnforde is chosen a brother into this house in the place of Walter Rydeot, deceased, and is sworn.

1 July 1645. This day William Hearne is chosen a brother into this house in the place of Mr Jonathan Penny, deceased, and is sworn. He paid his first 6s. 8d. 1 July 1646 and not before.

20 January 1646. This day Valentine Smith is chosen a brother into this house in the place of Mr Thomas Compton, deceased, and is sworn.

22 January 1649. This day Walter Lambert is chosen a brother into this house in the place of Richard Speed, deceased, and is sworn.

30 December 1651. This day John Eastmont, gentleman, formerly chosen a brother into this house in the place of Mr Richard Couth, deceased, was sworn.

15 March 1653. This day John Horne is chosen a brother into this house in the place of William Eares, deceased, and is sworn.

11 November 1653. This day Richard Oldes is chosen a brother into this house in the place of Robert Saunders, deceased, and is sworn.

11 November 1653. This day George Sterr, gentleman, is chosen a brother into this house in the place of William Lyford clerk, deceased, and is sworn.

2 May 1654. This day Nathaniel Highmore, doctor of physic, is chosen a brother into this house in the place of George Starr gentleman, deceased, and is sworn.

23 July 1655. This day Richard Voakes the younger (being formerly chosen a brother into this house in the place of Walter Lambert deceased) is sworn. On which day the account was passed by Mr John Eastmont and he then paid his first 6s. 8d. to the master.

20 January 1657. This day John Fisher is chosen a brother into this house in the place of Robert Whetcombe gentleman, deceased, and is sworn.

18 April 1657. This day John Saunders is chosen a brother into this house in the place of Nicholas Romayne gentleman, deceased, and was sworn the 21 July 1657 being the day the Master passed his account and he then paid his first 6s. 8d.

19 July 1659. This day Thomas Chase esquire (formerly chosen a brother into this house in the place of John Fisher deceased) was sworn and it being the day the Master passed his account the said Mr Chase then paid the said Master his first 6s. 8d.

13 October 1660. This day William Thorneton is chosen a brother into this house in the place of Henry Durneford gentleman, deceased, and is sworn.

6 December 1661. This day John Williams the elder is chosen a brother into this house in the place of Richard Avoake the elder, deceased.

26 April 1662. This day John Whetcombe the younger is chosen a brother into this house in the place of Valentine Smyth, deceased, and sworn.

27 July 1662. This day Robert Awse is chosen a brother into this house in the place of Thomas Chase esquire, deceased, and sworn.

23 September 1662. This day John Cooth is chosen a brother into this house in the place of Richard Voakes deceased. Sworn 15 April 1664.

15 April 1664. This day Joseph Barker, clerk, is chosen and sworn a brother into this house in the place of William Horne who has for many years absented himself from this town and place and house.

3 September 1664. This day Thomas Foyle is chosen a brother into this house in the place of Robert Awse, deceased, and is sworn.

30 August 1666. This day George Cunington is chosen a brother into this house in the place of Richard Oldes who is expelled the house and is sworn. And then paid the old master Thomas Sampson (who this day passed his account) his first 6s. 8d.

28 December 1666. This day Robert Morke is chosen a brother into this house in the place of Mr Josiah Cooth, deceased, and is sworn.

8 April 1669. This day Mr Hugh Hodges the younger is chosen a brother into this house in the place of Mr John Eastment, deceased, and is sworn.

31 May 1669. This day Mr William Martin is chosen a brother into this house in the place of John Martin, deceased, his late father and is sworn.

14 June 1669. This day Valentine Smyth is chosen a brother into this house in the place of John Cooth, deceased, and is sworn.

24 February 1670. This day Mr John Eastment is chosen a brother into this house in the place of Mr John Charmill, deceased, and is sworn.

24 May 1673. This day Mr John Fisher the younger is chosen a brother into this house in the place of Mr Hugh Hodges the elder, deceased, and is sworn.

16 January 1674. This day Mr Roger White is chosen a brother into this house in the place of John Williams who is expelled this company for refusing to attend the business of this house, and absenting himself from all assemblies of the said company, and having also made himself incapable of continuing of this corporation having not taken the oath nor made the subscription required by the late act of Parliament for preventing the growth of popery. And he the said Roger White is now sworn.

29 July 1674. This day Mr William Fisher is chosen a brother into this house in the place of James Wallis, deceased, and is sworn.

26 February 1676. This day Mr Robert Wyer is chosen a brother into this house in the place of Mr Thomas Sanson, deceased, and is sworn.

16 April 1677. This day William Coliar esquire is chosen a brother into this house in the place of Joseph Barker, deceased, and is sworn.

4 May 1677. This day John Oake is chosen a brother into this house in the place of William Colier esquire, deceased, and is sworn.

20 December 1682. This day Robert Dowding is chosen a brother into this house in the place of Roger White, who has left the town and refused any longer to continue of the company, and is sworn.

15 March 1683. This day Mr Henry Durnford is chosen a brother into this house in the place of Thomas Foyle, who is disfranchised the company for having left the town and the service of this society, and is sworn.

15 March 1683. This day Mr Robert Whetcomb is chosen a brother into this house in the room of Mr John Durnford who is disfranchised for he has for many years last past left his inhabitancy in this town, and very rarely frequents the service of this house, and is sworn.

24 January 1685. This day Raynold Pond is chosen a brother into this house in the place of Mr William Sansom, deceased, and is sworn.

24 January 1685. Mr Alexander Williams is chosen a brother into this house in the place of Mr John Whetcomb senior, deceased, and is sworn.

11 April 1685. Mr John Luckis is chosen a brother into this house in the place of Dr Nathaniel Highmore deceased, and is sworn.

14 December 1685. Mr Harry Hooper is chosen a brother into this house in the place of Mr John Saunders deceased, and is sworn.

3 April 1686. Mr John Thornton is chosen a brother into this house in the place of Mr William Thornton his father, deceased, and is sworn.

17 June 1686. Mr John Partridge is chosen a brother into this house in the place of Valentine Smith, deceased, and is sworn.

8 September 1687. Mr Baruck Fox chosen a brother into this house in the place of Robert Dowding, who resigned because of leaving the town, and is sworn.

8 September 1687. Mr Samuel Napper is chosen a brother into this house in the place of Mr Robert Whetcomb, deceased, and is sworn.

6 October 1688. Mr Cary Boucher is chosen a brother into this house in the place of Mr William Martin, deceased, and is sworn.

19 March 1690. Mr John Plowman is chosen a brother into this house in the place of Mr John Horne, deceased, and is sworn.

11 August 1691. Mr Thomas Mansell is chosen a brother into this house in the place of John Thornton, deceased, and is sworn.

15 September 1693. Hugh Hodges esquire is chosen a brother into this house in the place of Henry Durnford, deceased, is sworn.

22 September 1693. John Abington esquire is chosen a brother into this house in the place of Hugh Hodges esquire, lately deceased, and is sworn.

10 March 1694. George Keate esquire is chosen a brother into this house in the place of Henry Hooper, deceased, who is sworn.

19 September 1695. Abraham Forrester, gentleman, is chosen a brother into this house in the place of Mr George Connington, who is disfranchised from the company for leaving the town and the service of this house, who is now sworn.

22 August 1696. Mr Thomas Hobbs is chosen a brother into this house in the place of John Whetcomb who, having refused to attend the service of the house is expelled from this company and the said Mr Hobbs is sworn.

16 December 1696. Memorandum John Oake junior is chosen a brother into this house in the place of Alexander Williams who declines the company and refuses to attend the service of this house and is therefore expelled the company and the said John Oake is sworn.

6 April 1699. Memorandum Cary Boucher is again chosen as a brother into this house (he being formerly become irregular for not signing the Act of Association as he was not in London or in this county at the time when it was to be done) and it is agreed that he shall not begin to pay his nobles over again but only to pay his arrears: He is sworn. [*Nobles: coins valued at* 6s. 8d.]

6 April 1699. Thomas Dunham is now chosen a brother into this house in the room of George Keate, deceased, who is sworn.

29 January 1700. Mr George Cooper is now chosen a brother into this house in the room of John Abington esquire who deserted the company.

18 October 1700. William Samson is now chosen a brother into this house, in the room of Mr Thomas Hobbs who deserted the company, and is sworn.

18 December 1700. William Wickham is now chosen a brother into this house, in the room of Thomas Dunham who hath deserted the company, and is sworn.

16 October 1702. Thomas Crane, gentleman, is now chosen a brother into this house in the room of William Fisher, gentleman, who desired to leave the company by reason of his indisposition and weakness.

20 October 1703. Samuel Lambert is chosen a brother into this house in the room of Mr John Partridge deceased.

19 June 1705. Thomas Hobbs, gentleman, is again chosen as a brother into this house in the room of Mr Robert Wyer deceased, it is agreed that he shall not begin to pay his nobles over again but only to pay what is in arrears, and he is sworn.

7 February 1708. Francis Fisher gentleman is now chosen a brother into this house in the room of John Fisher gentleman, deceased, and is sworn.

7 February 1708. John Allambridge gentleman is chosen a brother into this house in the room of Mr John Plowman who has been for a considerable time out of the Kingdom.

December 1708. Mr James Lacy, vicar of Sherborne, is chosen a brother into this house in the room of Mr George Cooper who upon his own request is dismissed the company on account of his being removed out of the town and his great indisposition of body.

26 April 1712. Mr Robert Avoake junior is this day chosen a brother into this house in the place of William Wickham who is expelled this company for not giving in his account as warden of the school according to the order of this company, and is sworn.

15 May 1712. Mr Robert Avoke junior, not having qualified himself according to the Act of Parliament called the Test Act, is expelled this society.

22 May 1712. Mr Robert Avoke is again chosen a brother into this house and is sworn.

26 June 1712. Mr John Wickham is chosen a brother into this house in the place of Hugh Hodges esquire, deceased, and is sworn.

16 December 1713. Mr George Abington is chosen a brother into this house in the place of Mr Thomas Hobbs, deceased, and is sworn.

1 January 1715. Mr Elias Hosey is chosen a brother into this house in the room of Mr Robert Avoke senior, deceased, and is sworn.

29 December 1715. Mr Christopher Ryall is chosen a brother into this house in the room of Mr George Abington, who is expelled this company for not qualifying himself according to the rules of this house, and is sworn.

5 January 1717. Mr Joseph Staveley is this day chosen a brother into this house in the room of Mr John Luckas, deceased, and is sworn.

12 April 1718. Mr William Oldys is this day chosen a brother into this house in the room of Mr Thomas Crane, deceased, and is sworn.

17 September 1719. Carew Hervey Mildmay esquire is chosen a brother into this house in the room of Carey Boucher esquire, deceased, and is sworn.

17 September 1719. Mr Walter Foxe is chosen a brother into this house in the room of Mr John Oke junior, deceased, and is sworn.

17 September 1719. Mr Baruch Foxe is chosen a brother into this house in the room of his father Mr Baruch Foxe, deceased, and is sworn.

28 December 1719. Mr John Cooke is chosen a brother into this house in the room of Mr John Oke senior, deceased, and is sworn.

29 December 1719. Mr John Glover is chosen a brother into this house in the room of Mr John Allambridge, deceased, and is sworn.

27 December 1721. Mr Henry Oke is chosen a brother into this house in the room of Mr Robert Avoake, deceased, and is sworn.

27 December 1721. Mr Thomas Poole is chosen a brother into this house in the room of Mr William Oldys, deceased, and is sworn.

14 December 1722. Mr Samuel Napper is chosen a brother into this house in the room of Mr Samuel Napper his father, deceased, and is sworn.

14 December 1722. Mr William Toogood junior is chosen a brother into this house in the room of Mr William Samson, deceased, and is sworn.

[no date] Mr John Hutchins was chosen a brother into this house in the room of John Eastmont esquire, deceased.

25 August 1724. Mr Hutchins (being sent for by Mr Samuel Napper and Mr William Toogood two of the members of this house) refused to come and accept the trust, for he had so much business of his own that he could not attend at the usual meetings, upon whose refusal Mr John Parsons is chosen a brother into this house, in the room of Mr Hutchins, and is sworn.

2 October 1724. Mr William Foote was chosen a brother into this house in the room of Mr Walter Foxe, deceased, and is sworn.

16 March 1727. Mr William Sampson was chosen a brother into this house in the room of Mr Reynold Pond, deceased, and is sworn.

16 March 1727. Mr William Samson was chosen a brother into this house in the room of Mr Christopher Ryall, who is expelled, and is sworn.

11 August 1729. Mr Thomas Lambert was chosen a brother into this house and sworn in the room of Mr Francis Fisher, deceased.

11 August 1729. Mr John Wickham was chosen a brother into this house and sworn in the room of Mr Thomas Mansell, deceased.

2 May 1732. Mr William Toogood was chosen a brother into this house in the room of Mr William Toogood his late father, deceased, and sworn.

2 May 1732. Mr Samuel Wilkinson was chosen a brother into this house in the room of Mr Samuel Lambert senior, deceased, and sworn.

15 October 1733. Mr George Parsons was chosen a brother into this house in the room of Mr William Sansom, deceased, and sworn.

6 November 1735. Mr Richard Wickham was chosen a brother into this house in the room of Mr Baruch Fox, deceased, and is sworn.

14 April 1738. Mr Thomas Samson was chosen a brother into this house in the room of Mr Samuel Wilkinson, deceased, and is sworn.

21 January 1742. The Reverend Mr Digby Shuttleworth was chosen a brother into this house in the room of Mr William Foote, deceased, and is sworn.

3 June 1742. Dr Abel Moysey is chosen a brother to this house in the room of Mr Joseph Stavely, deceased, and is sworn.

3 June 1742. Mr Thomas Rodber is chosen into this house in the room of Mr John Parsons, deceased, and is sworn.

3 June 1742. Mr John Pearse is chosen into this house in the room of Mr Thomas Fooke, deceased, and is sworn.

24 July 1744. The Reverend Mr John Loop is chosen into this house in the room of the Reverend Mr James Lacy, deceased, and is sworn.

24 July 1744. Mr Thomas Hulbert is chosen into this house in the room of Mr Thomas Samson, deceased, and is sworn.

8 November 1744. Mr John Toogood is chosen into this house in the room of Mr Thomas Hulbert, deceased, and is sworn.

2 May 1745. Mr John King is chosen into this house in the room of Mr Samuel Napper, deceased, and is sworn.

14 January 1746. Mr James Blackmore is chosen into this house in the room of Mr Abraham Forrester, deceased, and is sworn.

3 January 1749. Reverend Mr Peter Smith is chosen into this house in the room of Mr ~~Richard~~ James Blackmore, deceased, and is sworn.

3 January 1749. Mr Benjamin Bastard was chosen into this house in the room of Mr Richard Wickham, deceased, and is sworn.

3 January 1749. Mr Isaac Toogood junior was chosen into this house in the room of Thomas Lambert esquire, deceased, and is sworn.

3 January 1749. Mr Samuel Jeffrey was chosen into this house in the room of Dr Abel Moysey and is sworn.

17 April 1750. Reverend Mr Henry Sampson, vicar of this town, is chosen into this house in the room of the Reverend Mr Loop, deceased, and is sworn.

17 April 1750. Mr Abraham Bragg is chosen into this house in the room of Mr John Pearce, deceased, and is sworn.

17 April 1750. Mr John Deering is chosen into this house in the room of Mr William Sampson, deceased, and is sworn.

6 November 1755. Mr John Foot is chosen a brother of this house in the room of Mr John Wickham senior, deceased.

27 December 1756. Dr Foot is chosen a brother of this house in the room of Mr Henry Oke, deceased, and is sworn.

28 February 1757. Mr John Chaffie is chosen a brother of this house Carew Harvey Mildmay esquire who has resigned, and is sworn.

28 August 1758. Mr William Burnett is chosen a brother of this house in the room of Mr Samuel Jeffrey who has resigned.

8 November 1759. Mr John Oke of Acreman Street is chosen a brother of this house in the room of Mr Shuttleworth.

27 December 1759. Mr Robert Goadby is chosen a brother of this house in the room of Mr John Cook who has refused to attend the business of the house.

3 April 1761. Thomas Hutchings esquire is chosen a brother of this house in the room of Mr John Wickham who has refused to attend the business of the house for some years.

3 April 1761. Mr John Fooks is chosen a brother of this house in the room of Mr Abraham Bragg who has resigned.

3 April 1761. Mr Simon Pretor is chosen a brother of this house in the room of Mr Peter Smith who has refused to attend the business of the house.

30 March 1763. Mr Samuel Hart is chosen a brother of this house in the room of Mr Elias Hosey, deceased.

15 January 1765. Reverend Mr George Hutchings is chosen a brother of this house in the room of his brother Thomas Hutchings esquire.

15 January 1765. Reverend James Parsons is chosen a brother of this house in the room of Mr John King, deceased.

15 January 1765. Mr William Sampson is chosen a brother of this house in the room of Mr Rodber who has refused to attend the business of the house for several years past.

15 January 1765. Mr John Thorne is chosen a brother of this house in the room of Mr Benjamin Bastard who has also refused to attend the business of the house for several years past.

15 January 1765. Mr Bartholomew Watts is chosen a brother of this house in the room of Mr Simon Pretor who has resigned.

11 August 1766. Mr Sampson Boys is chosen in the room of Mr Goadby who has resigned.

28 December 1767. Mr James Stidston is chosen a brother of this house in the room of Mr James Parson who has resigned.

27 December 1768. Mr William Toogood the younger is chosen a brother in this house in the room of Mr George Parsons, deceased.

27 December 1769. Mr William Willmott is chosen a brother in this house in the room of Mr Samuel Hart, deceased.

27 March 1771. Mr William Hewlett is chosen a brother in this house in the room of Mr Charles Hutchings who is gone to reside at Maiden Newton and left this place.

26 [no month or year] Mr Thomas Bastard is chosen a brother in this house in the room of Mr William Hewlett, deceased.

The same day Reverend Mr Charles Toogood is also chosen a brother in this house in the room of Dr Foot, deceased.

The same day Mr Thomas Cooth is also chosen a brother in this house in the room of Mr William Sansom, deceased.

28 December 1772. Reverend Mr Loop is chosen in the room of Mr William Hewlett, deceased.

28 December 1772. Mr Thomas Pittard is chosen in the room of Mr William Damson, deceased.

9 August 1773. The Reverend Mr Edward Cotes is chosen in the room of the Reverend Mr Sampson, deceased.

26 January 1779. Dr Johnson is chosen in the room of Mr William Cruttwell who has left the town and removed to Bath.

[no day] April 1780. Mr Robert Winter is chosen in the room of Mr John Glover, deceased.

26 September 1780. Mr Charles Bull Hart is chosen in the room of Mr Isaac Toogood, deceased.

15 November 1780. Reverend Mr Nathaniel Bristow is chosen in the room of the Reverend Mr Cotes, deceased. [Entry crossed out using X X]

27 September 1781. Mr Sweet Hart is chosen in the room of the Reverend Mr Cotes – The Reverend Mr Bristow, not being eligible, having refused to accept the office.

27 September 1781. Mr George Moore is chosen in the room of Mr William Toogood the elder who has resigned.

27 September 1781. Mr George Allambridge is chosen in the room of Mr William Toogood the younger who has also resigned.

27 December 1781. Mr Warwick is chosen in the room of Mr John Oke, deceased.

17 May 1782. Mr Sampson Boys junior is chosen in the room of Mr Warwick who has refused to accept the office.

[*Undated*] Mr John Oke is chosen in the room of the Reverend Mr Charles Toogood who has left Sherborne.

16 December 1782. Reverend Mr John Chafie is chosen in the room of Mr George Allambridge, deceased.

27 December 1785. Mr John Mellyar is chosen in the room of Mr John Oke, deceased.

1 December 1789. Mr Peter Batson is chosen in the room of Mr Deering, deceased, and is sworn.

[*Undated*] Mr John Fooke junior is chosen in the room of Mr Willmott, deceased, and is sworn.

[*Undated*] Mr William Harbin is chosen in the room of Mr George Moore, deceased, but declined to qualify.

[*Undated*] Mr William Hart is chosen in the room of ~~John Oke, deceased,~~ Mr Winter who has been expelled, and is sworn.

[*Undated*] Mr James Hoddinott is chosen in the room of the Reverend Mr Loop who has resigned.

20 June 1790. Mr Michael Pretor Gill is chosen in the room of Mr Sampson Boys, deceased, and is sworn.

20 June 1790. Mr Anthony Holms Smyth is elected in the room of Mr William Hart, deceased, and is sworn.

13 July 1795. Mr Brice is elected in the room of Dr Johnson.

13 July 1795. Mr Ridout is elected in the room of Mr Sampson Boys, deceased.

13 July 1795. Mr Tucker is elected in the room of Mr John Toogood, deceased.

13 July 1795. Mr Samuel Foot is elected in the room of Mr Gill.

13 July 1795. Mr Burge is elected in the room of Mr Pittard.

August 1800. Mr Charles Bristed is elected in the room of Mr Chafie.

August 1800. Mr James Jeffrey is chosen in the room of Mr Fooks.

August 1800. Mr James Langdon is chosen in the room of Mr Hutchings.

August 1800. Mr Joseph Burnett is chosen in the room of Mr Mellyar.

August 1800. Mr Thomas Fooks is chosen in the room of the Reverend Mr John Chaffey.

10 August 1801. Mr Thomas Willmott is chosen in the room of Mr Smith.

1 January 1805. Reverend John Parsons is elected in the room of the Reverend Charles Bristed who has left the town of Sherborne.

1 January 1805. Mr James Cruttwell is elected in the room of Mr James Stidston, deceased.

1 January 1805. Mr Charles Winter is elected in the room of Mr Bartholomew Watts who has left the town of Sherborne.

1 January 1805. Mr Robert Lewis is elected in the room of Mr George Moore, deceased, Mr William Harbin having declined to qualify.

The above four persons 1 January 1805 qualified by taking the necessary oath.

3 June 1806. Dr Pew is elected in the room of Mr Joseph Burnet who has left the town.

1 July 1806. Dr Richard Pew qualified by taking the necessary oath.

3 July 1821. John Melliar esquire is elected a brother of this house in the room of Mr Charles Bull Hart, deceased, sworn 15 August 1821.

Samuel Pretor Esquire is also elected a brother in the room of Mr James Cruttwell, deceased, sworn 7 August 1821.

Mr Charles Langdon is also elected a brother in the room of Mr Robert Lewis, deceased, sworn 7 August 1821.

1 February 1825. Mr Edward Turner is elected a brother of this house in the room of Mr John Malliar, resigned, and is sworn.

1 February 1825. Mr John Thorne is elected a brother in the room of Reverend John Tucker, deceased; and is sworn.

1 February 1825. Mr William Naish Allford is elected in the room of Mr Henry Smith Brice, deceased, and is sworn.

6 July 1830. Mr James Langdon, who ceased to be a brother of this house by having quitted his residence at Sherborne is now re-elected upon his return to the town in the room of his son Mr Charles Langdon, who has ceased to be a brother of the house by leaving the town, and residing at Ryme Intrinseca.

7 February 1832. Mr Nathaniel Highmore is elected a brother of this house in the room of the late Mr James Jeffrey and is sworn.

7 February 1832. Mr Thomas Ensor is elected a brother in the room of Mr Samuel Foot who is removed from Sherborne and is sworn.

7 February 1832. Mr James Ridout the younger is also elected a brother in the room of Mr Charles Winter who is also removed from Sherborne and is sworn.

5 August 1834. Mr George Warry is elected a brother of this house in the room of Mr Samuel Pretor, resigned, and has been sworn.

5 August 1834. Mr Henry Charles Goodden is elected a brother of this house in the room of the late Dr Richard Pew, deceased, and is sworn.

5 August 1834. Mr Thomas Warren Kempthorne is elected a brother of this house in the room of Mr Thomas Wilmott, deceased, and is sworn.

6 December 1836. Mr Charles Hutchings is elected a brother of this house in the room of Mr James Ridout.

2 December 1839. Mr William Fooks is elected a brother of this house in the room of Mr John Mills Thorne, who has ceased to reside at Sherborne, and is sworn.

7 September 1841. Mr Ernest Fussell is elected a brother of this house in the room of Mr Thomas Warren Kempthorne, who has removed from Sherborne, and is sworn.

21 March 1843. Mr Edward Turner is elected a brother of this house in the room of Mr Edward Turner, his late father, and is sworn.

6 May 1845. Mr William Thorne is elected a brother of this house in the room of Mr James Langdon, deceased, (never qualified).

6 May 1845. Mr John Young Melmoth is elected a brother of this house in the room of Mr Batson, deceased, and is sworn.

6 May 1845. Mr Thomas Fooks is elected a brother of this house in the room of Mr Fooks his late father, and is sworn.

1 February 1848. John Frederick Falwasser esquire, Mr John Street Mansford, Mr William Highmore and Mr James Hoddinott were this day elected brethren of this house in the rooms of governors deceased.

7 March 1848. Mr Falwasser, Mr William Highmore and Mr James Hoddinott this day attended and were sworn.

2 December 1851. Mr Robert Willmott, Mr Robert Longman and Mr Cornish Henley were this day elected brethren of this house in the room of governors deceased. They were sworn on the 2 January 1852.

1 August 1854. Mr William Parsons and Mr John George Bergman were this day elected brethren of the Almshouse in the room of those deceased. They were sworn on the 10 of August 1854.

7 November 1854. Reverend Edward Haiston was this day elected a brother of the Almshouse in the room of the Reverend John Parsons, deceased, and was sworn on this 5 day of December 1854.

10 June 1856. George Digby Wingfield esquire of Sherborne Castle was this day elected a brother of the Almshouse, and was sworn on 14 June 1856.

27 December 1860. Reverend Thomas James was this day elected a brother of the Almshouse and was sworn.

6 January 1863. Mr Charles Leftinch Oldfield Bartlett and Mr Edward Benthall having been elected brethren of the Almshouse, were this day sworn.

Almshouse Admissions, 1582-1866. Folio 181, loose folios D-K, followed by G-U, then folios 182-205.

5 May 1582. John Chepman is chosen into this house by the voice of Lawrence Swetnam, Thomas Barton, Bryan Colle, Hugh Whetcombe, Edmund Lane, John Wynnyff, Henry Stevens, Thomas Swetnam, John Molleyns, Jasper Fridlock and John Whetcombe.

1 July 1582. Agnes Stone is chosen into this house by the voice of Lawrence Swetnam, Thomas Barton, Bryan Colle, William Pope, Hugh Whetcombe, Edmond Lane, Henry Stephens, Thomas Swetnam, Richard Bawnton, John Moleyns and John Whetcombe.

20 December 1582. Agnes Carpenter was admitted into the house and the house is to have with her 26s. 8d. by the year.

17 May 1583. Ancrese Leve was chosen into the house in the place of Agnes Dampeer and brings with her [blank].

26 May 1583. Agnes Lewes was chosen into this house in the place of Anne Carpenter, deceased, John Newman gives 2s. to the house each year during her life.

9 December 1583. John Forte was chosen in the place of Richard Scoper into this house.

5 May 1584. William Fowke is chosen and admitted into this house upon the death of John Lightfote. William Fook refused the room, was discharged, and Walter Soper was chosen into his room.

11 October 1584. Joan Reade was elected into the house upon the death of Agnes Lewes.

5 December 1584. Katherine Elis was chosen in the room of Ancrese Leve.

6 January 1586. Joan Skoper, widow, was chosen in the room of Agnes Stone.

[blank] October 1585. [blank] Okeley, widow, was chosen in the room of [blank].

[blank] June 1586. Thomas Hayne was chosen into this house in the room of [blank] Cullens.

18 January 1588. Thomas Camell was chosen into this house in the room of [*blank*] Wheydon.

6 February 1588. William Poole was chosen into this house in the room of John Anderson and is to bring with him into the house a bed, a white gown, a platter, a pottinger, a saucer, a spoon, a dish, a coverlet, a blanket, a sheet and a wood hook.

24 August 1588. John Burges was chosen instead of John Towgood and brought in [*blank*].

12 January 1589. Anthony Lyne was chosen instead of Thomas Hayne and brought in [*blank*].

24 February 1589. Alice Lambert was received into this house by the gift of £50 by William Masters of Sherborne. [*The first to benefit from William Masters' gift.*]

25 March 1589. Agnes Bollyn was taken into this house upon the death of widow Okely.

9 July 1589. Thomas Grenewaie is presented by Peter Game, and received by the master and brethren of this house in consideration Peter Game's gift of £50, according to a writing thereof made. [*The first to benefit from Peter Game's gift.*]

23 December 1589. John Mogge is chosen into this house in the room of Walter Soper deceased.

1 December 1590. Robert Wase is chosen into this house in the room of Anthony Line who refused his place and was dismissed as appears in the register.

16 March 1591. Thomas Pouncefote is chosen into this house in the place of William Poole and is to bring with him into this house his bed, two sheets, two good shirts, a platter, a pottinger, a saucer, a spoon, a dish, 4*d*. in money, a bolster and a pillow.

[*No date*] Margaret Browne [*remainder of this entry blank*].

[*No date*] William Lockett is chosen into this house in the place of John Leycost alias Cutler, deceased, and will bring into this house 10*s*. in money John Locket his son is his pledge that the money shall be paid at Michaelmas.

September 1591. Walter Hynde is this day chosen a poor man of this house in the place of William Weare deceased and brings with him a coverlet a blanket one sheet, a bolster, a dish and spoon, 2 shirts new, which Walter and Richard his sons have promised to perform, and to discharge the town of his wife their mother.

28 March 1591. Thomas Riall is chosen a poor man into this house in the room of William Wever, and brought with him a saucer, a coverlet, a blanket and a saucer.

28 March 1591. Walter Long was chosen into this house in the room of Michael Berwick and brought a coverlet.

29 April 1591. Katherine Baker is chosen a poor woman into this house in the room of Alice Bedman, deceased, bringing with her a bad feather bed, a feather bolster, a feather pillow, an old blanket, a coverlet, a little pot, two little kettles, a platter, a pottinger, a candlestick, sufficient woollen and linen, a good sheet and a bad sheet.

29 April 1591. Alice Chamberlayne, late housewife of this house was chosen a poor woman into this house in the room of Katherine Ellis, deceased, and brought with her a feather bed two bolsters and a pair of blankets.

29 April 1591. Elizabeth Buisshop, widow, was chosen a poor woman into this house in the room of Joan Lambert, deceased, and brought with her a bed-tie of canvas, a platter, a pottinger, and a saucer a pair of sheets, a blanket, a shred coverlet, a bolster, a pillow, and a candlestick.

14 March 1592. Emma Callowe, widow, was chosen a poor woman into this house in the room of Elizabeth Buisshopp, widow, and brought with her [*blank*].

26 April 1592. John Buckingham, a late inhabitant of this town, for as much as no other inhabitant of this town has required this Almshouse is received (saving always that this be no precedent for any other such choice) and has brought with him 4s. 6d. in money, a kettle of three quarts, a bolster and blanket, a trencher, dish, and a spoon.

4 May 1592. Agnes Smyth, an inhabitant of this town, is admitted into this house in the place of mother Bishopp and brought with her six pewter dishes, a brass pot of three quarts, a candlestick, a sheet and a coverlet.

1 March 1593. Robert Blobell, an inhabitant of this town, is admitted into this house in the place of John Fose, deceased, and brings with him a new white gown of the livery of this house, one other gown of cloth, a featherbed, a bolster of flock, a pillow of feathers, a pair of blankets, a coverlet, a platter, a candlestick and saucer. Mr Ashbourne has given his word for the gown upon mistress Tillie's promise.

21 January 1594. William Bennett an inhabitant of this town, is admitted into this house and brought in a featherbed, a bolster, one feather pillow, a pair of blankets, a pair of sheets, his best coverlet, a platter, a pottinger, a saucer, a candlestick, a spoon, a dish, a cup and all his other goods if he survives his wife.

26 May 1594. William Russell, an inhabitant of this town, is admitted into this house to make the full number of men and has brought with him a pottenger, a pillow, and 18*s.* in money being the rent of his house.

28 June 1594. William Jervis, cardmaker, an inhabitant of this town, is admitted into this house in the place of William Bennett, deceased, and brought nothing and afterwards wilfully departed.

16 December 1594. Alice Parham, widow, an inhabitant of this town, is chosen into this house in the place of Agnes Bollen, deceased, and brought with her a coverlet, a pair of blankets, two feather pillows, a platter, a candlestick, a cup, a trencher, a dish and reasonable apparel.

10 May 1595. Richard Roberts alias Woodall, an inhabitant of this town, is admitted into this house in the place of Walter Long, deceased, and brought with him into this house a featherbed, a feather bolster, a feather pillow, coverlet, a quilt, a pair of blankets, a pair of sheets, a pottinger, he is to provide a livery gown and reasonable apparel.

10 February 1596. John Dier, an inhabitant of this town, is admitted into this house upon the voluntary departure of William Jervis, and brought with him a flock bed, a coverlet, a pair of sheets, a flock bolster, a feather pillow, a pottinger, a cup, a dish, a trencher, a spoon, 5*s.* 6*d.* in money and reasonable apparel.

6 December 1596. Robert Sexton, an inhabitant of this town, is chosen and sworn into this house upon the death of John Buckingham and brought with him a feather bed, a feather and flock bolster, a pillow, a pair of blankets, a coverlet, three sheets, 4*d.*, shirts with convenient apparel and [*blank*] towards a new gown, a pottinger and a candlestick.

23 January 1597. Thomas Ladbroke, an inhabitant of this town, is chosen and sworn a poor man into this house in the place of Robert Applyn, deceased, and brought with him a caddow, a bolster, blankets, a pillow, a pair of sheets, three shirts, two pairs of hose, a doublet, two coats, a candlestick, a platter, a rug-gown and a new gown.

23 January 1597. Katherine Symonds the new wife of John Symonds inhabitant of this [*manuscript torn*] and in treaty of her, and consent of her said husband is [*manuscript torn*] in the place of Agnes Smyth, deceased, and brought with [*manuscript torn*] petticoat.

23 January 1597. Ambrose Chetmyll, an inhabitant of this town, is chosen a poor man into this house in the place of John Mogge, deceased, and brought with him a

bed of [*blank*], a flock bolster, a bad coverlet, a blanket, a pair of sheets, a platter, a candlestick, reasonable clothes, a new gown, two shirts, 4*d*., and shirt bands.

[*no day or month*] 1597. John Davis is chosen into this house in the place of William Russell, deceased, and brings with him a flock bed, a pair of blankets, one sheet, a flock bolster, a coverlet, a platter, a candlestick, a dish, a spoon, a new gown, a coffer and 20*s*. given as a benevolence.

8 August [*no year*] John Rouswell, an inhabitant of this town, is chosen into this house in the place of Robert Blobell, deceased, and brought with him a pair of sheets, a rug gown, a dish, a spoon, a candlestick and some clothes to his body.

11 December 1598. Agnes Bartlet, widow, an inhabitant of this town, is chosen into this house in the place of Alice Perham and brought with her three pottingers, three saucers, and certain old bedding in the presence of John Thorne, Mr George Udale gentleman, Henry Meer, gentleman, Thomas Barton, Jasper Fridlock, Edmund Lane, Henry Stevens, John Coper, John Gardner, Ambrose Banwell, Richard Oringe, Peter Game, Richard Downton and James Compton, gentleman.

December 1598. Elizabeth Hudd is chosen into this house in the place of Katherine Wilkins, deceased, and brought a bolster and a blanket.

7 March 1599. Thomas Lodge, an inhabitant of this town, is chosen into this house in the place of John Chapman, deceased, in the presence of John Thorne master and fourteen others.

5 February 1600. John Mute, an inhabitant of this town, is chosen for one of the poor men of this house in the place of Thomas Ladbrooke, deceased, in the presence of George Uvedale, gentleman, master and twelve others and brought in a tin platter.

22 February 1600. William Sansom, an inhabitant of this town, is chosen for a poor man of this house in the place of Richard Roberts, deceased, in the presence of George Uvedale, gentleman, master and twelve others and brought in a tin platter, a brass candlestick.

22 February 1600. ~~Christian Davis~~ Avis Gaste, widow, is chosen a poor woman in the place of Joan Scopes, deceased, in the presence of George Uvedale, gentleman, master and fourteen others and gave in a tin charger.

15 May 1600. John Cleyhill, a decayed and ancient inhabitant of this town, is chosen into this house in the place of Robert Sexton, deceased, in the presence of George Udale, gentleman, master and ten others and brought in a pair of sheets, one blanket, a bolster, a pillow, a platter, a pottinger, a saucer and a candlestick.

8 July 1600. Walter Camell by the appointment of Peter Game was chosen into this house in the place of John Grenewaye, deceased, in the presence of George Uvedale, gentleman, master and nine others.

17 January 1601. John Pricket by the appointment of Peter Game was chosen into this house in the place of Water Carmell, deceased, [*manuscript torn*] and brought in with him a coverlet, a sheet, a bolster, a blanket, a pottinger, a saucer and a candlestick in the time of Henry Stevens [*master*].

6 February 1601. Simon Soper was chosen into this house in the room of Thomas Riall and brought with him a platter, a sheet and a bolster.

6 February 1601. John Keines was chosen in the room of John Ladbroke and brought with him a coverlet, one sheet, a blanket, a platter and a candlestick.

20 March 1602. William Maunfell is chosen in this house in the room of John Keines and brought with him a coverlet, a sheet, a pillow, a pottinger, clothes, a dish and a spoon and was sworn.

25 April 1603. John Newman is chosen into this house upon the death of William Sampson and brought with him a feather bed, a bolster, a pair of new sheets and a coverlet.

28 July 1603. Richard Bolleyn is chosen into this house upon the death of John Roswell and brought with him, a coverlet of shreds, a platter, a candlestick, a bolster of feathers and a saucer.

3 August 1603. Agnes Baller is chosen into this house upon the death of Elizabeth Hudd and brought with her a flock bed, two pairs of sheets, a bolster, two coverlets, one blanket, 4*d*., partlet, three aprons, a neckerchief, two head kerchiefs, three smockettes, a waistcoat, one gown, two petticoats, one hat, one pottinger, two pairs of shoes, one pair of hose and a coffer.

September 1603. William Michell is chosen in the room of Nicolas Bollin, who left this house without cause, and brought with him a cup, a platter, a pottinger, a spoon, a dish and a trencher.

29 January 1604. Clement Richman is chosen into this house in the room of Simon Soper, deceased, and brought with him, a dust bed, a feather pillow, a coverlet, a pair of sheets, a brass pot, two pottingers and a candlestick.

8 February 1606. John Luckes is chosen into this house in the room of John Dyer deceased and brought with him a platter, a sheet, a pillow, a dish and a spoon. Luke

Luckes his son has promised and given his word to Mr John Cupper to give this house 20*s.* at Lady Day 1607 to be spent on a new gown for his father.

22 February 1606. Henry Chapline alias Raynolds is chosen into this house in the room of Thomas Lodge. Deceased. and brought with him a brass pot worth 5*s.* one dish, a spoon and a trencher.

23 June 1606. Richard Dunham is chosen into this house in the room of John Newman, deceased, and brought with him a coverlet, two blankets and 6*s.* in money.

16 July 1606. Richard Gillam is chosen into this house in the room of Henry Raynolds alias Chapline, deceased, and brought in with him in money 10*s.*, a bed and a bolster, a pair of sheets, a coverlet, a platter, a dish, a spoon and a trencher.

22 September 1607. Anstye Freeman is chosen into this house in the room of Alice Chamberlayne, deceased, and brought with her into this house two petticoats, a gown, a good hat and a worse a pair of sheets, three smocks four good partlets and two others, two aprons, three single head clothes and a double kerchief, a good coffer, one bolster and one pillow.

1 February 1608. Agnes Sansom is chosen into this house in the room of Agnes Bartlett, deceased, and will bring with her a caldron, a bolster, one good gown and other apparel.

30 May 1608. Alice Fooke, widow, is chosen into this house in the room of Anstye Freeman, deceased, and will bring with her a feather and flock bed, a pair of blankets, two pairs of sheets, a coverlet, one pillow, one bolster, one kettle, one platter, one pottinger and one basin.

16 August 1608. Thomas Ivatt is chosen into this house in the room of John Prickett, deceased, by the appointment of Peter Game and will bring with him [*blank*].

9 December 1609. John Legcost is chosen into this house in the room of John Luccas, who has departed from this house having a living fallen into his hands, and brings with him a feather bed, a bolster, two coverlets, two sheets, an anvil, a pair of bellows, and all his working tools.

1 March 1610. William Geninges at this day is chosen in the room of John Dawe, deceased, and brings with him a blanket, a sheet and a pillow.

9 April 1610. Thomas Grayle, a poor man, is chosen in the place of Clement Richman, deceased, and brings with him a bed of feathers and flock, a bolster, a pillow, a pair of sheets, a blanket, a coverlet, a pewter dish, a brass candlestick, a dish, a spoon,

the apparel on his back, three shirts and a pair of shoes.

9 April 1610. Joan Dowle, widow, is chosen a poor woman into this house in the place of Agnes Longe and brings with her a bolster, a pair, of blankets one sheet, a coverlet, a pewter dish, a dish, a spoon, a cup and two sets of clothes of linen and woollen.

1 May 1610. Thomas Winchell is chosen a poor man into this house in the place of Richard Gillam, deceased, and brings with him, a pair of blankets and 20s. in money (the gift of John Winchell his brother).

31 May 1610. John Newman is chosen into the house in the room of Richard Dinham, deceased, and brings in nothing.

16 July 1610. John Tankyns is chosen into this house in the room of [*blank*] and brought with him one featherbed, a feather bolster, three feather pillows, one pair of blankets, one pair of sheets, one coverlet, one platter, one pottinger, one saucer and one brass candlestick, and is sworn.

[*torn*] September 1610. Robert Pawley is chosen into this house in the room of William Mitchell (late expelled for contempting to be ordered by the master and brethren of this house and often admonished to that purpose) and brought with him one blanket, one sheet and 5s. in money, and is sworn.

The same day Margaret Browne is chosen into this house in the room of Jane Dowle, deceased, and brings with her a dustbed, a bolster, two feather pillows, a coverlet, three sheets and a brass candlestick, and is sworn.

7 October 1610. Robart Manfeld is chosen into this house in the room of John Cleye, deceased, and brings with him a dish, a spoon, a trencher and a pottinger, and is sworn.

7 October 1610. John Hexe is chosen into this house in the room of John Mace, deceased, and brings with him a pair of sheets, a blanket and a bolster stuffed with straw, and is sworn.

30 October 1610. John Phelps alias Dagell is chosen into this house in the room of Robert Pawley, deceased, and brings with him one pair of sheets, one blanket, a pillow, a platter, a pottinger, a dish and a spoon, and is sworn.

20 June 1611. Christian Lodwine is chosen into this house in the room of Alice Fook, deceased, and being now housewife of this house brings with her all her bedding in which she now lies, and is sworn.

16 December 1611. Agnes Hopton, widow, is chosen housewife into this house upon the departure of Christian Ladwine, and is sworn.

2 January 1612. John Tissard is chosen into this house in the room of John Hext (lately expelled this house) and is now sworn, he brings with him a coverlet, a blanket and a sheet.

5 March 1612. Joan Rawlyns, widow, a long time inhabitant in this town is chosen into this house for a poor woman upon the death of Christian Ladwyn and is sworn. She brings with her a bed of feathers and flocks, a blanket, a coverlet, a bolster, a pair of sheets, a platter, a dish and a spoon.

24 March 1612. Thomas Vyncent is chosen a poor man into this house in the place of Thomas Grayle, expelled, and brings bedding full of furnished woollen and linen, a cloak and two sets of clothes. He relinquishes all his goods to his kinswoman Primrose Vyncent according to his deed.

10 April 1612. Steven Beaton is chosen a poor man into this house in the place of Thomas Wynchell, deceased, and brings with him a bad coverlet, a bolster, a pillow, a little brass pot, a platter, a pottinger and two sheets.

31 August 1612. Eleanor Daye is chosen a poor woman into this house in the place of Christian Davye, deceased, and brings with her a brass pot, a flock bed, a pillow, a coverlet, a blanket, one sheet, a dish and a spoon.

6 March 1613. John Gorman is chosen a poor man into this house in the place of Thomas Vincent, deceased, and brings with him a brass kettle, a spoon and a dish.

27 December 1613. John Coxe is chosen a poor man into this house in the place of Thomas Ivett, deceased, and brings with him a coverlet, a sheet, a bolster, a coffer, a spoon and a dish.

18 June 1615. Anthony Donnome is chosen a poor man into this house in the place of Robert Manfild, deceased, and brings with him a feather bed, a bolster, a pillow, a pair of sheets and a pair of blankets.

13 August 1615. Susan Ralings, widow, is chosen a poor woman into this house in the place of Agnes Baller, deceased, and brings with her a flock bed, a flock bolster, a feather pillow, two pairs of sheets, one coverlet, one blanket and a white rug.

11 March 1616. Margaret Browne is chosen a poor woman into this house with the consent of her husband in the place of the widow Susan Rawlinges deceased, and brings in no goods with the consent of her husband.

11 March 1616. Joan Baker is chosen a poor woman into this house in the place of Katherine Symons, deceased, being the room of a poor woman allowed by the house to William Masters, and brings in goods.

26 March 1616. William Weare the elder is this day chosen a poor man into this house in the place of John Dagle alias Phelpes and brings with him into this house a pair of sheets, a bolster, a platter and a coffer.

22 April 1616. Motley Pownfor is this day chosen a poor man into this house in the place of Antony Dunham, deceased, and has brought with him into this house a bolster and two pewter vessels.

18 January 1617. Robert Burgise this day is chosen a poor man into this house in the place of William Manfyld, deceased, and brings with him a coverlet, a blanket, a sheet and [manuscript torn].

27 April 1617. At this day Giles Stone is chosen a poor man into this house in the room of John William Loket, deceased, and brought in his carpentry tools, and is sworn.

6 May 1617. At this day Robert Ashwater is chosen a poor man into this house in the room of John Gorman, deceased, brings a platter, a dish and a spoon.

14 June 1617. At this day John Tabut is chosen a poor man into this house in the room of Motley Pounfer, deceased, and the 27 of [manuscript torn] following was sworn.

27 June 1617. At this day Joan Lane, widow, is chosen a poor woman into this house in the room of Joan Rawling, deceased, and brought in with her a [manuscript torn] featherbed, one bolster, one platter, one pottinger and one sheet and a blanket, and is sworn.

19 December 1617. At this day Christopher Richman is chosen a poor man into this house in the room of Robert Burges, deceased, and brought in with him one sheet and one pottinger.

9 February 1618. At this day Elizabeth Porter is chosen a poor woman into this house in the room of Eleanor Daye, deceased.

1 July 1618. At this day John Eredy Oredy is chosen a poor man into this house in the place of [manuscript torn] Hynde, deceased, and brings with him two [illegible] of clothes, a pair of sheets and [manuscript torn] shirts.

16 August 1618. This day Joan Mathew, widow of Thomas Mathew, is chosen a poor woman into this house in the room of Margaret Browne, deceased, and brought with her a pair of sheets, a feather ~~bolster~~ pillow, one dish, a spoon and a pair of blankets.

23 December 1618. This day David Castelman is chosen a poor man into this house in the room of Robert Ashwater, deceased, and brought in with him one flock bed, a bolster, one coverlet, a pair of sheets, a dish, a spoon and a trencher.

9 March 1619. Elizabeth Mamfild is chosen a poor woman into this house in the place of Joan Baker, deceased, a feather bed, a feather pillow, a coverlet, a blanket, a cup, a dish, a spoon, her linen and woollen clothing and one chest.

19 September 1619. This day George Browne is chosen a poor man into this house in the room of John Talbutt, deceased, and brought in with him 22d. and 2s. more is promised by John Taylor of Chilton and on 21 September he was sworn.

1 November 1621. This day Michael Maye is chosen a poor man into this house in the room of John Tankins, deceased, and brought in with him a flock bed, a coverlet, a bolster, a sheet, a blanket, a dish, a spoon, a hook and a spade, and is sworn.

22 April 1622. This day Robert Fort is chosen a poor man into this house in the room of William Jennings, deceased, and brought in with him a flock bed, a blanket, a sheet, a pillow and a kettle ~~and is sworn.~~

14 March 1623. This day Richard Edwards is chosen a poor man into this house in the room of Robert Forte, deceased, and brought with him a coverlet, a blanket, one sheet, a bolster, a pottinger, a hook and a pair of cuffs, and is sworn.

22 March 1623. This day John Shakell is chosen ~~into~~ a poor man into this house in the room of Ambrose Chetmell, deceased, and brings in with him one feather bolster, a blanket, a platter, a pottinger, a pressing iron and sheets.

5 April 1623. This day Thomas Bryne is chosen a poor man into this house in the room of Michael May, deceased, and brought in with him three pillows, two pairs of sheets, one blanket, a coverlet, a brass pot, a woodhook, a dish and a spoon.

9 November 1624. This day Bryant Dewe is chosen a poor man into this house in the room of John Newman, deceased, and brought in with him a coverlet, a pair of sheets, a blanket, a bed, a bolster, a pewter dish, a cup, a dish and a spoon, and is sworn.

26 December 1624. This day Henry Martyn is chosen a poor man into this house in place of Stephen Beaton, deceased, and brought in with him a blanket, a wooden beetle and six iron wedges, an axe a woodhook, a dish and a spoon, and is sworn.

9 January 1625. The said day Thomas Glover is chosen a poor man into this house in the place of David Castleman, deceased, and brought in with him a bed, a bolster, a blanket, a pair of sheets, one pillow, a coverlet, a dish and a spoon, and is sworn.

5 September 1625. The said day William Chesocke, an inhabitant of this town, is chosen a poor man into this house in the place of Christopher Rytchman, deceased, and brought in with him a pair of sheets, a coverlet, one pewter dish, a dish and a spoon, and is sworn.

7 November 1625. The said day William Bownde, an inhabitant of this town and born in the same, is chosen a poor man into this house in the place of Lawrence Williams, deceased, and brought with him one sheet, one hatchet, a dish and a spoon, and is sworn.

17 January 1626. The said day John Phelpes alias Daggle, an inhabitant of this town and born in the same, is chosen a poor man into this house in the place of Thomas Bryne, deceased, and brought with him a feather pillow, a blanket, a sheet, a platter, a dish, and a spoon, and is sworn.

10 February 1627. The said day Eleanor Heath, widow, an inhabitant of this town and born in the same, was chosen a poor woman into this house in the place of Margaret Porter, deceased, and brought with her one flock bed, a bolster, a pair of sheets, a coverlet, a pottinger, a dish and a spoon, and is sworn.

20 March 1627. The said day Anne Sheane, widow, an inhabitant of this town, was chosen a poor woman into this house in the place of Joan Lane, deceased, and brought in with her a dust bed, two feather pillows, a coverlet, one blanket, a pair of sheets, a pottinger, a dish and a spoon, and is sworn.

[*Manuscript torn*] William Ponde an inhabitant of this town, being seven weeks there, is chosen a poor man into this house [*manuscript torn*] deceased, having been in addition to the founder number was this day sworn and brought in with him [*manuscript torn*] flock bed, a pair of sheets, a pillow, a blanket and a coverlet.

15 October 1627. [*Manuscript torn*] man into this house and brought in a bedstead, a bed, a bolster, a pair of blankets, a coffer and cloak, and is sworn.

22 October 1627. This day Agnes Lawrence is chosen a poor woman into this house by way of addition to the former number and brings in a pottinger, one sheet, one pillow, a dish and a spoon and is sworn.

9 December 1628. At this day William Harris is chosen into this house in the room of John Tissard and brings into the house a pair of sheets and a platter and is sworn.

9 December 1628. Edith Lambe widow is admitted instead of Ann Shere, deceased, and brings into the house a couple of feather pillows, a platter, a pair of sheets and a coverlet.

9 March 1629. At this day John Marshall is chosen a poor man into this house in the place of Henry Martyn, deceased, and brought in with him a bolster, a blanket, a sheet, a dish and a spoon, and is sworn.

30 November 1629. This day Edith Rawlens, widow, is chosen into this house as housewife in the room of Agnes Hopton, deceased, and is sworn.

30 November 1629. Mary Whitehead, widow, is chosen a poor woman into this house in the room of Elizabeth Manfeilde, deceased, and is sworn. She brought in a little featherbed, a bolster, one pair of sheets, a coverlet, a pottinger, a dish and a spoon.

31 December 1629. This day Joan Illarye, born in this town, is chosen a poor woman into this house in the place of Fortune Davy, deceased, and brought in a blanket, a pair of sheets, a bolster, a pottinger, a chest, a dish and a spoon, and is sworn.

4 September 1630. This day John Parkens, dwelling in this town, is chosen a poor man into this house in the place of John Greedye, deceased, and brought in a woodhook, a dish and a spoon, and is sworn.

28 February 1631. This day Robert Parham, born in this town, is chosen a poor man into this house in the place of John Shackell and brought in a woodhook, a hatchet, a dish and a spoon.

28 May 1632. This day Sampson Cawpin is chosen a poor man into this house in the place of John Marshall, deceased, and brought in a blanket, a sheet, a dish and a spoon, and is sworn. It is ordered that forthwith, with the consent of the company, he shall be and execute the office of Prior of the house.

21 June 1632. This day John Martyn is chosen a poor man into this house in the place of Sampson Cawpin, deceased, and brought in a coverlet, a blanket, a dish, spoon and a bolster and is sworn.

21 June 1632. This day John Mitchell was chosen a poor man into this house in the place of Giles Stone, deceased, and brought in a sheet, a blanket, a bolster, a coverlet and a feather pillow, and was sworn.

28 December 1632. This day Julian Raller alias Davie and Slade are now chosen as poor women into this house (by virtue of Mr Wood's gift), and Julian Davy will bring with her a dust bed, a feather bolster, a pair of blankets and a coverlet, and is sworn.

28 December 1632. This day John Bealy is chosen a poor man into this house (by virtue of Mr Wood's gift). He is to be Prior and brought in with him a desk, a chair, a cushion and a pillow [*manuscript torn*] and is sworn.

January 1633. The said day Mary Callowe is chosen a poor woman into this house (by virtue of Mr Wood's gift), being a long time inhabitant of this town, and brought bedding for her own use, and is sworn.

3 February 1633. This day Thomas Rawlins is chosen a poor man into this house in the place of Richard Edwards, deceased, and is to bring in a bed, a coverlet, a sheet, a blanket, a dish and a spoon. He is to execute the office of the Prior of this house and is sworn.

17 July 1633. Elizabeth Dawe, widow, was this day chosen a housewife into this house and is sworn.

30 July 1633. This day Steven Towgood is chosen a poor man into this house in the place of William Harris, deceased, and brings a wood hook, a dish, a spoon, a cup and a trencher, and is sworn.

30 July 1633. The said day Richard Mitchell a poor man is chosen into this house, by way of addition to the former number or improvement of the revenues, in the place of William Pond, deceased, and brings in a sheet, a platter, a dish, a spoon and a trencher, and is sworn.

30 July 1633. The same day John Illary is chosen a poor man into this house in the place of John Martyn, deceased, and brings in a flock bed, a blanket, a sheet, a bolster, a dish, a spoon, a ~~platter~~ and a cup, and is sworn.

20 August 1633. The said day Elizabeth Greedye is chosen a poor woman into this house in the place of Joan Matthew, deceased, and brought in a pair of sheets, a dish and a spoon, and is sworn.

9 November 1633. The said day John Cole is chosen a poor man into this house in the place of George Browne, deceased, and brought in a sheet, a platter and a spoon, and is sworn.

11 February 1634. The said day Urath Barnard, widow, born in this town, is chosen a poor woman into this house in the place of Eleanor Hearth, widow, deceased and brought in a coverlet, a blanket, a pair of sheets, a feather pillow, a feather bolster, a dish, a spoon and a cup, and is sworn.

18 June 1635. The said day William Illery, a poor man and an ancient inhabitant of this town, was chosen into this house in the place of Brian Dew, deceased, and brings in a mattock, a spade, one pottinger, a dish and a spoon, and is sworn.

13 October 1635. The said day Cuthbert Ribby a poor man, born in this town, was [*manuscript torn*] this house in the place of John [*manuscript torn*], deceased, and brings a pair of [*manuscript torn*].

16 February 1636. [*Manuscript torn and entry missing*].

6 April 1636. The said day William Chafin, an inhabitant and born in this town, is chosen a poor man into this house in the place of William Illarye, deceased, and brings in with him a new bed, a feather pillow, a sheet, a half bedstead, a pewter platter, a dish and a spoon.

30 August 1636. This day John Sampson, an inhabitant and born in this town, is chosen a poor man into this house in the place of ~~William~~ Robert Perham and brings in him a flock bed, a bolster, a sheet, a blanket, a coverlet, a dish and a spoon.

10 October 1636. This day Michael Dewey, an inhabitant in this town, is chosen a poor man into this house in the place of Thomas Rawlins and brings in with him a blanket, a platter, a dish, a spoon and a cup.

2 January 1637. This day John Barnard, an inhabitant of this town, is chosen a poor man into this house in the place of John Cox, being nominated by William Game with Thomas Caller and William Dodge, and John Barnard brought into the house with him a bed furnished for his lodging, a platter, a dish and a spoon.

December 1637. This day Tamsin Poule, widow, an inhabitant in this town is chosen a poor woman into this house in the place of Urith Barnard, deceased, and brought into the house a feather bolster, three feather pillows, two coverlets, a pair of sheets, one dish, a spoon and a cup.

March 1638. This day John Okely, an ancient inhabitant of this town, is chosen a poor man into this house in the place of John Sampson and brings in with him a bed furnished for himself with a half headed bedstead, a cord and a mat, a flock bed, a flock bolster, a pillow and pillowbere, a blanket, a coverlet, a pair of sheets, a bearded cup, a dish, a trencher, a spoon and a coffer with lock and key.

24 March 1638. This day Alice Phelips, widow, an ancient inhabitant in this town, is chosen a poor woman into this house in the place of Marie Callway, deceased, and brought in with her a sheet, a pillow, a blanket, a pottinger, a cup, a dish and a spoon.

25 February 1639. This day Thomasine White, widow, an ancient inhabitant of this town, is chosen a poor woman into this house in the place of Edith Rawlins, widow, deceased, and brings in a cup, a dish and a spoon, and is sworn.

20 April 1639. This day William Dodge, a inhabitant of this town, is chosen a poor man into this house in the place of John Okely, deceased, and brings in a sheet, a coverlet, a platter, a dish and spoon, and is sworn.

20 April 1639. The same day Jane Cuffe is chosen a poor woman into this house, being an inhabitant of this town, in the place of Agnes Lawrence and brought in a flock bed, a pair of sheets, a coverlet, two pillows, a blanket, a platter, a dish and a spoon, and is sworn.

30 October 1639. This day Jane Hassedge, an old woman and born in this town, is chosen a poor woman into this house in the place of Elizabeth Greedy, widow, deceased, and brings in with her two blankets, a pillow, a dish, a spoon and an old bedstead, and is sworn.

May 1639. Edmund [*manuscript torn*], an inhabitant of this town, is chosen a poor man into this house in the place of John [*manuscript torn*] dish and spoon.

[*Manuscript torn*] inhabitant of this town, is chosen a poor man into this house in the place of William [*manuscript torn*] a coverlet, a pair [*manuscript torn*].

3 June 1640. This day Thomas Callow, an ancient inhabitant of this town, is chosen a poor man into this house upon the death of William Chessick and brings in a dish, a spoon, a pressing iron and a pair of tailor's shears, and is sworn.

6 July 1640. This day John Daniell, an ancient inhabitant being born in this town, a poor man is chosen into this house in the place of William Chaffyn, who voluntarily left his place about three weeks since without any leave or licence, and brings in a feather bed, a feather bolster, a feather pillow, a coverlet, a pair of blankets, a pair of sheets and other things, and is sworn.

13 July 1640. This day Edward Fudge an ancient inhabitant of this town is chosen a poor man into this house in the place and upon the death of John Perkins and brings in a pair of blankets, one sheet, a coverlet, a bolster, a pewter dish and a spoon, and is sworn.

21 August 1640. This day John Glyde, an ancient inhabitant of this town, is chosen a poor man into this house in the place of Thomas Callow and upon his death, and brings in a dish, a spoon, a trencher and a cup, and was sworn the 26 October 1640.

21 July 1641. This day Joan Bollen, wife of Henry Bollen, is chosen a poor woman in the place of Edith Lame, deceased, and brings into this house a dish, a spoon and a cup, and sworn.

21 July 1641. This day Agnes Morly, the wife of William Morlye, is chosen a poor woman into this house in the place of Steven Toogood, who was expelled for his great misdemeanour of drunkenness and other misdemeanours and has often been admonished and refuses to be reformed. This was done in the presence of Robert Sander master, Mr Lyford, Richard Cooth, Robert Whetcombe, Richard Speele, John Chitmyll, Nicholas Rowman, James Wallis, William Sansome, Thomas Sansome and John Martin and she brings into this house [*blank*].

16 February 1642. This day Mary Appleby, a widow born in this town, was chosen to the housewife's place for this house (or if not performing that service she is to be admitted into this house as a poor woman in the place of Joan Whittle, deceased) and brings a bed-tye, a sheet, a coverlet, a dish, a spoon and a cup, and she was sworn 10 March 1642.

10 March 1642. This day Christian Chaplyn, widow, is chosen a poor woman into this house in the place of Jane Hassidge, deceased, and brings in a sheet, a pair of blankets, a dish and a spoon, and she is sworn

23 October 1642. This day Dorothy Cowarde, widow, is chosen a poor woman into this house in the place of Jane Cuffe, deceased, and brings in a coverlet, one blanket, one sheet, one bolster, one pillow, one half sheet, a pottinger, a dish and a spoon.

23 November 1642. This day Henry Stone, an inhabitant of this town, is chosen a poor man into this house in the place of John Illarye and brings a straw bed for his continual lodging, a pair of blankets, one bolster, one pillow, one platter, a dish and a [*manuscript torn*].

23 October 1643. At this day Anne Justins, widow, was chosen a poor woman into this house in the room of Tamsin White, deceased, and brought in with her a brass kettle, one pair of sheets, a rug, a feather pillow, a dish and a spoon, and is sworn.

21 May 1644. At this day John Burges, a poor man born in this town, is chosen into this house in the room or place of William Browne, deceased, and brings in a flock bed, a bolster, a blanket, a sheet, a dish, a spoon and a cup, and is sworn.

1 July 1645. At this day Thomas Hobbs, a poor man of this town, is chosen into this house in the room or place of Edward Fudge, deceased, and brings in a pottinger, a dish, a spoon and a cup, and is sworn.

1 July 1645. The same day Alice Cole, widow, a poor woman of this town, is chosen
into this house in the room of Joan Bollen, deceased, and brings in a bed, a sheet,
a coverlet, a coffer, a dish and a spoon, and is sworn.

13 October 1645. At this day John Locket is chosen a poor man into this house and
brings in with him a bolster, a blanket, two sheets, a dish and a spoon, and is sworn
and came into this house in the room of Michael Dewe, deceased.

20 January 1646. The same day Richard Symes, a poor man of this town, is chosen
into this house in the room of Thomas Glover, deceased, and brings in one pewter
platter, a pottinger, one cup, a dish, a spoon and a pillow.

10 April 1646. The same day Edward Lane, a poor man and a continual inhabitant of
this town, is chosen into this house in the place of Richard Mitchell, deceased, and
brings in one flock bed, a bolster, a pillow, one pair of blankets, a coverlet, a pair of
sheets, a cup, a dish and a spoon, and is sworn.

30 November 1646. At this day Thomas Davy, a poor man and continual inhabitant
of this town, is chosen into this house in the place of John Lockett, deceased, and
brings in a coverlet, a sheet, a blanket, a feather bolster pillow, a dust bolster, a straw
bed, a dish, a spoon and a trencher, and is sworn.

1 May 1647. At this day Margery Snow, widow, a poor woman of this town, is chosen
into this house in the place of Margaret Palmer, widow, deceased and brings in a
feather pillow, a blanket, a dish, a spoon and a cup, and is sworn. By the gift of Mr
William Woodd.

6 September 1647. At this day Lawrence Way, a poor man of this town, was chosen
into this house in the place of John Bealy, deceased, and brings in a coverlet, a
platter, a dish, a spoon and a pillow, and is sworn.

[*Undated*] At this day Joan Ponne, widow, a poor woman of this town, was chosen in
the place of Mary Callow, deceased, and brings in a feather bed, a bolster, a rug, a
blanket, a pair of sheets, a pewter dish and a spoon, and is sworn. [*Marginal note:*
upon Mr Wood's gift.]

[*Undated*] Mary Callow was chosen a poor woman into this house 29 January 1632 and
upon her death nobody else was chosen so that place was void until Joan Ponde,
widow, was now chosen by the gift of Mr William Wood.

[*Undated*] The same day Peter Freeman, an ancient inhabitant of this town, was
chosen a poor man into this house upon the death of a poor man who died long
since. In regard that the provisions for the maintenance of the poor people has

been extraordinarily dear and the rents abated by reason of the late wars none was chosen until this present and the said Peter Freeman brings in 20s. and [*blank*].

[*Undated*] The same day William Baller an ancient inhabitant of this town was chosen a poor man and for his ~~allowance~~ maintenance is allowed 10d. per week and is not to be taken into this house.

1 March 1648. This day Robert Harvy was chosen into this house, being an ancient inhabitant in this town, upon the death of Richard Symes to live by the alms thereof. He brings in a coverlet, a sheet, a dish, and a spoon and was chosen in the presence of Thomas Samsone master, Richard Cooth, Robert Whetcombe, Josiah Cooth, John Martine, Richard Speede Richard Avoakes, Nicholas Romayne, James Wallis, William Eares, John Chetnole, Robert Sanders and John Durnford.

5 June 1648. This day John Soper was chosen into this house, being an ancient inhabitant of this town, upon the death of Peter Freeman, deceased, to live by the alms thereof. He brings in a pair of sheets, a bolster, a dish and a spoon and was chosen in the presence of Thomas Samson master, Mr Richard Cooth, Mr Robert Whetcombe, Robert Sanders, John Martine, Richard Speed, Richard Avoke, John Chetmell. William Sansom. James Wallice, John Durnford. Valentine Smith and William Hone.

25 November 1648. This day was John Pope chosen into this house, being an ancient inhabitant of this town, there being a place void to live by the alms thereof. He brings in a sheet, a blanket, a coverlet, a dish, a spoon and a cup and this done in the presence of Richard Speed, Robert Saunders, John Chetmill, Roger Morten, Richard Vokes, Nicholas Romayne, Hugh Hodges, James Wallis, Thomas Sansom, Valentine Smyth and William Hone.

21 January 1650. This day Alice Bealy was chosen into this house, being an ancient inhabitant in this town, in the place of Agnes Morley, deceased, to live by the alms of this house. She brings in a flock bed, a coverlet, two blankets, two sheets, a dish and a spoon and this was done in the presence of Mr Lyford, Richard Cooth, Robert Whetcombe, Robert Saunders, John Morton, Richard Voke, John Chetmill, Hugh Hodges, William Sansom, James Wallis, Valentine Smyth and Walter Lambert, and is sworn.

15 May 1650. This day Elizabeth Warren, widow, was chosen into this house, being an ancient inhabitant in this town, in the place of Elizabeth Daw, widow, deceased, to live by the alms of this house. She brings in a blanket, a sheet, a bolster, a coverlet, a dish and a spoon and this done in the presence of John Cooth master, Mr Lyford, Richard Cooth, Robert Whetcombe, Robert Saunders, John Morten, John Chetmill,

Nicholas Romayne, Hugh Hodges, James Wallis, William Sansom, William Horne, Valentine Smyth and Walter Lambert, and is sworn.

3 July 1650. This day Charles Rawlens was chosen into this house, being an ancient inhabitant in this town, to live by the alms of this house and brings in a flock bed, a feather bolster, a feather pillow, a bedstead, a platter, a dish a spoon and a cup.

16 September 1650. This day Christopher Marten was chosen into this house, being an ancient inhabitant in this town, to live by the alms of this house in the place of Lawrence Way and brings in a sheet, a pillow, a pottinger, a dish and a spoon.

16 September 1650. The same day John Lock is chosen into this house, being an ancient inhabitant in this town, to live by the alms of this house and brings in a coffer, a dish and a spoon.

10 March 1651. This day Richard Nott is chosen into this house, being an ancient inhabitant in this town (and his sight very bad), to live by the alms of this house and brings in a skillet, a dish and a spoon.

9 May 1651. This day Christian Mitchel being an ancient, poor woman and inhabitant of this town born, is chosen into this house to live by the alms thereof and brings in a blanket, a pillow, a dish and a spoon.

8 March 1652. This day Thomas Whetcombe, a poor man, was chosen into this house to live by the alms thereof in the presence of John Martine master, Robert Whetcombe, Josiah Cooth, John Chetnole, John Whetcombe, William Sansome, James Wallis, Thomas Sansom, Valentine Smith, William Horne, Nicholas Rumayne and John Eastmont. Thomas Whetcombe brings in a dust bed, a rug, two sheets, two bolster cloths, two sheets [*sic*], a dish and a spoon, and is sworn.

Upon a view at the Almshouse the 25 of April 1586 there were found accounts for the regnal years:

19 Henry VI (1 Sep. 1440–31 Aug. 1441)
10 Edward IV (4 Mar. 1470–3 Mar. 1471)
1 Richard III (26 Jun. 1483–25 Jun. 1484)
11 Henry VII (22 Aug. 1495–21 Aug. 1496)
29 Henry VIII (22 Apr. 1537–21 Apr. 1538)
7 Edward VI (28 Jan. 1553–6 Jul. 1553)
3 Philip and Mary (Mary: 6 Jul. 1555–5 Jul. 1556)/(Philip: 25 Jul. 1556–24 Jul. 1557)
1-9 Elizabeth I (17 Nov. 1558–16 Nov. 1567)
11-28 Elizabeth I (17 Nov. 1568–1586)

29 May 1652. This day was chosen into this house Gawen Downton in the place of
Thomas Dawe, deceased, in the presence of John Martin master, Robert Whetcombe,
Robert Sanders, Richard Avoxe, John Whetcombe, James Walles, William Eares,
William Horne, Valentine Smith, Walter Lambertt and John Estment and he brings
into the house a sheet, a bolster, a dish and a spoon, and is sworn.

25 August 1652. This day Joan Illary, widow, was chosen into this house in the place
of good wife [*Elizabeth*] Warren to live by the alms thereof. She brought in a sheet,
a blanket, a rug and ~~a pewter dish~~ bolster.

12 April 1653. This day John Flower was chosen into this house in the place of John
Soper and brings into the house [*blank*].

10 January 1654. This day Grace Danyell was chosen into this house in the place of
Margery Snow and brings in a flock bed, a bolster, a pair of sheets, a blanket, a dish
and a spoon.

2 May 1654. This day Thomas Fort was chosen into this house in the place of Gawen
Downton and brings in a dish, a spoon and a cup.

3 September 1654. This day Henry Bollen was chosen into this house in the place of
William Dodge and brings in a feather pillow, a straw bed, an old coverlet, a dish, a
spoon, a cup and an old pair of sheets.

9 September 1654. This day Joan Farant, widow, was chosen into this house in the
place of Alice Cole, widow, and brings in a flock bed, a flock bolster, two blankets, a
pair of sheets, a coverlet, a sheet, a box, a platter, a dish, a spoon and a cup.

18 September 1654. Henry Castleman was chosen into this house in the place of
Thomas Whetcombe and brings in a rug, a dish, a spoon and a cup.

13 July 1655. This day Joan Culleford is chosen into this house in the place of Joan
Farant [*remainder of this entry is in a different hand*] sworn, and her daughter has sent
her a petticoat to wear, it is consented that her daughter shall have it again after
her death.

13 July 1655. The same day Mary Chaplin alias Rayndel is chosen into this house in
the place of the widow Justins.

22 January 1656. The said day William Game of Haydon nominated Robert Dowle,
Robert Forrest and William Selby to the company upon the death of John Bernard
and of them the company made the choice of Robert Dowle who has nothing to
bring into the house. Sworn.

22 July 1656. The said day Alexander Chaunt was chosen into this house in the place of John Burges and brings in a dish and spoon. Sworn.

20 January 1657. The said day Grace Lambe, widow, is chosen into this house in the place of Mary Chaplyn alias Reynolds and brings in a straw bed, a bolster and sheet, a dish and a spoon. Sworn.

18 April 1657. This day John Trew was chosen into this house in the place of Robert Harvey and brings in a coverlet, a pillow, a sheet, a cup, a dish and spoon, and is sworn.

14 November 1657. This day Dorothy Hebditch, widow, was chosen into, this house a cup in the place of Grace Danyell, widow, and brings in a pair of sheets, two blankets, two pillows, a cup, a dish and a spoon, and is sworn.

6 September 1658. This day Thomas Michell was chosen into this house in the place of Edmund Kyppen and brings in one coverlet, one bolster, a cup, a dish and a spoon, and is sworn.

9 February 1659. This day Robert Forrest was chosen into this house in the place of John Lock and brings in one flock pillow, a blanket, a cup, a dish and spoon, and is sworn.

12 February 1659. This day Eleanor Thresher was chosen into this house in the place of Grace Lambe, widow, and brings in one sheet, a dish and spoon, and is sworn.

26 April 1659. This day Antony Mathew was chosen into this house in the place of John Glyde and brings in a blanket, a cloak cup, dish and spoon, and is sworn.

16 December 1659. This day Walter Richman was chosen into this house in the place of John Glover, deceased, and brings in a sheet, a pair of blankets, a bolster, a dish, a spoon and a platter.

28 January 1660. This day Edmond Whetcombe was chosen into this house in the place of Charles Rawlins, deceased, and brings in a bed, a dish and a spoon.

1 June 1660. This day William Selby was chosen into this house in the place of Thomas Fort, deceased, and brings in a dish and a spoon, and is sworn.

20 October 1660. This day John Gill was chosen into this house in the place of Thomas Michell, deceased, and brings in a blanket, a cup, a dish and a spoon.

2 May 1661. This day Ambrose Lambert was chosen into this house in the place of John Gill, deceased, and brings into the house a coverlet, a little bed and one sheet.

19 June 1661. This day William Edwards was chosen into this house in the place of Alexander Chant, deceased, and brings in a blanket, a dish, a spoon and a cup.

27 September 1661. This day Mary Lane was chosen into this house in the place of the widow Coward, deceased, and brings into the house a dust bed, two sheets, a blanket, a dish, a spoon and a bolster.

28 November 1661. This day Thomas Slade was chosen into this house in the place of William Edwards, deceased, and brings into the house a pewter dish, a skillet, a dish and a spoon.

6 December 1661. This day William Game nominated Peter Keepin, Augustine Forrest and John Hadd to the company upon the death of Robert Dowle and the company chose John Hadd who brings into the house one bed, one sheet, one blanket, one dish and one spoon.

6 December 1661. This day Augustine Forrest was chosen into this house in the place of Cuthbert Rybby, deceased, and brings in one flock bed, one dish, one spoon, one trencher and one drinking cup.

28 December 1661. This day Margaret Kinge, widow, was chosen into this house in the place of Dorothy Dodge, deceased, and brings in one bed, bedstead, coverlet, blanket, sheet, dish, spoon, cup, trencher and bolster.

1 April 1662. This day Elizabeth Hopkins, widow, was chosen into this house in the place of Dorothy Hebditch, deceased, and brings in one feather bed, one feather pillow, a dust pillow, two blankets, one coverlet, one sheet, a bolster, a cloth, one dish, a spoon and a cup.

26 April 1662. This day Henry Bernard was chosen into this house in the place of Augustine Forrest, deceased, and brings in a feather pillow, a blanket, a dish, a spoon and a cup.

24 May 1662. This day Giles Stoney was chosen into this house in the place of Robert Forrest, deceased, and brings in a dust bed, a flock pillow, a coverlet, a sheet, a dish, a spoon and cup.

27 July 1662. This day John Symonds was chosen into this house in the place of Walter Richman, deceased, and brings in a feather bolster, a feather pillow, a blanket, a pewter dish, a dish, spoon and a cup.

27 September 1662. This day Stephen Hill was chosen into this house in the place of Thomas Slade, deceased, and brings in a feather pillow, a rug, a sheet, a dish, a spoon and a cup.

23 December 1662. This day Alice Stickland was chosen into this house in the place of Mary Lane, deceased, and brings in one sheet, a dish, a spoon and a cup.

22 August 1663. This day Thomas Bishopp was chosen into this house in the place of William Selby, deceased, and brings in a bed, a blanket, one sheet, a rug, a dish, a spoon and coverlet, and is sworn.

15 April 1664. This day Robert Smyth was chosen into this house in the place of Thomas Hobbs, deceased, and brings in one bed blanket, one sheet, one dish, one spoon and one drinking cup, and is sworn.

23 May 1664. This day Ann Baker, widow, was chosen into this house in the place of Elizabeth Painter and brings in a good sheet, a pillow, a coverlet, a dish and a spoon, and is sworn.

3 September 1664. This day Thomas Hopton was chosen into this house in the place of Giles Stoney, deceased, and brings in a blanket, a bolster, a dish, a spoon and a cup, and is sworn.

25 July 1666. This day William Soper was chosen into this house in the place of Christopher Marten, deceased, and brings in a flock bed, a sheet, an old blanket, a flock pillow, a dish, a spoon and cup.

24 April 1667. This day Mary Charles was chosen into this house in the place of Alice Stickland, deceased, and brings in one straw bed, a dust pillow, a feather pillow, a blanket, a sheet, a coverlet, a cup, a dish and a spoon.

27 May 1667. This day Anne Selby, widow, was chosen into this house in the place of Margaret Kinge, deceased, and brings in one sheet, a dish, a spoon and a cup. She also yields up in the hands of the master and brethren her rights in her house and garden at Horsecastle to buy her a bed and other necessaries.

25 May 1665. This day William Game nominated John Churchill, John Weare and John Marshall to the company upon the death of John Hudd and of them the company made the choice of John Marshall. [*This entry is out of sequence and in a different hand.*]

10 July 1667. This day Alice Swetnam, widow, was chosen into this house in the place of Anne Selby, widow, deceased, and brings in one feather bed, one feather bolster,

one feather pillow, a coverlet blanket, a pair of sheets, a bed mat, a cup, a dish and a spoon, and is sworn.

16 September 1667. This day Jane Hobbs, widow, is chosen a poor woman into this house in the place of Joan Pond, widow, deceased, and brings in a sheet, a blanket, a platter, a cup, a dish and a spoon, and is sworn.

October 1667. This day Jane Ryall, widow, is chosen into this house in the place of Christian Michell, widow, deceased, and brings in part of a rug, a pillow-tye, a cup, a dish and a spoon. And is sworn.

January 1668. This day John Linkhorne was chosen into this house in the place of Thomas Byshopp, deceased, and brings in a bolster, a rug, a dish and a spoon, and is sworn.

10 March 1669. This day Robert Baller was chosen into this house in the place of Antony Mathew, deceased, and brings in a flock bed, a bolster, a rug, a dish and a spoon, and was sworn.

27 March 1669. This day Ambrose Bollen was chosen into this house in the place of Henry Casement and brings in ~~an old rug,~~ a cup, a dish and a spoon, and was sworn.

3 August 1669. This day Henry Spurrier was chosen into this house in the place of John Pope and brings in a coffer, a cup, a dish and a spoon, and was sworn.

8 February 1670. This day Joan Ellis, widow, was chosen into this house in the place of Jane Hobbs, widow, and brings in a dish, a spoon a platter and one pillow, and was sworn.

9 March 1670. This day William Richmond was chosen into this house in the place of Robert Baller and brings in a sheet, a pillow, a platter, a dish and a spoon, and was sworn.

9 March 1670. William Willis was chosen into this house in the place of Richard Nott and brings in a dust bed, a blanket, a sheet, a rug and a bolster, a dish and a spoon, and was sworn.

5 December 1670. The same day Edward Scott was chosen into this house in the place of Thomas Hopton and brings in a dust bed, a blanket, a sheet, a coverlet, a bolster, a dish and spoon, and is sworn.

2 January 1671. The same day Alexander Illary was chosen into this house in the place

of William Richmond and brings in a feather pillow, a sheet, a coverlet, a dish, a spoon and a cup, and is sworn.

31 January 1671. This day Thomas Coward was chosen into this house in the place of Edward Whetcombe and is to bring into this house a rug, a blanket, a sheet, a cup, a dish and a spoon. Coward was sworn 16 March 1671.

4 April 1671. This day William Senior was chosen into this house in the place of Henry Bollen deceased, and brings in one blanket, one sheet, one dish, a spoon and cup, and is sworn.

6 May 1671. John Amans was this day chosen into this house in the place of John Trew, deceased, and brings in one straw bed, one bolster, one blanket, one sheet, a dish, a spoon and a cup, and is sworn.

8 August 1671. This day Margery Pond was chosen into this house in the place of Mary Charles, deceased, and brings in a rug, a pair of sheets, a bolster, a dish, a spoon and a cup, and is sworn.

20 January 1672. This day Thomas Stephens was chosen into this house in the place of Edward Scott, deceased, and brings in, a bed, a coverlet, a blanket, a sheet, a pillow, a dish, a spoon and a cup.

30 January 1672. Andrew Dowsy was chosen a poor man into this house in the place of Alexander Illery and brought into this house a bed, a sheet, a blanket, a bolster, a dish and a spoon.

14 February 1672. John Weare was this day chosen into this house in the place of Thomas Coward, deceased, and brought in a dust bed, a pillow, a sheet and a blanket, and is sworn.

4 March 1672. Edward Vowell was this day chosen into this house in the place of Andrew Dowsy deceased and brought into the house a feather bed, a pillow, a sheet, a coverlet, a cup, a dish, a spoon and a coffer. And is sworn.

1 April 1672. Robert Hide was this day chosen into this house in the place of Ambrose Lambert, deceased, and brought in, a flock bed, a pillow, a sheet, a blanket, a coverlet, a cup, a dish and a spoon, and is sworn.

31 May 1672. Gawen Gold was this day chosen into this house in the place of Robert Smith, deceased, and brought in one flock bed, one flock bolster, one feather pillow, one old rug, one old coverlet, two old sheets, a cup, one wooden platter, a spoon and a coffer. And is sworn.

20 December 1672. John Daw was this day chosen into this house in the place of Ambrose Bollen, deceased, and brought in one pair of sheets, one rug, one bolster, one coffer, one dish, one spoon and one cup, and is sworn.

12 April 1673. Joan Phillips, widow, was this day chosen into this house in the place of Joan Ellis, deceased, and brought in one flock bed, two feather pillows, one pair of sheets, one flock bolster, one rug, one blanket, one coffer, a box, a dish, a spoon, a cup and one brass candlestick. Petronella Jones, widow, the present housewife desired to be eased of that employment and Joan Phillips, widow, is now also made choice of to succeed her, and is sworn.

27 September 1673. Edith Chaunt was this day chosen into this house in the place of Joan Gulliford and brought in one coverlet, one pillow, one sheet, a little bed, one coffer, one dish, one spoon and one cup. And is sworn.

20 October 1673. Phillip Jones was this day chosen into this house in the place of Henry Barnard and brought in one sheet, one pillow, one dish, one spoon and one cup. And is sworn.

7 December 1675. Richard Toogood was this day chosen into this house in the place of Stephen Hill, deceased, and brought in one straw bed, one dust bolster, one sheet, one blanket, a piece of a rug, one dish, a spoon and a cup, and is sworn.

10 December 1675. William Loden was this day chosen into this house in the place of Edward Vowell, deceased, and brought in one blanket, one dish, a spoon and a cup. And is sworn.

24 January 1676. Temperance Sheare was this day chosen into this house in the place of Petronella Jones, deceased, and brought in, one feather bolster, one pillow, a pillow-tye, one pair of sheets, one coverlet, one blanket, one dish [*item erased*] and a cup. And is sworn.

1 January 1677. Mary Dober was this day chosen into this house in the place of Alice Swetnam deceased and brought in one feather pillow, one sheet, one dish and spoon and a cup. And is sworn.

24 June 1677. Sybil Andrews, widow, was this day chosen into this house in the place of Elizabeth Hopkins, deceased, and brought in one flock bed, one coverlet, one blanket, a pair of sheets, one bolster, one pillow, one dish, one spoon and one cup. And is sworn.

8 December 1677. Roger Lamb was this day chosen into this house in the place of William Senyer, deceased, and brought in one sheet, one blanket, one dish, one

spoon and one cup. And is sworn.

13 April 1678. Matthew Phelps alias Daggle was this day chosen into this house in the place of John Daw, deceased, and brought in one flock bed, a pair of sheets, one coverlet, one blanket, one bolster, one pillow, one pewter platter, one spoon, one cup, one porridge dish and one trencher. And is sworn.

7 June 1678. Leonard Whittle was chosen into this house in the place of John Weare, deceased, and brought in a straw bed, a bolster, a flock pillow, a coverlet, one sheet, a dish, a spoon and a cup. And is sworn.

20 September 1678. John Dunham was this day chosen into this house in the place of William Loden, deceased, and brought in one bolster, one pillow, one sheet, one blanket, one dish, one spoon and a cup. And is sworn.

9 November 1678. William George was this day chosen into this house in the place of John Symonds, deceased, and brought in, one feather bolster, one sheet, one pewter platter, one dish, one spoon and one cup. And is sworn.

11 February 1679. George Hannam was this day chosen into this house in the place of Henry Spurrier, deceased, and brought in one feather bed and bolster, one pillow, one coverlet, one blanket, one sheet, one dish, one spoon and one cup. And is sworn.

5 March 1679. Oliver Fitz-Jarrard was this day chosen into this house in the place of John Linkhorne, deceased, and brought in, one bolster, one sheet, one blanket, a dish, a spoon and a cup, and is sworn.

10 March 1679. John Gullifer was this day chosen into this house in the place of John Amans, deceased, and brought in, one dust bed, one coverlet, one pair of blankets, one sheet, one bolster, one pillow, one dish, a spoon and a cup. And is sworn.

21 June 1679. Thomasine Symonds was this day chosen into this house in the place of Margery Pond, turned out for lunacy, and brought in one feather and flock bed, one feather bolster, one blanket, one sheet, one coverlet, one dish, one spoon, one cup. And is sworn.

1 July 1680. William Chetnoll was this day chosen into this house in the place of Richard Togood, deceased, and brought in one sheet, one dish, a spoon, a cup and a pewter platter. And is sworn.

27 January 1682. James Jeffery was this day chosen into this house in the place of Leonard Whittle, deceased, and brought in one sheet, one pewter dish, one spoon, one cup, one pillow and pillow-tye. And is sworn.

17 July 1682. Thomas Hull was this day chosen into this house in the place of James Jeffary deceased and hath brought in one flock bed, one coverlet, one blanket one pillow bolster, one dish, one spoon and a cup. And is sworn.

11 June 1683. Joan Bartlett alias Haicot was this day chosen into this house in the room of Edith Chaunt, deceased, and brought in a bed, a bolster, a rug, a sheet, a dish, a spoon and a cup, and is sworn.

11 August 1683. John Purchase was this day chosen into the house in the place of Gawen Gold, deceased, and brought in one sheet, a bolster, one blanket, one dish, one spoon and one cup. And is sworn.

27 December 1683. Richard Stoney was this day chosen into the house in the place of Oliver Fitz-Jarrard, deceased, and brought in one flock bed, one bolster, one rug, one blanket, one sheet, one dish, one spoon and a cup. And is sworn.

15 March 1684. William Coxall was this day chosen into this house in the place of William George, deceased, and brought in a dish, a spoon and a trencher, and is sworn.

29 March 1684. William King was this day chosen into this house in the place of William Soper, deceased, and brought in one flock bed, a feather bolster, one rug, one platter, one spoon and a cup. And is sworn.

16 June 1684. Mary Grove, widow, was this day chosen into this house in the place of Anne Parham alias Baker, deceased, and brought in one rug, one sheet, one bolster, one cup, one dish and a spoon. And is sworn.

7 July 1684. Richard Chaunt was this day chosen into this house in the place of Roger Lamb, deceased, and brought in one feather bed, one feather bolster, two sheets, two blankets, one coverlet, one cup, one dish and one spoon. And is sworn.

11 August 1684. Stephen Denford was this day chosen into this house in the place of Matthew Daggle, deceased, and brought in one bolster, one pillow-tye, one blanket, one sheet, one cup, one dish and one spoon. And is sworn.

6 February 1685. Richard Mitchell was this day chosen into this house in the place of Thomas Stephens, deceased, and brought in one flock bed, one bolster, one pillow, one sheet, one rug, a pillow-tye, a cup, one dish and one spoon. And is sworn.

9 December 1686. George Yearsely was this day chosen into this house in the place of William Coxall, deceased, and brought in one sheet, one pillow, one cup, one dish, a spoon and one trencher. And is sworn.

8 April 1687. Joan Parsons, widow, was this day chosen into this house in the place of Jane Ryall, deceased, and brought in one flock bed, one sheet, one coverlet, one blanket, one pillow, one bolster, two bolster cloths, a trencher, one dish, one spoon and a cup, and is sworn.

28 November 1687. This day Thomas Pope was chosen into this house in the room of John Purchase, deceased, and brought in, one flock-bed, a bolster, one rug, one blanket, two sheets, one dish, one spoon and a cup. And is sworn.

21 March 1688. This day Thomas Game nominated Thomas Ridout, Abraham Hopkins and George Hebditch senior to the company in the room of John Marshall, deceased. Thomas Ridout was chosen and brought in, a dust bed, one flock bolster, one feather pillow, one sheet, one rug, one blanket, one dish, one spoon and one cup. And is sworn.

21 April 1688. This day Elizabeth Perham, widow, was chosen into this house in the room of Thomasine Symonds, widow, deceased, and brought in, one blanket, one sheet, one bad rug, one feather pillow, one coffer, one dish, one spoon and one cup. And is sworn.

6 July 1688. This day Elizabeth Mitchell was chosen into this house in the room of Temperance Sheare, deceased, and brought in, one feather pillow, one pillow-tye, one bolster cloth, a sheet, a pewter platter, a dish, a spoon and a cup. And is sworn.

6 July 1688. Susannah Hodder, widow, was chosen into this house in the room of Mary Grove, deceased, and brought in, one bed of feathers and flocks, one feather bolster, one pillow, a coverlet, one dish, one spoon and one cup. And is sworn.

6 July 1688. Edward Beauchamp was chosen into this house in the room of Thomas Pope, deceased, and brought in, one flock bed, one pillow, one dish, one spoon and one cup. And is sworn.

31 August 1688. Walter Kemp was chosen into this house in the room of William Wills, deceased, and brought in one flock bed, one pillow, one bolster, one blanket, one sheet, one rug, one dish, one spoon and one cup, and is sworn.

17 August 1689. Walter Ridout was chosen into this house in the room of William King, deceased, and brought in one bed-tache, one pillow, one sheet, one dish, one spoon and one cup. And is sworn.

1 February 1690. Samuel Hoddinott was chosen into this house in the room of Thomas Hull, deceased, and brought in one flock bed, one bolster, a dish, a spoon and a cup. And is sworn.

13 May 1690. Edward Scot was chosen into this house in the room of Edward Beauchamp, deceased, and brought in a sheet, a bolster, a dish, spoon and a cup. And is sworn.

16 June 1690. Samuel Mandfield was chosen into this house in the room of Robert Hide, deceased, and brought in one flock bed, a bolster, a pillow, one rug, two blankets, a pair of sheets, a dish, a spoon and a cup. And is sworn.

5 July 1690. Hugh Brooke was chosen into this house in the room of George Yearsley, deceased, and brought in one flock bed, a bolster, one coverlet, one sheet, a dish a spoon and a cup. And is sworn.

26 October 1690. Walter Hooper was chosen into this house in the room of Walter Ridout, deceased, and brought in one flock bed, a flock bolster, one coverlet two blankets, a pair of sheets, one dish, one spoon and a cup.

10 December 1690. Jane Buglar, widow, was chosen into this house in the room of Joan Parsons, widow, deceased, and brought in one feather bed, one flock bolster, two feather pillows, one pair of sheets, one rug, a pair of blankets, one coffer, two pewter dishes, one cup and one spoon, and is sworn.

1 January 1691. Anne Hutchins, spinster, aged 70 or near abouts, was chosen into this house in the room of Jane Phillips, deceased, and brought in one flock bed, one rug, one bolster, one blanket, one pair of sheets, one pewter platter, one cup and one spoon, and is sworn.

5 February 1691. John Jolliffe was chosen into this house in the room of Phillip Jones deceased, and brings in, one feather bed, a bolster, one pillow, one rug, one blanket, one pair of sheets, a dish, a spoon, a cup and a trencher, and is sworn.

11 February 1691. This day Richard Lane is chosen into this house in the room of George Hanham, deceased, and brings in one flock bed, a flock bolster, one rug, one pillow, one iron pot, a dish, a spoon and a cup, and is sworn.

10 September 1691. This day Christopher Knight is chosen into this house in the room of Richard Stoney, deceased, and brings in a flock bed, a flock bolster, one rug, one pillow, a pillow-tye, one blanket, a pair of sheets, a dish, a cup and a spoon, and is sworn.

3 January 1693. This day John Bulchard was chosen into this house in the room of John Dunham, deceased, and brought in, a flock bed, two bolsters, one flock pillow, one sheet, one coverlet, one blanket, one cup, one dish, one spoon and one trencher, and is sworn.

7 March 1693. This day Ursula Jaffary, widow, was chosen into this house in the room of Sybil Andrews, deceased, and brought in one flock bed, two sheets, one coverlet, one blanket, two pillows, one dust bolster, one earthen platter, one cup, one dish, one spoon and one trencher, and is sworn.

12 April 1693. This day Katharine Morris, widow, was chosen into this house in the room of Anne Hutchins, deceased, and brought in one canvas sheet, one coverlet, one blanket, one pillow, one bolster, one box, two earthenware dishes, one cup, one dish and one spoon, and is sworn.

4 May 1693. This day Richard Chaunt was chosen into this house in the room of Thomas Ridout, deceased, and brings in a flock bed, a feather bolster, a pair of canvas sheets, a striped rug, a bolster cloth, an earthenware platter, one cup, one dish, one spoon and one trencher, and is sworn.

7 November 1693. John Speed was chosen a poor man into this house in the room of Hugh Brooke, lately deceased, and brings in one feather bed, a feather bolster, one rug, one pair, of blankets, one pair of sheets, one pillow, a bolster cloth, a dish, a spoon and a cup, and is sworn.

20 April 1694. Jasper Hutchins was chosen a poor man into this house in the room of Richard Mitchell, deceased, and brings in one flock bed, one pillow, one sheet, a dish, a spoon and a cup, and is sworn.

28 April 1694. Alice Oliver, widow, was chosen a poor woman into this house in the room of the widow Hodder, deceased, and brings in one bed, a bolster, one sheet, one rug, a dish, a spoon and a cup, and is sworn.

26 May 1694. Roger Baker was chosen a poor man into this house in the room of Richard Chant, deceased, and brings in one rug, a blanket, one pillow, one box, one chair, a dish, a spoon, a trencher and a cup, and is sworn.

22 February 1695. Nicholas Stone was chosen in a poor man into this house in the room of Jasper Hutchins, deceased, and brings in one flock bed, a flock bolster, one coverlet, one blanket, one sheet, a dish, a spoon and a cup, and is sworn.

6 December 1695. Deborah Lambert was this day chosen a poor woman into this house in the room of Mary Dober, widow, lately deceased, and brings in one flock bed, a flock bolster, a feather pillow, one pair of blankets, one pair of sheets, two rugs, one coffer, one earthenware platter, a dish, a spoon, a cup and all her apparel, and is sworn.

27 December 1695. Robert Hyde was this day chosen a poor man into this house in the room of Nicholas Stone, lately deceased, and brings in a flock bed, a feather bolster, a feather pillow, a coverlet, a pair of blankets, a pair of sheets, a dish, a spoon and a cup, and is sworn.

7 March 1696. John Amans was this day chosen a poor man into this house in the room of John Jolliffe, deceased, and brings in a flock bed, a flock bolster a sheet, a blanket, a dish, a spoon and a cup, and is sworn.

13 April 1696. Lydia Stoney was this day chosen a poor woman into this house in the room of Elizabeth Michell, lately deceased, and brings in a feather bed, a feather bolster, a feather pillow, one pillowbere, one bolster cloth, one coverlet, one blanket, one sheet, a dish, a spoon and a cup, and is sworn.

25 April 1696. Andrew Newman was this day chosen in a poor man in the room of Christopher Knight lately deceased and brings in a flock bed, one rug, one blanket, one sheet, a dish, a spoon and a cup, and is sworn.

19 May 1696. Mary Balson was this day chosen in a poor woman in the room of Alice Oliver, lately deceased, and brings in one flock bed, one coverlet, a pair of sheets, a flock bolster, two bolster cloths, a dish, a spoon and a cup, and is sworn.

19 September 1696. John Hud was this day chosen in a poor man into this house in the room of Walter Hooper, deceased, and brings in a feather pillow, one dust bolster, one blanket, one sheet, a dish, a spoon and cup, and is sworn.

16 December 1696. John Weare was this day chosen a poor man into this house in the room of Stephen Denford, deceased, and brings in a rug, a blanket, a sheet, a bed, a bolster, a dish, a spoon and a cup, and is sworn.

23 December 1696. Robert Greene was this day chosen a poor man into this house in the room of William Chetnoll, deceased, and brings in a dust bed, a coverlet, a blanket, a sheet, a feather pillow, a dish, a spoon and a cup.

15 March 1697. Mathew Bartlet was chosen in a poor man into this house in the room of Samuel Manfield, deceased, and brings in a kettle, two wedges, one axe, one box, one coffer, a dish, a spoon and a cup, and is sworn.

20 April 1697. Anne Vincent was chose in a poor woman into this house in the room of Elizabeth Baker, deceased, and brings in one feather bed, a feather bolster, a feather pillow, one pair of sheets, one blanket, one rug, one dish, one spoon and a cup, and is sworn.

13 May 1697. Francis Bartlet was chosen a poor man into this house in the room of Richard Lane, lately deceased, and can bring nothing into this house by reason of his poverty, and is sworn.

10 December 1697. Thomas Hand was chosen a poor man into the house in the room of Roger Baker, lately deceased, and brings in a bed blanket, a sheet, a bolster, a dish, a spoon and a cup and is sworn.

27 December 1697. Anne Browne was chosen a poor woman into this house in the room of Debora Lambert, deceased, and brings in one feather bed, a feather bolster, one rug, one blanket, one sheet, one pillow, a dish, a spoon and a cup, and is sworn.

7 June 1698. Jasper Walter was chosen a poor man into this house in the room of John Gullifer, deceased, and brings in one feather bed, and feather bolster, two feather pillows and pillow-tyes, one rug, a pair of blankets, a pair of sheets, a coffer, a dish, a spoon and a cup, and is sworn.

2 June 1699. Joan Knight, widow, was chosen a poor woman into this house in the room of Joan Bartlet, widow, deceased, and brings in one flock and featherbed, a feather bolster, a feather pillow, one rug, one blanket, one sheet, one pillow-tye, a dish, a spoon and a cup, and is sworn.

20 October 1699. Joan the wife of William White was chosen a poor woman into this house in the room of Lydia Stony, deceased, and is so poor that she brings nothing.

19 December 1699. Anne Williams was chosen a poor woman into this house in the room of Joan Knight, deceased, and brings in one flock bed, three flock pillows, one coverlet, one blanket, one pair of sheets, a dish, a spoon and a cup, and is sworn.

20 September 1700. Thomas Glover was chosen a poor man into this house in the room of Edward Scot, deceased, and by reason of his poverty he is not able to bring in any thing but a dish, a spoon and a cup, and is sworn.

18 October 1700. Thomas Game nominated Robert Phelps, John Coward and John Jacob to the company in the room of Richard Chant. Robert Phelps is chosen by the company and brings in one flock bed, two feather bolsters, one coverlet, two blankets, two sheets, a dish, spoon and a cup, and is sworn.

26 October 1700. John Coward was chosen in this house in the room of Francis Bartlet, deceased, and brings in one pewter platter, one hook, one spade, a dish, a spoon and a cup, and is sworn.

27 November 1700. John Jacob was chosen a poor man into this house in the room of Thomas Glover, deceased, and brings in one flock bed, a flock bolster, one coverlet, a blanket, one sheet, a dish, a spoon and a cup, and is sworn.

18 December 1700. William Dampier was chosen a poor man into this house in the room of Robert Greene, deceased, and being very poor brings in only a dish, a spoon and a cup.

18 December 1700. Anne Dunham was chosen a poor woman into this house in the room of Joan Whitehead, deceased, and is sworn.

1 January 1701. Margaret Linckorne was chosen a poor woman into this house in the room of Jane Buglar, deceased, and brings in a blanket, a sheet, a dish, a spoon and a cup, and is sworn.

1 February 1701. Charity Hodges, widow, was chosen a poor woman into this house in the room of Margaret Linckorne, deceased, and is so poor that she cannot bring in anything, and is sworn.

5 May 1701. Elizabeth Hardy, widow, was chosen a poor woman into this house in the room of Margaret Linckorne and brings into this house a feather and flock bed and half a sheet, and is sworn.

2 March 1702. William White was chosen a poor man into this house in the room of John Jacob, deceased, and brings into the house a flock bed, a sheet, a cup, a dish and a spoon, and is sworn.

31 March 1702. Nominated to the company: David Ford, John Vincent and George Watts in the room of Robert Phelps, deceased. The company chose John Vincent who brings in a feather bed and bolster, a rug, a blanket, a sheet, a cup, a dish and a spoon, and is sworn.

9 September 1702. John Martin was chosen a poor man into this house in the room of John Amary, deceased, and brings in a crock, a cup, a dish and a spoon, and is sworn.

9 September 1702. George Watts was chosen a poor man into this house in the room of John Coward, who is expelled the house for his saucy and abusive language to the master and brethren and for not obeying the orders of the house to which he was sworn. George Watts brings in a cup, a dish and a spoon, and is sworn.

23 March 1703. William Hoddinot was chosen a poor man into this house in the room of George Watts, deceased, and brings in a dust bed, a feather bolster and pillow, a sheet, a coverlet, a cup, a dish and a spoon, and is sworn.

15 April 1703. William Simonds was chosen a poor man into this house in the room of Mathew Bartlet, deceased, and brings in a flock bed, a flock bolster, a rug, a blanket, a cup, a dish and a spoon, and is sworn.

28 May 1703. Charity Pouncefoot was chosen into this house in the room of Ann Vincent, deceased, and brings into the house a flock bed, a feather bolster, a rug, a blanket, a pair of sheets, a cup, a dish and a spoon, and is sworn.

18 June 1703. Thomas Moores was chosen a poor man into this house in the room of Samuel Hoddinot, deceased, and brings in a bed, a sheet, a cup, a dish and a spoon, and is sworn.

20 January 1704. Richard Bennet is chosen a poor man into this house in the room of John Martin, deceased, and brings into the house a flock bed, a flock bolster, a feather pillow, a bed mat, a coverlet, a blanket, two sheets, a cup, a dish, a spoon and a skillet, and is sworn.

25 April 1704. Robert Randal is chosen a poor man into this house in the room of Andrew Newman, deceased, and brings in a flock bed and bolster, a cup, a dish and a spoon, and is sworn.

30 July 1704. Margaret Mathew is chosen a poor woman into this house in the room of Elizabeth Hardy, who is turned out for several offences, and brings in a flock bed, a rug, a sheet, a blanket, a box, a cup, a dish and a spoon, and is sworn.

1 August 1704. Philip Elloway is chosen a poor man into this house in the room of John Weare, deceased, and brings in a dust bed, a blanket, a sheet, a coverlet, a flock bolster, three shirts, a cup, a dish and a spoon, and is sworn.

26 August 1704. Joan Plowman is chosen a poor woman into this house in the room of Ann Dunham, deceased, and brings in a chest, and is sworn.

27 December 1704. George Pope is chosen a poor man into this house in the room of William White, deceased, and brings in a flock bed, a rug, a sheet, a dish, a cup and a spoon, and is sworn.

8 March 1705. Ann Loden, widow, is chosen a poor woman into this house in the room of Ann Browne, deceased, and brings into the house a flock bed and bolster, a coverlet, a blanket, a pillow and a pair of sheets, and is sworn.

13 June 1705. Jeremiah Lodge is chosen a poor man into this house in the room of Thomas Hall, deceased, and brings in a flock bed and bolster, a coverlet, a blanket and a sheet, and is sworn.

13 June 1705. Roger Lamb is chosen into this house in the room of John Speed, deceased, and brings in a flock bed, a coverlet, a blanket and a sheet, and is sworn.

19 June 1705. Joan Bartlet is chosen a poor woman into this house in the room of Charity Pouncefoot, deceased, and brings in a feather and flock bed, a rug, a bolster and a sheet, and is sworn.

26 July 1705. Henry Dunham is chosen a poor man into this house in the room of Jasper Walter, deceased, and brings in a feather pillow, a bed and a coverlet, and is sworn.

28 November 1705. Elizabeth Mathews is chosen a poor woman into this house in the room of Ann Williams, deceased, and brings in a bed-tye, a rug, a cup, a dish and a spoon, and is sworn.

2 September 1706. Robert Morris is chosen a poor man into this house in the room of Walter Kamp, deceased, and brings in a bed, a rug, a sheet, a bolster, a cup, a dish and a spoon, and is sworn.

23 May 1707. Mary Holland is chosen a poor woman into this house in the room of Katherine Morris, widow, and brings in a flock bed, a feather pillow, a sheet, a cup, a dish and a spoon, and is sworn.

2 August 1707. Joseph Keynes is chosen a poor man into this house in the room of John Belchard, deceased, and brings in a flock bed, a rug, a bolster, a sheet, a cup, a dish and a spoon, and is sworn.

20 July 1708. Bishop Day is chosen a poor man into this house in the room of William Simonds, deceased, and brings in a feather and flock bed, a coverlet, a sheet, a bolster, a dish and a spoon, and is sworn.

26 October 1708. Walter Fook is chosen a poor man into this house in the room of Henry Dunham, deceased, and brings in a flock bed, a coverlet, a pillow, a dish and a spoon, and is sworn.

6 January 1709. Richard Pouncefoot is chosen a poor man into this house in the room of William Dampier, deceased, and brings in a feather bed and bolster, a rug, a blanket, two sheets, a dish, a spoon and a tin chamber pot, and is sworn.

9 March 1709. Mary Marshall, widow, is chosen a poor woman into this house in the room of Elizabeth Mathews, deceased, and brings in a flock bed, a feather pillow, a rug, a blanket, a sheet, a dish and a spoon, and is sworn.

8 April 1709. John Williams is chosen a poor man into this house in the room of William Dampier, deceased, and brings in a flock bed, and is sworn.

28 July 1709. Ellis Weare is chosen a poor man into this house in the room of John Hudd, deceased, and brings in a feather bed, a coverlet, two pillows, a blanket and a sheet, and is sworn.

20 December 1709. Thomas Stevens is chosen a poor man into this house in the room of Jeremiah Lodge, deceased, and brings in a flock and feather bed, a feather pillow and bolster, a pair of sheets, a pair of blankets and a rug, and is sworn.

3 February 1710. Sarah Dunham, widow, chosen a poor woman into this house in the room of Charity Hodges, deceased, and brings in a feather and flock bed, a pair of blankets, a pair of sheets, a bolster, a pillow and a rug, and is sworn.

30 June 1710. Francis Dunham is chosen a poor man is chosen into this house in the room of Robert Rendall, deceased, and brings in a feather bed, bolster and pillow, a coverlet, blankets and sheet, and is sworn.

26 July 1710. James Glover is chosen a poor man into this house in the room of Philip Elwell, deceased, and brings in a flock bed and bolster, a rug, a blanket, a pair of sheets and a bedstead, and is sworn.

21 November 1710. Charity Stone, widow, is chosen a poor woman into this house in the room of Ursula Jeffery, deceased, and brings in a bed, a bolster, two pillows, two blankets, a rug and a pair of sheets, and is sworn.

24 January 1712. Stephen Bound is chosen into this house in the room of Richard Bennet, deceased, and brings in a sheet, a pillow, a cup, a dish and a spoon, and is sworn.

24 January 1712. Miriam Vowell is chosen a poor woman into this house in the room of Joan Hancocke, deceased, and brings in a flock bed, a pillow, a sheet, two rugs and two bolster cloths, and is sworn.

15 May 1712. Robert Hodges is chosen a poor man into this house in the room of Thomas Moores, deceased, and brings in a flock bed and bolster, a coverlet, a sheet, a dish, a spoon and a cup; and is sworn.

22 May 1712. John Cooke senior is chosen a poor man into this house in the room of Roger Lambe, deceased, and brings in a dust bed, a bolster, a coverlet, a dish, a spoon and a cup, and is sworn.

29 May 1712. Richard Clarke is chosen a poor man into this house in the room of Robert Hyde, deceased, and by reason of his poverty he is not able to bring anything into this house but a dish, spoon and cup, and is sworn.

12 May 1712. John Sturmey is chosen a poor man into this house in the room of George Pope, deceased, and brings in a bed stuffed with wool, a bolster, a coverlet, a sheet, a blanket, a dish, a spoon and a cup, and is sworn.

11 September 1712. John Pyke is chosen a poor man into this house in the room of Thomas Stevens, deceased, and brings into the house a flock bed, a bolster, a pillow, a coverlet, one sheet, a dish, a spoon and a cup, and is sworn.

29 November 1712. Mary Scott widow is chosen a poor woman into this house in the room of Margery Matthews, deceased, and brings into the house a feather bed, a bolster, a pillow, a coverlet, a dish, a spoon and a cup, and is sworn.

18 December 1712. Richard Vinsant is chosen a poor man into this house in the room of John Sturmey, deceased, and brings into the house a flock bed, two pillowberes, a blanket, a sheet, a rug, a dish, a spoon and a cup, and is sworn.

17 March 1713. William Bragge is chosen a poor man into this house, in the room of Ellis Weare, deceased, and brings into the house a bed filled with feathers and flocks, a sheet, a bolster, a coverlet, a dish, a spoon and a cup; and is sworn.

17 March 1713. Mary Hodder is chosen a poor woman into this house in the room of Charity Stone, deceased, and brings in a dust bed, a coverlet, a sheet, a bolster, a dish, a spoon and a cup, and is sworn.

17 June 1713. Samuel Manfield is chosen a poor man into this house in the room of John Cooke, deceased, and by reason of his poverty he brings in only a coverlet, a dish, a spoon and a cup, and is sworn.

16 April 1714. John Miller is chosen a poor man into this house in the room of William Hoddinott, deceased, and by reason of his poverty he brings into the house only a dish, a spoon and a cup, and is sworn.

26 August 1714. Joseph Kenney is chosen a poor man into this house in the room of Walter Fooke, deceased, and brings into the house a flock bed, a feather bolster, a feather pillow, a blanket, a pair of sheets, a coverlet, a dish, a spoon and a cup, and is sworn.

7 February 1716. Grace Cooke, widow, is chosen a poor woman into this house in the room of Mary Holland, deceased, and brings into the house a flock bed and pillow,

a coverlet, a dish and a spoon, and is sworn.

23 February 1716. Thomas Game nominated to the company George Bishop, Thomas Jeffrey and James Toogood in the room of John Vincent, deceased. The company chose George Bishop who brings in a feather bed, a bolster, a pillow, sheets, blankets, a rug, a dish, a spoon and a cup, and is sworn.

6 April 1716. Thomas Game nominated to the company Thomas Jeffrey, James Toogood and Thomas Pinkard in the room of George Bishop, deceased. The company chose Thomas Pinkard who brings in a flock bed, a bolster, a pillow, a rug, a dish and a spoon, and is sworn.

[*Two small documents are pinned to this page as follows:*]

[*Document* 1.]

23 February 1715.
Gentlemen, I have according as formerly presented three men for you to put one of them into your hospital or Almshouse in Sherborne their names are as follows: George Bishop, Thomas Jafery and James Toogood.
Your friend Thomas Game

[*Document* 2.]

6 April 1716
Gentlemen, I have now presented to you three men of your parish and town of Sherborne for you to place one of them in the hospital or Almshouse in Sherborne their names are as follows:
Thomas Jafery (a lame and crippled man), James Toogood and Thomas Pinkard.
Your friend Thomas Game

[*On reverse of this note:*]

Yes	No
Mr Ryall	Mr Hosey
	Mr Avoake
	Mr [*blank*]

12 April 1717. James Toogood is chosen a poor man into this house in the room of John Pyke, deceased, and brings in a flock bed, a bolster, a pair of blankets, a pair of sheets, a rug, a dish, a spoon and a cup and is sworn.

12 April 1717. Robert Barber is chosen a poor man into this house in the room of John Williams, deceased, and by reason of his poverty is to have one of the beds in house and brings in a coverlet, a blanket, a dish, a spoon and a cup, and is sworn.

7 May 1717. Amy Gerrard, widow, is chosen a poor woman into this house in the room of Miriam Vowell, widow, deceased, and brings in a flock bed, a blanket, a rug, a dish, a spoon and a cup, and is sworn.

18 December 1717. Edward Scott is chosen a poor man into this house in the room of Richard Vincent, deceased, and brings in a flock bed a pillow, a rug, a dish, a spoon and a cup, and is sworn.

12 March 1719. John West is chosen a poor man into this house in the room of Bishop Day, deceased, and brings in a flock bed, a bolster, a blanket, a rug, a dish, a spoon and a cup, and is sworn.

12 March 1719. James Gent is chosen a poor man into this house in the room of Robert Hodges, who has this day left the house having inherited an estate on which he can subsist without the charity, and James Gent brings in, a rug, a sheet, a blanket, a bolster, a bolster cloth, a fire box, a dish, a spoon, a cup and two trenchers, and is sworn.

17 September 1719. Henry White is chosen a poor man into this house in the room of Edward Scott, deceased, and brings in a flock bed, a bolster, a sheet, a rug, a blanket, a dish, a spoon and a cup, and is sworn.

29 December 1719. Thomas Game nominated to the company Richard Bennet, George Hibditch and Phillip Loaden in the room of Thomas Pinkard, deceased. The company chose Richard Bennet who by reason of his poverty has nothing to bring into the house, and is sworn.

11 January 1720. Phillip Loaden is chosen a poor man into this house in the room of James Glover, deceased, and brings in a flock bed, a bolster, a pillow, one sheet, a blanket, a rug, a dish, a spoon and a cup, and is sworn.

8 July 1720. Thomas Hodder is chosen into this house in the room of Francis Denham, deceased, and brings in a dust bed, a blanket, a sheet, a rug, a coffer, a dish, a spoon and a cup, and is sworn.

8 July 1720. George Hibditch is chosen a poor man into this house in the room of Robert Morris, deceased, and brings in a flock bed, a blanket, a rug, a coffer, a dish, a spoon and a cup, and is sworn.

18 August 1720. Elizabeth Collins, widow, is chosen into this house in the room of Grace Cooke, widow, deceased, and brings in a flock, a bed, a sheet, a blanket, a dish, a spoon and a cup, and is sworn.

26 August 1720. The said Elizabeth Collins this day expelled this house for 'contemning' its alms.

26 August 1720. Phillipa Pride is chosen a poor woman into this house in the room of Elizabeth Collins and brings in a flock bed, a blanket, a dish, a spoon and a cup, and is sworn.

14 June 1721. Eleanor Vowell, widow, is chosen a poor woman into this house in the room of Mary Scott, deceased, and brings in a feather bed, a bolster, a pillow, two blankets, a pair of sheets, a rug, a box to put her clothes in, a dish, a spoon and a cup, and is sworn.

10 July 1721. William Olliver is chosen a poor man into this house in the room of Joseph Kaynes, deceased, and brings in a feather bed, a bolster, a pillow, a blanket, a dish, a spoon and a cup, and is sworn.

7 August 1722. Elizabeth Smith, widow, is chosen a poor woman into this house in the room of Joan Plowman, deceased, and brings in a flock bed, a bolster, a sheet, a blanket, a coverlet, a dish, a spoon and a cup, and is sworn.

18 September 1722. Elizabeth Hitchins, widow, is chosen a poor woman into this house in the room of Anne Loaden, deceased, and brings in a flock bed, a bolster, a rug, a coffer, a dish, a spoon, a trencher and a cup, and is sworn.

6 March 1724. Mary Loaden, widow, is chosen a poor woman into this house in the room of widow Marshall, deceased, and brings in a bed mixed with flocks and feathers, one sheet, a pair of blankets, a rug, a bolster, a pillow, a dish, a spoon and a cup, and is sworn.

17 April 1724. William Moon is chosen a poor man into this house in the room of Stephen Bound, deceased, and brings in a flock bed and bolster, a blanket, a sheet, a rug, a dish, a spoon and a cup, and is sworn.

11 June 1724. Daniel Weed is chosen a poor man into this house in the room of William Miller, deceased, and brings in a rug, a sheet, a chair, a dish, a spoon and a cup, and is sworn.

25 August 1724. Jeremiah Hebditch is chosen a poor man into this house in the room of William Bragg, deceased, and by reason of his wife being aged and almost blind

brings only a blanket, a sheet, a dish, a spoon and a cup, and is sworn.

15 October 1724. William West is chosen a poor man into this house in the room of John West, deceased, and by reason of his poverty has nothing to bring into this house, but is sworn.

25 November 1724. Thomas Purchase is chosen a poor man into this house in the room of Henry White, deceased, and brings in a canvas sheet, a pillow and pillow-tye, a dish and a spoon, and is sworn.

18 April 1726. Margaret Sturgiss, widow, is chosen a poor woman into this house in the room of Eleanor Vowell, deceased, and brings in a rug, a blanket, a pillow, a sheet, a dish, a spoon and a cup, and is sworn.

26 May 1726. John Loaden is chosen a poor man into this house in the room of William Moon, deceased, and brings in a flock bed and bolster, a pillow, a pair of sheets, a coverlet, a dish, a spoon and a cup, and is sworn.

22 August 1726. John Burrow senior is chosen a poor man into this house in the room of James Toogood, deceased, and brings in a rug, a sheet, a dish, a spoon and a cup, and is sworn.

2 February 1727. Thomas Chant is chosen a poor man into this house in the room of James Gent, deceased, and by reason of his poverty brings in only a dish, spoon and cup, and is sworn.

7 March 1727. Thomas Braxstone is chosen a poor man into this house in the room of William Olliver, deceased, and brings in a rug, a blanket, one sheet, a dish, a spoon, a cup and a box, and is sworn.

16 October 1727. Peter Hyde is chosen a poor man into this house in the room of Joseph Kenney, deceased, and brings in a flock bed, a blanket, two sheets, one rug, one oak chair, a dish and spoon, and is sworn.

18 December 1727. George Towell is chosen a poor man into this house in the room of Robert Barber, deceased, and is sworn.

2 February 1728. Mathew Stoodly is chosen a poor man into this house in the room of Phillip Loaden, deceased, and brings in a bed of flock and feathers, a bolster, a rug, a blanket and a sheet, and is sworn.

2 February 1728. Anne Parsons, widow, is chosen a poor woman into this house in the room of Emma Gerrard, deceased, and brings in a dust bed, a feather bolster, a

pillow, a coverlet, a pair of blankets and a pair of sheets, and is sworn.

26 August 1728. William Upshall is chosen a poor man into this house in the room of Mathew Stoodly, deceased, and brings in a feather bed, a pillow, a rug and a sheet, and is sworn.

17 September 1728. William Osmond is chosen a poor man into this house in the room of Peter Hyde, deceased, and brings in a dish, a spoon and a cup, and is sworn.

17 December 1728. Thomas Chapman a poor man is chosen into this house in the room of William Upshall, deceased, and brings in one flock bed, a pillow, a rug, a sheet and a dish, and is sworn.

4 February 1729. George Odry senior is chosen a poor man into this house in the room of Richard Clark, deceased, and brings in one flock bed, one sheet and one coverlet, and is sworn.

23 September 1729. William Rydout is chosen a poor man into this house in the room of Thomas Hodder, deceased, and brings in one flock bed, one pillow, one rug, a blanket and a sheet, and is sworn.

4 November 1729. Elizabeth Dunning, widow, is chosen a poor woman into this house in the room of Elizabeth Smith, deceased, and brings in a rug, a blanket and a sheet, and is sworn.

24 February 1730. John Chafey senior is chosen a poor man into this house in the room of Jerome Hibditch, deceased, and brings in a sheet, a feather bolster and a blanket, and is sworn.

9 December 1730. William Hibditch is chosen a poor man into this house in the room of John Chaffey, deceased, and brings in a rug and a pillow, and is sworn.

9 December 1730. William Sturmy is chosen a poor man into this house in the room of Samuel Manfield, deceased, and brings in a flock bed, a flock bolster, a flock pillow, one sheet and a blanket, and is sworn.

23 April 1732. Thomas Morrice a poor man is chosen into this house in the room of Thomas Purchase, deceased, and brings in a sheet and a blanket, and is sworn.

5 October 1732. John Vowell a poor man is chosen into this house in the room of Daniel Weed, deceased, and brings in a rug, a blanket, a sheet and a bolster, and is sworn.

5 October 1732. John Crew a poor man was chosen into this house in the room of Thomas Bragstone, deceased, and brought into the house a blanket and a pillow, and is sworn.

23 November 1732. Richard Rydout a poor man was chosen into this house in the room of John Loaden, deceased, and brings in one hop bolster, one feather pillow, one green rug, one sheet and one bolster cloth, and is sworn.

1 January 1733. John Crees a poor man was chosen into this house in the room of George Towell, deceased, and brings in a bed of flocks and wool, and is sworn.

8 January 1733. Henry Sturmy a poor man was chosen into this house in the room of William Osmond, deceased, and brings in two feather pillows, one sheet and one blanket, and is sworn.

8 February 1733. John Wear a poor man was chosen into this house in the room of William West, deceased, and brings in a bolster, a blanket and one sheet, and is sworn.

21 February 1733. Anne Leach, widow, is chosen a poor woman into this house in the room of Mary Hodder, deceased, and brings in one feather bed, one feather bolster, one rug, a blanket and a pair of sheets, and is sworn.

26 June 1733. Elizabeth Hodder, widow, a poor woman is chosen into this house in the room of Elizabeth Hutchings, widow, deceased, and brings in a feather pillow, a bolster and an old blanket, and is sworn.

13 December 1733. Susannah Purchase, widow, a poor woman is chosen into this house in the room of Phyllis Pride, widow, deceased, and brings in one blanket, one sheet, an old rug, one pillow and a pillow-tye, and is sworn.

27 December 1733. John Rapson a poor man is chosen into this house in the room of Richard Ridout, deceased, and brings in a flock bed, one rug and one blanket, and is sworn.

14 May 1734. Robert Hodder a poor man is chosen into this house in the room of John Vowell, deceased, and brings in a bolster, a rug, a blanket, a sheet and a bed, and is sworn.

25 July 1734. Samuel Game nominated the following three persons: Thomas Down, John Higgens and James Jeffery to be elected into the Almshouse in the room of Richard Bennet, deceased. The company chose John Higgens who brought in one rug, and is sworn.

[Loose, but previously pinned, document between the folios at this point]

To the masters of the Almshouse in Sherborne:

Gentlemen, I nominate the three poor persons under named for you to choose one of them into the Almshouse in the room of Richard Bennet, deceased: 23 July 1734. Thomas Down, John Higgens and James Jeffery.

Samuel Game

4 September 1734. Mary Corp, widow, a poor woman is chosen into this house in the room of Margaret Sturgis, widow, deceased, and brings in one feather pillow, one quilt, one sheet and one blanket, and is sworn.

31 October 1735. James Jeffery a poor man is chosen into this house in the room of John Borrow, deceased, and brings nothing into this house, and is sworn.

29 January 1736. William Mullender a poor man is chosen into this house in the room of Thomas Chant, deceased, and brings with him a blanket, a sheet, a dish and a spoon, and is sworn.

23 November 1736. Mary Loaden, widow, a poor woman is chosen into this house in the room of Sarah Denham and brings in a feather bed, a pillow, a sheet, a blanket and a bolster, and is sworn.

11 July 1737. Mary Justins, widow, a poor woman is chosen into this house in the room of Mary Loaden, deceased, and brings into the house one sheet, and is sworn.

14 December 1738. Joan Pope, widow, a poor woman is chosen into this house in the room of Susannah Purchase, deceased, and brings in one feather bed, two blankets, one pillow and a sheet, and is sworn.

2 March 1739. Thomas Parris a poor man is chosen into this house in the room of William Rydout, and is sworn.

26 June 1739. William Bragg a poor man is chosen into this house in the room of George Odry deceased, and is sworn.

27 July 1739. Moses Lamb a poor man is chosen into this house in the room of William Sturmy, deceased, and brings in a bolster and a blanket, and is sworn.

24 January 1740. Walter Justins a poor man is chosen into this house in the room of George Hibditch, deceased, and brings into the house a flock bed, a rug, one blanket, one sheet and one pillow, and is sworn.

5 February 1740. Mary Symonds, widow, a poor woman is chosen into this house in the room of Mary Corpe, deceased, and brings in a sheet, and is sworn.

14 February 1740. Samuel Dampier a poor man is chosen into this house in the room of Walter Justins, deceased, and brings in a rug, a sheet and a bolster, and is sworn.

11 August 1740. John Glide a poor man is chosen into this house in the room of Thomas Chapman, deceased, and brings in a flock bed and a feather pillow, and is sworn.

5 March 1741. Robert Hanham a poor man is chosen into this house in the room of John Wear, deceased, and is sworn.

20 May 1741. Thomas Mathews a poor man is chosen into this house in the room of John Crees, deceased, and brings in a bed, and is sworn.

12 October 1741. John Justins a poor man is chosen into this house in the room of Robert Hodder, deceased, and is sworn.

22 October 1741. Samuel Game nominated the following three poor persons: William Lovick, Joseph Dampier and Samuel Hamblen to be elected into this house in the room of John Higgens who is turned out of this house. Samuel Hamblen is chosen in the room and is sworn.

10 December 1741. Elizabeth West, widow, is chosen into this house in the room of Anne Parsons, deceased, and brings into the house a featherbed, a rug, a pillow and a blanket, and is sworn.

15 February 1742. It is agreed that John Rapson the present Prior is discharged on account of his indisposition and Samuel Hamblen is chosen Prior in his room.

15 March 1743. Joseph Dampier a poor man is chosen into this house in the room of John Crew deceased, and brings in a wool bed, and is sworn.

15 March 1743. Peter Davis a poor man is chosen into this house in the room of James Jeffery, deceased, and is sworn.

15 March 1743. William Lovick a poor man is chosen into this house in the room of Moses Lamb, deceased, and is sworn.

15 March 1743. Elizabeth Painter widow a poor woman is chosen into this house in the room of Anne Leach widow, deceased, and is sworn.

19 May 1743. William Rogers a poor man is chosen into this house in the room of Henry Sturmy, and is sworn.

19 May 1743. John Manfield a poor man is chosen into this house in the room of John Rapson, and is sworn.

6 October 1743. John Cooke a poor man is chosen into this house in the room of John Glyde and has brought in a bed, two blankets and a rug, and is sworn.

6 October 1743. Joseph Hanam a poor man is chosen into this house in the room of Robert Hanham and brought in one bed, and is sworn.

10 April 1744. Mary Hodder a poor woman is chosen into this house in the room of Mary Loaden, deceased, and brought into the house a blanket and a sheet, and is sworn.

17 May 1744. Thomas Hoddinot a poor man is chosen into this house in the room of Thomas Paris, deceased, and brought to the house one featherbed, a bolster, a rug and one sheet, and is sworn.

28 June 1744. Margaret Baker, widow, a poor woman was chosen into this house in the room of Elizabeth Hodder, deceased, and brings with her a feather pillow.

24 July 1744. William Stephens a poor man is chosen into this house in the room of Joseph Hanham, deceased, and brought in a flock bed and a pillow, and is sworn.

[*Undated*] Robert Odry a poor man is chosen into this house in the room of Thomas Hoddinott, deceased, and is sworn.

19 February 1745. Alexander Williams a poor man is chosen into this house in the room of William Hibditch, deceased, and is sworn.

2 May 1745. John Chaffey a poor man is chosen into this house in the room of William Bragg, deceased, and brings with him a flock bed, and is sworn.

27 December 1745. Francis Slidston a poor man is chosen into this house in the room of John Cooke, deceased, and is sworn.

2 April 1746. John Battis a poor man is chosen into this house in the room of Samuel Hamblin, deceased, and is sworn.

2 April 1746. William Jeffery a poor man is chosen into this house in the room of Samuel Dampier and brings in a flock bed, a rug, a sheet and a blanket, and is sworn.

9 July 1746. Samuel Penny a poor man is chosen into this house in the room of William Lovick and has brought in nothing, and is sworn.

9 July 1746. Daniel Weed a poor man is chosen into this house in the room of William Rogers, who is expelled the house for frequent drunkenness, and has brought in a rug and a pillow, and is sworn.

29 October 1746. Thomas Plowman a poor man is chosen into this house in the room of Thomas Mathews, deceased, and has brought in with him a featherbed and a rug, and is sworn.

7 April 1747. Unity Hopkins a poor woman is chosen into this house in the room of the widow Pope, and is sworn.

28 December 1747. Rebecca Justins a poor woman is chosen into this house in the room of Elizabeth West, deceased, and has brought in a bed, a bolster, a pillow, a blanket and a sheet, and is sworn.

29 March 1748. Mary Symonds a poor woman is chosen into this house in the room of Elizabeth Paynter, deceased, and is sworn.

19 July 1748. Samuel Pyke a poor man is chosen into this house in the room of John Chaffey and brought with him [*blank*], and is sworn.

3 November 1748. Jane Sug a poor woman is chosen into this house in the room of Margaret Baker, deceased, and brings with her a bed, a rug, a bolster, a blanket and a sheet, and is sworn.

23 May 1749. Martha Bartlet a poor woman is chosen into this house in the room of Elizabeth Dinning, deceased, and brings with her a featherbed, a blanket, one sheet, a pillow and a bolster, and is sworn.

4 May 1750. John Talbot a poor man is chosen into this house in the room of Thomas Morris, deceased, and brings with him a bed, a blanket, a rug, a sheet and a bolster.

25 June 1750. Thomas Noake a poor man of this town is chosen in the room of John Mandefield, deceased, and brought nothing into the house.

8 February 1753. George Pike a poor man of this town is chosen into this house in the room of William Mullinder, deceased, and brings nothing into the house.

8 June 1753. Martha Shepherd a poor woman is chosen into this house in the room of Mary Simonds, deceased, and brings with her one bed, a bolster and a pillow.

13 February 1754. Christopher Drodge a poor man of this town is chosen into this house in the room of John Justins, deceased, and brings into the house a bed, a blanket, a sheet, a rug, a bolster and a pillow, and Christopher Drodge is accordingly sworn.

30 May 1754. Sybil Rapson a poor woman of this town is chosen into this house in the room of Mary Symonds, deceased, and brings in nothing, and is sworn.

30 October 1754. Thomas Pride a poor man is chosen into this house in the room of Daniel Weed, deceased, and Thomas Pride is sworn accordingly.

September 8 1755. Mary Ridout, widow, a poor woman is chosen into this house in the room of [*blank*] Justins, widow, deceased, and is sworn.

6 November 1755. Thomas Pope a poor man is chosen into this house in the room of William Stephens, deceased, and is sworn.

17 February 1756. Mary Lamb a poor woman is chosen into this house in the room of Mary Hodder, deceased, and is sworn.

30 March 1756. Robert Reeves a poor man is chosen into this house in the room of Thomas Pope, deceased, and is sworn.

4 June 1756. Thomas Hebditch a poor man is chosen into this house in the room of William Jeffery, deceased, and is sworn.

24 January 1757. Walter Justins a poor man is chosen into this house in the room of Joseph Dampier, deceased, and is sworn. He brings in one bed, etc.

24 January 1757. John Hurfits is chosen into this house in the room of Francis Slidston, deceased, and is sworn. He brings in one bed, etc.

20 May 1757. Elizabeth Hearne a poor woman is chosen into this house in the room of Rebecca Justins, deceased, and is sworn.

22 June 1757. Martha Pope a poor woman is chosen into this house in the room of Mary Lamb, deceased, and is sworn. She is to bring in a blanket and pillow.

28 August 1758. John Symonds a poor man is chosen into this house in the room of Thomas Plowman, deceased, and is sworn.

13 February 1759. Thomas Tucker a poor man is chosen into this house in the room of Alexander Williams, deceased, and is sworn.

13 February 1759. George Hardy a poor man is chosen into this house in the room of Peter Davis, deceased, and is sworn.

28 May 1759. Elizabeth French a poor woman is chosen into this house in the room of Sybil Rapson.

8 November 1759. Mary Piddle, widow, a poor woman is chosen into this house in the room of widow Sug, deceased.

27 December 1759. Hugh Philips a poor man is chosen into this house in the room of John Symmonds and is sworn.

21 February 1760. Andrew Newman a poor man is chosen into this house in the room of Samuel Penny, deceased, and is sworn.

4 March 1760. Deborah Pride a poor woman is chosen into this house in the room of Mary Ridout, deceased, and is sworn. She brings in one feather bed, a bolster, a pillow, one blanket and a rug.

17 April 1760. James Howill a poor man is chosen into this house in the room of Samuel Pyke, deceased, and is sworn, but he brings nothing into this house.

17 April 1760. William Ridout a poor man is chosen into this house in the room of John Talbott, deceased, and is sworn. He brings in a bed, a bedstead, a blanket and a sheet.

17 April 1760. John Collier a poor man is chosen into this house in the room of Hugh Phillips, deceased, and is sworn. He brings in a bed and a blanket.

13 July 1761. Edward Bartlett a poor man is chosen into this house in the room of George Hardy, deceased.

2 March 1762. George Hebditch a poor man is chosen into this house in the room of Thomas Noake, deceased.

29 June 1762. John Manfield a poor man is chosen into this house in the room of George Hebditch, deceased, and is sworn.

11 August 1762. William Phillips a poor man is chosen into this house in the room of John Battis, deceased, and is sworn. He brings in one bed, etc.

14 October 1762. Israel Moores a poor man is chosen into this house on the nomination of Samuel Game, the representative of Peter Game a benefactor of this

house, in the room of Walter Justins, deceased, and is sworn.

27 December 1762. Thomas Chapman a poor man is chosen into this house in the room of Robert Odery, deceased, and is sworn.

27 June 1763. Thomas Hoffe a poor man is chosen into this house in the room of George Speke, deceased, and is sworn.

13 March 1764. Edward Parsons a poor man is chosen into this house in the room of Thomas Pride, deceased, and is sworn.

13 March 1764. Mary Hoddinott a poor woman is chosen into this house in the room of Martha Pope, deceased, and is sworn.

26 October 1764. Martha Day a poor woman is chosen into this house in the room of Hannah Bartlett, deceased, and brings in one bed, etc.

10 October 1765. Thomas Stephens a poor man is chosen into this house in the room of Robert Hebditch, deceased.

10 October 1765. Hannah Manfield a poor woman is chosen into this house in the room of Judith Gent, deceased.

3 December 1765. Thomas Heathman a poor man is chosen into this house in the room of Andrew Newman, deceased.

3 July 1766. William Vowell a poor man is chosen into this house in the room of Christopher Drodge, deceased.

27 December 1766. Joseph Burbidge a poor man is chosen into this house in the room of William Phillips who was turned out for his misbehaviour.

27 December 1766. John Carter a poor man is chosen into this house in the room of Thomas Hoffe who was turned out also for his misbehaviour.

17 March 1767. Martha Justins a poor woman is chosen into this house in the room of Martha Shepherd, deceased.

29 July 1767. Joseph Jeffery a poor man is chosen into this house in the room of William Hellyar, deceased.

29 July 1767. John Mullett a poor man is chosen into this house in the room of Thomas Heathman, deceased.

29 July 1767. Thomas Chant a poor man is chosen into this house in the room of James Howell, deceased.

5 October 1767. Elizabeth Hearne one of this house is chosen housewife in the room of Unity Hopkins, deceased.

5 October 1767. Ann March a poor woman is chosen into this house in the room of Elizabeth Hearne.

28 December 1767. Joseph Cole a poor man is chosen into this house in the room of Joseph Jeffrey, deceased.

28 December 1767. Mary Hellyar a poor woman is chosen into this house in the room of the widow French, deceased.

23 February 1768. Thomas Symonds a poor man is chosen into this house in the room of Thomas Chapman, deceased.

15 December 1768. John Maggs a poor man is chosen into this house in the room of Joseph Burbidge, deceased.

13 January 1770. Bernard Hebditch a poor man is chosen into this house in the room of Joseph Cole, deceased.

2 April 1770. William Mitchell a poor man is chosen into this house in the room of Robert Reeves, deceased.

2 April 1770. Ann Kemp a poor woman is chosen into this house in the room of Deborah Pride, deceased.

21 May 1770. Richard Vincent a poor man is chosen into this house in the room of Thomas Tucker, deceased.

25 July 1770. James Gent a poor man is chosen into this house in the room of Edward Parsons, removed.

12 October 1770. Jeremiah Gent, a poor man is chosen into this house in the room of John Carter, deceased.

16 November 1770. Thomas Lodge a poor man is chosen into this house in the room of James Gent, deceased.

6 December 1770. Michael Bowne a poor man is chosen into this house in the room of Thomas Lodge who has left the house.

6 December 1770. Francis Hobbs a poor man is chosen into this house in the room of John Hurfit, deceased.

28 February 1771. [*blank*].

12 March 1771. John Moore a poor man is chosen into this house in the room of John Collier.

30 May 1771. Catherine Parsons a poor woman is chosen into this house in the room of Ann Kemp.

26 September 1771. ~~Susannah Symonds a poor woman is chosen into this house in the room of Mary.~~

[*undated – presumably the same day*] Elizabeth Hoffe a poor woman is chosen into this house in the room of Mary Hellyar, deceased.

26 March 1772. Henry Short a poor man is chosen into this house in the room of Jeremiah Gent, deceased.

9 March 1773. Samuel Game nominated the following three persons: Thomas Pope Richard Perram and John Willis to be elected into the Almshouse in the room of Israel Moores, deceased. Thomas Pope was elected.

27 March 1773. Robert Swyer a poor man is chosen into this house in the room of William Ridout, deceased.

1 July 1773. Elisha Mitchell a poor man is chosen into this house in the room of John Moore, deceased.

9 August 1773. John Williams a poor man is chosen into this house in the room of Edward Bartlett, deceased.

27 December 1773. Richard Ware a poor man is chosen into this house in the room of Richard Vincent, deceased.

21 April 1774. Susannah Symonds a poor woman is chosen in the room of Hannah Manfield, deceased.

8 August 1774. Ann Attwood a poor woman is chosen in the room of Ann March who is expelled for misbehaviour.

16 December 1774. John Hebditch a poor man is chosen in the room of Thomas Symonds.

27 December 1774. John Linckhorne a poor man is chosen in the room of Robert Swyer who is removed for misbehaviour.

1 August 1775. Mary Moors, widow, a poor woman is chosen in the room of Mary Hoddinott.

27 February 1776. Mary Grove, widow a poor woman is chosen in the room of Betty Hearne, deceased.

3 July 1776. Susannah Thomas a poor woman is chosen in the room of Martha Day, deceased.

27 November 1776. John Baker a poor man is chosen into the house in the room of Bernard Hebditch, deceased.

24 June 1777. Mary Denham a poor woman is chosen into the house in the room of Elizabeth Hoffe, deceased.

1 October 1777. Jephthah Newman a poor man is chosen into the house in the room of Thomas Stevens, deceased.

8 April 1778. Mary Higgins a poor woman is chosen into the house in the room of Mary Groves, deceased.

19 May 1778. Mary Moores a poor woman is chosen in the room of Mary Denham, deceased.

October 1778. Benjamin Whitehead a poor man is chosen in the room of John Williams, deceased.

2 November 1778. John Pope a poor man is chosen in the room of Jephtha Newman, deceased.

14 December 1778. John West a poor man is chosen in the room of John Linckhorne, deceased.

14 December 1778. Edward Grimes a poor man is chosen in the room of Elisha Mitchell, deceased.

24 August 1779. Mary Weare a poor woman is chosen in the room of Mary Moore, deceased.

10 November 1779. Richard Perham a poor man is chosen in the room of John Mullett, deceased.

10 November 1779. Henry Symonds a poor man is chosen in the room of John Manfield, deceased.

5 February 1780. Joseph Furlong a poor man is chosen in the room of Henry Mitchell, deceased.

7 March 1780. John Mathews a poor man is chosen into this house in the room of Henry Short, deceased.

21 April 1780. Edward Eason a poor man is chosen into this house in the room of John Maggs.

26 September 1780. James Waters a poor man is chosen into this house in the room of Benjamin White, deceased.

26 September 1780. John Reeves a poor man is chosen into this house in the room of Edward Grymes, deceased.

15 November 1780. Ann Glyde a poor woman is chosen into this house in the room of Catherine Parsons, deceased.

27 December 1780. Thomas Mathews a poor man is chosen into this house in the room of Richard Perram, deceased.

14 August 1782. Edward Pearce a poor man is chosen in the room of John Pope, deceased.

14 August 1782. Henry Newberry a poor man is chosen in the room of William Mitchell, deceased.

12 March 1783. Francis Denham a poor man is chosen in the room of Joseph Furlong, deceased.

30 March 1784. Joseph Justins a poor man is chosen in the room of Richard Weare, deceased.

30 March 1784. Thomas Weed a poor man is chosen in the room of John Baker, deceased.

7 April 1784. Mary Watts a poor woman is chosen in the room of Susannah Symonds, deceased.

21 December 1784. Christopher Ridout a poor man is chosen in the room of Michael Bowne, deceased.

24 November 1785. John Hyde a poor man is chosen in the room of John Hebditch, deceased.

24 November 1785. Elizabeth Cross, widow is chosen in the room of Mary Higgins, deceased.

27 December 1785. Jane Higgins, widow is chosen in the room of Mary Weare, deceased.

22 May 1786. Elizabeth Floyde, widow is chosen in the room of Hannah Glyde, deceased.

31 August 1786. Isaac Sherring is chosen in the room of Christopher Ridout, deceased.

[*Undated – presumably the same day*] Tristam Masters is also chosen.

27 December 1786. Jane Gent, widow a poor woman is chosen into this house in the room of Sarah Watts, deceased.

12 February 1787. William Busey a poor man is chosen into this house in the room of Edward Pearce, deceased.

12 February 1787. Elizabeth Ridout a poor woman is chosen in the room of Mary Moore, deceased.

31 July 1787. Joan Mitchell a poor woman is chosen in the room of Elizabeth Ridout, deceased.

20 December 1787. Ann Bragstone a poor woman was chosen in the room of Martha Justins, deceased.

1 February 1788. William Vowell a poor man was chosen in the room of John Matthews, deceased.

16 March 1789. Samuel Hodges a poor man was chosen in the room of Edward Eason, deceased.

1 May 1789. Ann Bragstone a poor woman was chosen in the room of Jane Gent, deceased.

20 January 1790. Mrs ~~Martin~~

~~6 July 1791. Thomas daughter of Champion Thomas was chosen in the room of~~ [blank]

~~Samuel Gent, son of Mary is chosen in the room of.~~ [*blank*]

[*No day or month*] 1791, Robert Fry was chosen.

16 January 1792, Thomas Sadler is chosen into this house in the room of Francis Hobbs, deceased.

16 January 1792. Mathew Tewsberry is chosen.

16 January 1792. Robert Rapson is chosen into this house in the room of William Vowell, deceased.

16 January 1792. Hannah Short is chosen into this house in the room of Jane Higgens, deceased.

16 January 1792. Richard Stidston is chosen into this house in the room of Henry Symonds, deceased.

22 May. [*No year*] Martha Mathews is chosen into this house in the room of Susannah Thomas, deceased.

[*Undated – presumably the same day*] Peter Lamb is chosen.

15 July 1793. Robert Burrow is chosen in this house in the room of John Reeves, deceased.

16 September 1793. John Eyres is chosen into this house in the room of Thomas Weed, deceased.

23 July 1794. George Hebditch is chosen into this house in the room of John Hyde, deceased.

23 July 1794. John Eldridge is chosen into this house in the room of James Painter, deceased.

25 September 1794. Richard Ellaway is chosen into this house in the room of Tristram Masters, deceased.

23 December 1794. Ambrose Bonnell is chosen into this house in the room of John Eyres, deceased.

31 October 1795. Mark Spragg is chosen into this house in the room of Robert Fry, deceased.

31 October 1795. George Hebditch is chosen Prior in the room of the said Mr Fry.

13 April 1797. John Stevens is chosen in this house in the room of Thomas Sadler.

13 April 1797. John Hanham is chosen in this house in the room of Isaac Sherring.

8 August 1797. Joseph Thomas is chosen in the room of James Waters, and is sworn.

8 August 1797. Charles Jestins is chosen in the room of Richard Stidston.

26 September 1797. Thomas Pearce is chosen in the room of William Bewsey, deceased.

26 September 1797. Catherine Parker is chosen in the room of Martha Mathews, deceased.

28 February 1798. Jacob Parsons is chosen in the room of John Stevens.

16 [*blank*] John Dowland a poor man is chosen in the room of Peter Lamb, deceased, and is sworn.

The same day Lucy Hoddinott a poor woman is chosen in the room of Mary Floyd, deceased, and is sworn.

The same day Sarah Rapson a poor woman is chosen into the house.

The same day Elizabeth Dampier a poor woman is chosen into the house.

1 November 1798. Charles Noake a poor man is chosen into the house in the room of Mark Spragg, deceased, and is sworn.

9 December 1799. Martha Moors, widow, is chosen into the house in the room of Hannah Short, deceased.

9 December 1799. James William is chosen into this house.

2 January 1800. Mary Bewsey is chosen in the room of Catherine Parker, deceased, and is sworn.

2 January 1800. Barnard Odhams is chosen in the room of Ambrose Bonnell, deceased.

20 February 1800. Elizabeth Pope is chosen in the room of Elizabeth Cross, deceased, and is sworn.

16 April 1800. Robert Symonds is chosen in the room of John Hanham, deceased, and is sworn.

16 April 1800. Peverel Hamblin is chosen in the room of Jacob Parsons, deceased, and is sworn.

16 April 1800. Mary Bettinson is chosen in the room of Ann Bragstone.

14 December 1801. Thomas Hamblin is chosen in the room of Samuel Jestins, and is sworn.

14 December 1801. John Parker is chosen in the room of Thomas Pearce, and is sworn.

14 December 1801. Bernard Odhams on a promise of his future good behaviour is re-chosen into this house.

6 November 1804. John Payne is chosen in the room of Richard Ellaway, deceased, and is sworn.

6 November 1804. James Hyde is chosen in the room of Charles Jestins, deceased, and is sworn.

5 February 1805. Daniel Thomas is chosen in the room of Bernard Odhams, deceased, and is sworn.

4 February 1806. George Chant is chosen in the room of John Eldridge, deceased, and is sworn.

19 January 1807. John Mance is chosen in the room of George Hebditch, deceased, and is sworn.

13 February 1807. Robert Garrett is chosen in the room of John Mance, deceased, and is sworn.

20 April 1807. Laurence Justins is chosen in the room of Charles Noake, deceased, and is sworn.

3 November 1807. Champion Thomas is chosen in the room of Samuel Hodges, deceased, and is sworn.

3 November 1807. Henry Miles is chosen in the room of Matthew Tewksbury, deceased, and is sworn.

28 December 1807. Elizabeth Wise is chosen in the room of Elizabeth Pope, deceased.

7 May 1808. Julia Fox is chosen in the room of Martha Moores, and is sworn.

21 June 1808. William Sharp is chosen in the room of James Williams, deceased, and is sworn.

7 February 1809. Abraham Hutchings is chosen in the room of Robert Burrows, deceased, and is sworn.

27 March 1809. Lucy Soper, widow, is chosen in the room of Joan Mitchell, deceased (aged 102), and is sworn.

27 March 1809. Sarah Knott, widow, is chosen in the room of Elizabeth Wise, and is sworn.

1 August 1809. Elizabeth Williams is chosen into this house in the room of Sarah Knott, deceased.

1 August 1809. John Dowland, elected in this house 20 February 1798 and afterwards chosen to be Prior, is this day deposed from his office for a breach of trust, but permitted to remain a member of this house, and to be placed as the junior.

1 August 1809. Samuel Justins is chosen Prior in the room of John Dowland.

15 August 1809. Roger Dicker is chosen in the room of Champion Thomas, deceased, and is sworn.

7 November 1809. James Mitchell is chosen in the room of John Dowland, who was expelled on 5 September for embezzling the property belonging to this house, and James Mitchell is sworn.

5 February 1811. Betty Farthing is chosen in the room of Mary Bewsy, deceased, and is sworn.

5 February 1811. Mary Short is chosen in the room of Ann Hardy, deceased; ~~and is sworn~~ and on the 18 June was expelled for refusing to take the oath and for disobeying the orders and rules of the house, as well as for great insolence to the governors.

5 March 1811. Ann Thomas is chosen in the room of Elizabeth Williams, deceased, and is sworn.

5 March 1811. Henry Cross is chosen in the room of Henry Miles, deceased, and is sworn.

6 May 1811. Charles Maber is unanimously chosen in the room of John Parker, deceased, and is sworn.

2 July 1811. Betty Guppy is chosen in the room of Mary Short, who was expelled for insolence and disobeying the orders of the house, and is sworn.

7 January 1812. Thomas Jeffrey is chosen in the room of James Hyde, deceased, and has been sworn.

3 October 1812. James Mitchell is chosen in the room of Peverell Hamlyn, deceased, and is sworn.

8 December 1812. Tristram Masters is chosen in the room of Daniel Thomas, deceased, and is sworn.

16 February 1813. John Hewlett is chosen in the room of Robert Garrett, deceased, and was sworn.

7 December [*blank*] James Linkhorne is chosen in the room of Thomas Jeffrey, deceased, and is sworn.

27 December [*blank*] John Harris is chosen in the room of Robert Simmonds, deceased (aged 84), and is sworn.

27 December [*blank*] Ann Parker is chosen in the room of Sarah Rapson, deceased, (aged 84), and is sworn.

2 April 1816. Thomas Justins is chosen in the room of Roger Dicker, deceased (aged 82) and is sworn.

2 April 1816. Herbert Moores is chosen in the room of Thomas Hamblin, deceased, and is sworn.

Thomas Justins is the Junior Member.

14 June 1816. William Hodges (aged 79) is chosen in the room of Samuel Justins, the Prior, deceased (whose age was 72), and is sworn.

10 December 1816. Elizabeth Mills (aged 67) is chosen in the room of Betty Farthing, deceased, and is sworn.

23 September 1817. George Miller (aged 66) is chosen into this house in the room of Tristram Masters, deceased, and is sworn.

3 February 1818. William Simmonds (aged 72) is chosen in the room of Joseph Thomas, deceased, and is sworn.

3 February 1818. Clifford Brackstone (aged 70) is chosen in the room of John Payne, deceased, and is sworn.

3 February 1818. Josiah Gander (aged 70) is chosen in the room of Charles Maber who, with expressions of gratitude for the benefits received during his residence in the house for upwards of 6 years past, now retires to live with his aged wife upon the request of his son George who had promised to provide for them both during the remainder of their lives. Josiah Gander is sworn.

3 March 1818. Ann Jeffrey (aged 68) is chosen in the room of Betty Farthing, deceased, and is sworn. [*The 10 Dec.1816 entry is correct. The parish register shows Betty Farthing's burial in December 1816. The error in the source is here.*]

7 April 1818. Jane Pearce (aged 79) is chosen in the room of Ann Thomas, deceased, and is sworn.

13 July 1819. Charlotte Amans (aged 56) is this day chosen housewife in the room

of Elizabeth Mills, deceased, and was sworn at the following meeting of the master and brethren on 3 August 1819.

7 December 1819. Anne Parker, widow of the late James Parker, aged 75 is this day chosen in the room of Lucy Hoddinott, deceased, and was sworn at this meeting.

4 January 1820. Sarah Ellaway, widow of the late John Ellaway, aged 67 is this day chosen in the room of Lucy Soaper, deceased (aged 74), and was sworn 1 February 1820.

1 February 1820. Robert Bond, aged 69, is this day chosen in the room of John Hewlett, deceased aged 87, and was sworn.

29 April 1820. John Ridout (aged 66) is this day chosen in the room of James Linkhorne, deceased aged 78, and was sworn.

17 May 1820. William Walters, aged 73, is this day chosen in the room of Herbert Moores, deceased aged 70, and was sworn.

21 October 1820. William Martin, aged 68, is this day chosen in the room of William Hodges, deceased aged 83, and was sworn.

5 December 1821. William Glyde (aged 70) is this day chosen in the room of Henry Cross, deceased aged 77, and was sworn.

4 June 1822. Mary Baunton, widow aged 68, is this day chosen in the room of Ann Parker, aged 77, and was sworn.

2 July 1822. Thomas Holmes, aged 76, is this day chosen in the room of Clifford Bragstone, aged 74, and was sworn.

7 January 1823. Davis Colly, aged 73, is this day chosen in the room of James Mitchell, deceased aged 85, and was sworn.

18 April 1823. John Bratcher (aged 67) is this day chosen in the room of Abraham Hutchings, deceased aged 85, and was sworn.

18 April 1823. Thomas Matthews, aged 75, is this day chosen in the room of William Simmonds, deceased aged 75, and was sworn.

3 June 1823. Robert Bull, aged 67, is this day chosen in the room of William Martin, deceased aged 70, and was sworn.

2 September 1823. Betty Hodder, aged 77, is this day chosen in the room of Julian Fox, deceased aged 82, and was sworn.

2 December 1823. William Parsons, aged 74, is this day chosen in the room of Josiah Gander, deceased aged 77, and was sworn.

3 October 1826. Jane Cornick, aged 70, is this day chosen in the room of Jane Pierce, deceased aged 86, and was sworn.

7 November 1826. Charles Pearce, aged 71, is this day chosen in the room of Thomas Holmes, deceased aged 80, and was sworn.

7 November 1826. John Wines, aged 70, is also chosen in the room of William Sharpe, deceased aged 81, and was sworn.

27 December 1826. Mary Burrough, widow aged 65, is chosen in the room of Ann Jeffrey, deceased aged 76, and was sworn.

9 January 1827. John Whitehead, aged 60, is chosen in the room of George Chant, deceased aged 87, and was sworn.

1 May 1827. James Hanham, aged 71, is chosen in the room of John Ridout, deceased aged 73, and was sworn.

[*Undated*] Mary Furlong aged, 80, is chosen in the room of Anne Parker, deceased aged 82, and was sworn.

19 October 1827. Isaac Buglar, aged 74, is chosen in the room of Charles Pearce, deceased aged 72, and was sworn.

1 January 1828. Job Pearce, aged 66, is chosen in the room of Robert Bond, deceased aged 76, and was sworn.

1 April 1828. John Pearce, aged 70, is chosen in the room of William Parsons, deceased aged 78, and was sworn.

2 June 1829. John Bartlett, aged 70, is chosen in the room of George Miller, deceased aged 78, and was sworn.

15 December 1829. John Bridle, aged 68, is chosen in the room of William Glyde, deceased aged 78, and was sworn.

2 February 1830. Nathaniel Hoddinott, aged 66, is chosen in the room of John Bridle, who died soon after his election aged 68, and was sworn.

2 March 1830. Biddy Miller, aged 62, is chosen in the room of Sarah Ellaway, deceased aged 77, and was sworn.

23 March 1830. William Hardy, aged 71, is chosen in the room of William Walters, deceased aged 83, and was sworn.

7 September 1830. James Mitchel, aged 70, is chosen in the room of James Mitchel (his father), deceased aged 91, and was sworn.

1 February 1831. Sarah the wife of John Bull, aged 67, is chosen in the room of Mary Baunton, deceased aged 76, and was sworn.

7 August 1832. Elizabeth, aged 81, widow of the late William Sharpe is chosen in the room of Betty Guppy, deceased aged 91, and was sworn.

8 January 1833. John Hyde, aged 72, is chosen in the room of Isaac Buglar, deceased aged 79, and was sworn.

20 September 1834. Obadiah Griffith, aged 86, is chosen in the room of William Hardy, deceased aged 66, and was sworn.

2 June 1835. William Chant, aged 65, is chosen in the room of Nathaniel Hoddinott, deceased aged 71, and was sworn.

6 October 1835. James Hamblin, aged 70, is chosen in the room of John Bartlett, deceased aged 76, and was sworn.

3 November 1835. William Sutton, aged 66, is chosen in the room of Obadiah Griffith, deceased aged 87, and was sworn.

28 December 1835. Israel Watts, aged 89, is chosen in the room of Thomas Justins, deceased aged 80, and was sworn.

7 June 1836. James Senior, aged 67, is chosen in the room of Israel Watts, deceased, and was sworn.

7 June 1836. Mary Dawe, aged 70, widow of Thomas Dawe is chosen in the room of Betty Hodder, deceased aged 90, and was sworn.

27 December 1836. Deborah Reeves, widow aged 78, is chosen in the room of Elizabeth Sharpe, deceased aged 85, and was sworn.

7 March 1837. Benjamin Scott, aged 72, is chosen in the room of John Whitehead, deceased aged 70, and was sworn.

22 March 1837. John Parker, aged 76, is chosen in the room of Thomas Matthews, deceased aged 89, and was sworn.

22 March 1837. William Hunt, aged 74, is chosen in the room of John Pearce, expelled aged 79, and was sworn.

7 November 1837. Stephen Bown, aged 70, is chosen in the room of John Harris, deceased aged 86, and was sworn.

8 February 1838. William Moore, aged 75, is chosen in the room of John Parker, deceased aged 77, and was sworn.

1 May 1838. Thomas Kennison, aged 68, is chosen in the room of Davis Colly, deceased aged 88, and was sworn.

7 August 1838. Thomas Heathman, aged 74, is chosen in the room of William Chant, deceased aged 68, and was sworn.

5 February 1839. Jane Ridout, aged 84, is chosen in the room of Mary Furlong, deceased aged 91, and was sworn.

2 April 1839. John Gardner, aged 79, is chosen in the room of John Hyde, deceased aged 78, and was sworn.

3 September 1839. Love Stephens, aged 70, is chosen in the room of Mary Dawe, deceased aged 73, and is sworn.

7 April 1840. Elizabeth Chant, aged 67, widow of George Chant, was chosen in the room of Love Stephens, deceased aged 70, and is sworn.

4 August 1840. Ann Heathman, aged 72 widow of John Heathman, is chosen into this house in the room of Charlotte Amans, deceased aged 75, and is sworn.

1 September 1840. Elizabeth Lanning, widow aged 62, is chosen into this house in the room of Sarah Bull, deceased aged 77, and is sworn.

2 November 1841. Joseph Hamblin, aged 81, is chosen into this house in the room of Job Pierce, deceased aged 77, and is sworn.

15 March 1842. Martha Noake, aged 75 widow of the late Charles Noake, is chosen into this house in the room of Mary Burrough, deceased aged 81, and is sworn.

4 October 1842. Charlotte Parker, widow aged 82, is chosen into this house in the room of Biddy Miller, deceased, and is sworn.

17 January 1843. Jane Sevil, widow aged 70, is chosen into this house in the room of Jane Cornick, aged 88 deceased, and is sworn.

7 February 1843. Thomas Walters, aged 70, is chosen into this house in the room of Thomas Heathman, deceased aged 78, and is sworn.

1 August 1843. George Penny, aged 78, is chosen into this house in the room of Robert Bull, deceased aged 87.

This man was unanimously chosen as one the nominees of Mr George Game of Poyntington.

[*Attached to the page is a note:*]

Mr George Game nominates the undermentioned persons to the masters of the Almshouse in Sherborne, one of whom they will be pleased to choose as a member of the establishment:
George Penny, Henry Roberts and Barter Chaffey
August 1st 1843]

5 December 1843. Barter Chaffey, aged 69, is chosen in the room of John Wines, deceased aged 87, and was sworn.

5 March 1844. Eleanor Chaffey, aged 70, is chosen in the room of Jane Ridout, deceased aged 89, and was sworn.

4 June 1844. Charles Lampard, aged 67, is chosen in the room of James Hanham, deceased aged 88, and was sworn.

6 August 1844. Grace, widow of Joseph Jeffrey aged 72, is chosen in the room of Charlotte Parker, deceased aged 84, and was sworn.

3 December 1844. John Sharpe, aged 66, is chosen in the room of James Senior, deceased aged 77, and was sworn.

1 April 1845. Jane Heathman, widow aged 76, is chosen in the room of Martha Noake, widow, deceased aged 78, and was sworn.

20 May 1845. Stephen Pearce, aged 68, is chosen in the room of John Gardner, deceased aged 84, and was sworn.

7 July 1846. John Game, aged 84, is chosen in the room of John Blacherd, deceased aged 90, and was sworn.

6 October 1846. John Bartlett, aged 78, is chosen in the room of William Moore, deceased aged 83, and was sworn.

28 December 1846. Isaac Baker aged 66, was elected in the room of William Sutton, deceased aged 77, and was sworn.

28 December 1846. William Jeffrey, aged 67, is chosen in the room of John Game, deceased aged 85, and was sworn.

2 February 1847. Jane Bown, aged 81 widow of William Bown, is chosen in the room of Ann Heathman, deceased aged 79, and was sworn.

12 April 1847. Henry Roberts, aged 71, is chosen in the room of Joseph Hamblin, deceased aged 87, and was sworn.

7 December 1847. Jeremiah Stacey, aged 76, is chosen in the room of James Mitchell, deceased aged 87, and was sworn.

1 February 1848. William Fear, aged 75, and Thomas Brown, aged 73, are chosen in the rooms of Barter Chaffey, deceased aged 74, and Benjamin Scott, deceased aged 83, and were sworn.

7 March 1848. George Reeves, aged 64, is chosen in the room of Thomas Kennison, deceased aged 78, and was sworn.

11 April 1848. Mary Reeves, aged 75, is chosen in the room of Elizabeth Chant, deceased aged 75, and was sworn.

4 July 1848. Jane Strickland, aged 72, is chosen in the room of Jane Bown, deceased aged 82, and was sworn.

5 September 1848. William Hodges, aged 70, is chosen in the room of William Hunt, deceased aged 85, and is sworn.

5 February 1850. Jane Dibsdall, widow aged 86, is chosen in the room of Grace Jeffrey, deceased aged 76.

2 April 1850. Elizabeth Cross, widow aged 72, is chosen in the room of Jane Heathman, deceased aged 83.

6 August 1850. Robert Penny, aged 76, is chosen in the room of Stephen Pearce, deceased aged 73, and was sworn.

20 May 1851. Peter Clarke, aged 78, is chosen in the room of Henry Roberts, deceased aged 74, and was sworn.

20 May 1851. James Foot, aged 75, is chosen in the room of James Hamblin, deceased aged 85, and was sworn.

2 March 1852. Elizabeth Gosney, aged 72, is chosen in the room of Deborah Reeves, aged 92, and was sworn.

13 April 1852. William Hammond, aged 67, is chosen in the room of Jeremiah Stacey, aged 81, and was sworn.

13 April 1852. John Miller, aged 70, is chosen in the room of John Bartlett, aged 84, and was sworn.

7 September 1852. Matthew Moores, aged 71, is chosen in the room of Charles Lampard, aged 75, and was sworn.

12 April 1853. Richard Morris, aged 71, is chosen in the room of Thomas Brown, aged 78, and was sworn.

8 February 1854. James Hewlett, aged 75, is chosen in the room of Peter Clarke, aged 81, and was sworn.

November 1854. Mary Gent is chosen in the room of Jane Dibsdall, deceased aged 84, and was sworn.

11 April 1854. James Bridle, aged 77, is chosen in the room of William Hodges, deceased.

8 January 1855. Ann Gillard, aged 75, is chosen in the room of Jane Sevill, deceased aged 81, and was sworn.

6 March 1855. Richard Tuffin, aged 68, is chosen in the room of William Hammond, deceased aged 69, and was sworn.

6 March 1855. James Reeves, aged 71, is chosen in the room of James Hewlett, deceased aged 76, and was sworn.

11 April 1855. Lizzy Gent, aged 78, is chosen in the room of Ann Gillard, aged 75, and is sworn.

17 July 1855. William Amans, aged 69, is chosen in the room of William Jeffrey, aged 78, and is sworn.

4 September 1855. Lucy Foot, aged 75, is chosen in the room of Elizabeth Cross, deceased aged 77, and is sworn.

2 October 1855. Elizabeth Thorne, aged 75, is chosen in the room of Jane Stickland, who was expelled on 4 September for drunkenness and other improper conduct, and was sworn.

1 April 1856. George Mills, aged 75, is chosen in the room of James Foot, deceased aged 79, and is sworn.

2 September 1856. Charlotte Mansfield, aged 70, is chosen in the room of Elizabeth Gosney, aged 75, and is sworn.

3 March 1857. John Parker aged 72 is chosen in the room of William Amans deceased aged [*blank*] and is sworn

4 October 1859. Richard Seville, aged 70, is chosen in the room of [*blank*], deceased, aged [*blank*], and is sworn.

4 October 1859. Samuel Durden, aged 71, is chosen in the room of [*blank*], deceased, and is sworn.

4 October 1859. William Carman, aged 76, is chosen in the room of [*blank*] deceased, and is sworn.

4 October 1859. Thomas Miles, aged 74, is chosen in the room of [*blank*] deceased, and is sworn.

4 October 1859. George Button, aged 70, is chosen in the room of [*blank*] deceased, and is sworn.

4 October 1859. Grace Hodges, widow, aged 79, is chosen in the room of [*blank*], deceased, and is sworn.

4 October 1859. Catherine Simmonds, spinster, aged 67, is chosen in the room of [*blank*], deceased, and is sworn.

4 October 1859. Jane Collins, widow, aged 72, is chosen in the room of [*blank*], deceased, and is sworn.

4 October 1859. Elizabeth Cames, aged 70, is chosen in the room of [*blank*], deceased, and is sworn.

7 February 1860. Edward Sly, aged 72, is chosen in the room of Richard Morris, deceased, and is sworn.

3 February 1861. George Gent [*this entry is inserted in pencil*].

7 February 1861. Ann Willis, widow, aged 65, is chosen in the room of Jane Collins deceased aged 73, and was sworn.

4 February 1862. Hannah Granger, widow, aged 74, is chosen in the room of Catherine Simmonds, discharged, and was sworn.

2 September 1862. Ann Foot, widow, aged 62, is chosen in the room of Lizzy Gent, deceased.

3 November 1863. James Miller, aged 75, is chosen in the room of Thomas Miles, deceased, and was sworn.

3 November 1863. Elizabeth Higgens, aged 74, is chosen in the room of Charlotte Mandsfield, deceased.

3 November 1863. Betsy Beale, aged 69, is chosen in the room of Grace Hodges, deceased.

3 May 1864. George Lamb, aged 72, is chosen in the room of John Parker, aged 78, deceased,

5 July 1864. John Pearce, aged 85, is chosen in the room of Stephen Bown, aged 97, deceased.

5 July 1864. Elizabeth Hoff, aged 80, is chosen in the room of Elizabeth Thorne aged 83.

6 March 1865. Elizabeth Button, aged 78, wife of George Button, was elected into the house in the room of Elizabeth Higgins, deceased.

6 March 1865. John Heathman, aged 74, was elected into the house in the room of William Fear, deceased.

2 May 1865. Joseph Easton, aged 70, is chosen in the house in the room of Richard Sevill, deceased.

6 March 1866. Thomas Hunt, aged 71, is chosen in the house in the room of Joseph Easton, who has discharged himself, and was sworn.

APPENDIX

Early Almspeople and Brethren (Named in other Sources)

Almspeople

In the original document recording the founders' statutes the names of the almspeople whose care was transferred from Dodill's Almshouse to Sherborne Almshouse on its foundation in 1437 are listed as the first almspeople to be accommodated under the new foundation. The list is not repeated in the copy which has been transcribed. How many of these almspeople survived from 1437 until the completion of the new building in 1448 is not recorded. Those named in the original document were:

Men: William Gore, John Salter, the elder, William Floure, John Dale, Henry Baret, Robert Coscombe, John Garland, John Whynne, John Whyppe, Richard Wellys, Thomas Vnwyn, John Whytlegh.

Women: Agnes Knyghttesse, Edith Merston, Julian Symmes, Alice Prior.

(DHC: D/SHA/CH2)

Brethren

The names of these brethren have been compiled from two sources, the foundation deed of 1437 and the early accounts of the masters. The list from the accounts is not exhaustive, since not all brethren became masters. Where names are the same as those included in the register of brethren transcribed in this book, they have been omitted from the accounts list unless there is certainty that they were known to have died before the first entry with that same name appears in the register. The date of the account each master submitted is included in the list, all preceding the change from the *Julian* calendar to the *Gregorian* calendar in 1582.

From the Foundation deed: John Brunyng, parson of the Grene, John Thirlewynd, priest, John Gotehill, priest, Roger Lyveden, John Bromlegh, John Kayleway, Richard Rochell, John Dene, John Wyllys, John Grenyng, Richard Deuyas, John Spadard, Thomas Donne, John Sadeler, Thomas Doget, Walter Weston, Stephen Lymyn, William Knaplok, Richard Hikkes, Thomas Sparowe.

(DHC: D/SHA/CH2)

From the Accounts: Richard Rochell (1439–47); William Smyth (1451–2); George Swetnam (1553–4); John Adams (1554–5); George Barton (1555–6); Brian Cole (1555–7); William Meyer (1555–7); Hugh Myer (1559–60); Thomas Wyneff (1561–2); John Southey (1563–4); Richard Cupper (1565–6); John Fry (1567–8); Thomas Maundfeld (1568–9).

(DHC: D/SHA/A)

GLOSSARY OF TERMS
IN THE SHERBORNE ALMSHOUSE REGISTER

Apparel	Ordinary clothing.
Artificer	Skilled workman.
Bargain and sale	Form of property transfer.
Barton	Farmyard.
Bed	Mattress only.
Bed-tye	Mattress case to contain the stuffing.
Beetle/Bittelle	Wooden hammer or mallet.
Bolster	Long, stuffed bed pillow.
Burgage	Substantial land holding with voting rights within a borough.
Chancery	Court of Chancery, with jurisdiction in civil disputes.
Colverhouse	Pigeon house or dovecot.
Copyhold	Form of manorial tenancy; land granted in the manor court.
Court roll	Record of the business of a manor court.
Croft	Enclosed area of land, usually pasture, not including a dwelling.
Demesne	The home farm of a manor.
Court of Arches	Religious court of the archbishopric of Canterbury.
Heriot	Death duty payable to the lord of a manor by his tenants.
Lady Day	Feast of the Annunciation of the Virgin held on 25th March.
Letters Patent	Royal grants recorded in the Patent Rolls.
Liberty	A local administrative area distinct from neighbouring territory and with a degree of independence.
Licence of mortmain	Licence granted by the Crown to give property to a corporation.
Messuage	House.
Noble	Coin, 6s. 8d., half a mark.
Obit	Gifts of land or money in return for regular, religious, remembrance of a deceased person.
Oblations	Religious offerings, particularly pre-Reformation.
Partlette	Woman's clothing to cover the neck and upper part of the chest.
Physick	Medicine.
Pillowbere	Pillowcase.
Prebend	Form of benefice providing income to religious institutions.

Relief	Payment made by freeholders to the lord of a manor when inheriting property.
Rood	A quarter of an acre.
Rother beast	Horned animal such as an ox or bullock.
Shambles	Market area, particularly for butchers shops.
Socage	Archaic form of land tenure.
Tenement	Landholding of indeterminate size sometimes including a dwelling.
Tithes	Tenth part of agricultural produce paid to the church.
Tithing	Civil administrative unit used for collecting taxes, military musters and enforcement of minor laws.
Toft	Small house.

BIBLIOGRAPHY

Bailey, B., *Almshouses* (London, Robert Hale, 1988).

Blaydon, A., 'Almshouse Rules and Regulations for Trustees and Almspeople with particular reference to Surrey', Chapter 9, in Goose, N., Caffrey, H. and Langley, A., (eds.) *New Perspectives in British Almshouse History, 1400-1914* (provisional title), (Family & Community Historical Research Society, forthcoming 2013).

Caffrey, H., *Almshouses in the West Riding of Yorkshire, 1600-1900* (Kings Lynn, Heritage Publications Ltd., 2006).

Clay, R. M., *The Mediaeval Hospitals of England*. (London, Methuen & Co., 1909).

Clark, A., 'Almspeople and their possessions: gleanings from an admissions register, Sherborne, 1582-1866', Chapter 12 in Goose, N., Caffrey, H. and Langley, A., (eds.) *New Perspectives in British Almshouse History, 1400-1914* (provisional title), (Family & Community Historical Research Society, forthcoming 2013).

Cockburn, E. O., *The Almshouses of Dorset* (Dorchester, The Friary Press Ltd, 1970).

Cox, B. G., *The Book of Blandford Forum* (Buckingham, Barracuda Books, 1983).

Fowler, J., *Mediaeval Sherborne*, (Dorchester, Longmans (Dorchester) Ltd., 1951).

Fripp, J., '*The Sherborne Riots of 1831: Causes, Characters and Consequences*', *Proceedings of the Dorset Natural History and Archaeological Society* (2006), Vol. CXXVII, pp. 21-30.

Fry, E. A., 'Dorset Chantries' Pt. 2, *Proceedings of the Dorset Natural History and Antiquarian Field Club* (1907), Vol. XXVIII, pp.12-29.

Gaydon, A. T. and Pugh, R. B. (eds.), *The Victoria County History: A History of the County of Shropshire: Vol. II* (London, 1973).

Gibb, J. H. P., *The Almshouse of SS. John, Sherborne* (Guide Book, 1990).

Gibson, J. M., *The Walthamstow Charities: Caring for the Poor 1500-1000* (Chichester, Phillimore, 2000).

Gillett, M., *Talbot Village: a Unique Village in Dorset 1850-1989* (Bournemouth, Bournemouth Local Studies Publications, 1989).

Gooden, C. P., *The Story of Sherborne Pageant* (Sherborne, 1906).

Goose, N. and Basten, S., 'Almshouse residency in nineteenth century England', *Family and Community History* (2009), Vol. XII, pp.65-76.

Goose, N. and Moden, L., *A History of Doughty's Hospital, Norwich, 1687-2009* (Hatfield, University of Hertfordshire Press, 2010).

Gourlay, A. B., *A History of Sherborne School* (Sherborne, Sowtells of Sherborne, 1971).

Hays, R. C. *et al.*, (eds) *Records of Early English Drama - Dorset* (Toronto, Toronto University Press, 1999).

Herber, M., *Ancestral Trails* (Stroud, Sutton Publishing/Society of Genealogists, 2004).

Higginbotham. P., *The Workhouse Encyclopedia* (Stroud, The History Press, 2012).

Hindle, S., *On the Parish? The Micropolitics of Poor Relief in Rural England, c.1550-1750* (Oxford, Clarendon Press, 2004).

Howson, B., *Almshouses: A Social and Architectural History* (Stroud, The History Press, 2008).

Hutchins, J., *The History and Antiquities of the County of Dorset*, 1861-74, 3rd edition, W. Shipp and J. W. Hodson, (eds), Vols. I, III. (Wakefield, E. P. Publishing Ltd., 1973).

Hutchins J. *The Annals and Iconography of Dorsetshire and Dorset Worthies* (Extra Illustrated Edition, Vol. XI. (London and Bridport, 1904).

Lewis, L., *A Requiem for Workhouses*, (Faversham, Lionel Lewis, 2006).

Machin, R., *Probate Inventories and Manorial Exerpts of Chetnole, Leigh and Yetminster* (Bristol, University of Bristol, 1976).

Mayo, C. H., *An Historic Guide to the Almshouse of St John the Baptist and St John the Evangelist, Sherborne* (Oxford, Oxford University Press, 1926 and 2nd ed. 1933).

McIntosh, M. K., 'Local responses to the poor in late medieval and Tudor England', *Continuity and Change* (1988), Vol. III, pp. 209-245.

Orme, N. and Webster, M., *The English Hospital, 1070-1570* (London, Yale University Press, 1995).

Page, W. (ed.), *The Victoria County History: A History of the County of Dorset: Vol. II* (London, 1908).

Page, W. (ed.), *The Victoria County History: A History of the County of Oxford: Vol. II* (London, 1907).

Royal Commission on Historical Monuments, *An Inventory of the Historical Monuments in the County of Dorset, Vol. I: West Dorset* (London, HMSO, 1952).

Slack, P., *Poverty and Policy in Tudor and Stuart England* (London, Longman, 1988).

West, J., *Town Records* (Chichester, Phillimore, 1983).

Wildman, W. B., *A Short History of Sherborne from 705 AD* (Sherborne, F. Bennett, 1902).

Wrightson, K., *Earthly Necessities: Economic Lives in Early Modern Britain, 1470-1750* (London, Penguin Books, 2002).

INDEX

This is an index of personal and place names, and selected subjects. Places are in Dorset unless otherwise stated.

DORSET RECORD SOCIETY PUBLICATIONS

Vol. 1 (1964) Weymouth and Melcombe Regis Minute Book 1625–1660, edited by M. Weinstock (out of print)

Vol. 2 (1964) Witchcraft at Toners Puddle, edited by Christina Hole (out of print)

Vol. 3 (1965) Thomas Rackett Papers, edited by H. S. L. Dewar (out of print)

Vol. 4 (1971) Dorset Lay Subsidy 1332, edited by A. D. Mills (out of print)

Vol. 5 (1971) Two 17th century inventories, edited by Lettice Ashley Cooper (out of print)

Vol. 6 (1980) Dorset Lay Subsidy 1327, edited by A. R. Rumble (out of print)

Vol. 7 (1981) The Case Book of Sir Francis Ashley 1614–1635, edited by J. H. Bettey. Ashley was Recorder, or borough magistrate, of Dorchester from 1610 until 1635.

Vol. 8 (1983) The Building Accounts of Mapperton Rectory 1699–1703, edited by R. Machin.

Vol. 9 (1985) Touchinge Witchcrafte and Sorcerye, edited by G. J. Davies (out of print)

Vol. 10 (1986) The Love Poems and Letters of William Barnes and Julia Miles, edited by C. H. Lindgren (out of print)

Vol. 11 (1988) Puddletown: House, Street and Family, edited by C. L. Sinclair Williams (out of print)

Vol. 12 (1991) William Whiteway of Dorchester: his diary 1618–1635 (out of print)

Vol. 13 (1993) Farming in 18th century Dorset: the diary of James Warne, 1758, with George Boswell's letters, 1787–1805 (out of print)

Vol. 14 (2006) Dorset Quarter Sessions Order Book 1625–1638, a Calendar. edited by Terry Hearing and Sarah Bridges. Hardback.

Vol. 15 (2009) Dorset in Wartime, the diary of Phyllis Walther 1941–1942. Mass Observation Diary. Illustrated with contemporary photos, edited by Patricia and Robert Malcolmson. Hardback.

Vol. 16 (2011) Birth, Marriage, Death and Taxes, the Lyme Regis Censuses 1695–1703, edited by Dr Judith Ford. Hardback.

DNHAS Occasional Paper no. 1 (2008) Early Years, recollections of life in Sturminster Newton in the early nineteenth century, by Robert Young, edited by Alan Chedzoy

DNHAS Occasional Paper no. 2 (2011) Dorset Manorial Documents: A guide for local and family historians. By Mark Forrest.

Further details of these volumes, prices and payment methods may be found on the website of the Dorset County Museum: http://research.dorsetcountymuseum. org/drspubs.html